WITHDRAWN

VICENTE HUIDOBRO
THE CAREERS OF A POET

Vicente Huidobro
The Careers of a Poet

René de Costa

CLARENDON PRESS · OXFORD
1984

Oxford University Press, Walton Street, Oxford OX2 6DP

London New York Toronto
Delhi Bombay Calcutta Madras Karachi
Kuala Lumpur Singapore Hong Kong Tokyo
Nairobi Dar es Salaam Cape Town
Melbourne Auckland

and associated companies in
Beirut Berlin Ibadan Mexico City

Oxford is a trade mark of Oxford University Press

Published in the United States by
Oxford University Press, New York

British Library Cataloguing in Publication Data
De Costa, René
Vicente Huidobro.
1. Huidobro, Vicente
I. Title
861   PQ8097.H8
ISBN 0-19-815789-4

Library of Congress Cataloging in Publication Data
Costa, René de.
Vicente Huidobro : the careers of a poet.
Bibliography : p.
Includes index.
1. Huidobro, Vicente, 1893-1948 — Biography — Careers.
2. Authors. Chilean — 20th century — Biography.
I. Title
PQ8097.H8Z636 1984   861 [B]   83-23643
ISBN 0-19-815789-4

Set by Hope Services, Abingdon
Printed in Great Britain
by Billing & Sons Limited, Worcester.

Author's note

Huidobro has been studied from a variety of perspectives. Several books and many lengthy studies exist already. What motivates my effort is not the desire to cover old ground or to uncover new errors in the existing body of criticism, but rather the need to fill in some of the gaps.

New research in the libraries and archives of France, Spain, Chile, and the United States, and most especially newly discovered documents among Huidobro's personal papers in Santiago now make it possible to present a more complete assessment of the man and his work.

Timely grants from the Social Science Research Council, the American Philosophical Society, and La Fondation Camargo, as well as a generous research leave from the University of Chicago have provided me with the time and the wherewithal to carry this project to completion. To these institutions, to my family, and to all those who have worked on Huidobro before me, I am grateful.

RdC

Acknowledgement

Grateful acknowledgement is made to the Huidobro family in Santiago de Chile, and most especially to the poet's son don Vicente García Huidobro Portales, for permission to use freely the published works of Vicente Huidobro and to reproduce the unpublished materials which inform this study.

Contents

Illustrations

Grateful acknowledgement is made to Carlos Hermosilla for
permission to reproduce his engraving of Vicente Huidobro,
and to the Huidobro family who have generously provided the
other iconographic material illustrating this book.

For Serpil and Alev

Introduction

Contemporary poetry begins with me.   1939

There are many facets to Huidobro. Perhaps too many. Novelist, poet, playwright, political militant, polemicist, screenwriter . . . At one time or another he seems to have tried his hand at practically everything. And most of the time he did rather well. Yet he was sometimes a failure too, and even at this he seems to have excelled. For his admirers, the failings are easily dismissed: Huidobro was always way ahead of his time, hence misunderstood at every step of the way. For his detractors, he is rather out of step, hamstrung by contradictions and inconsistencies. The truth as usual, is to be found somewhere between these two extremes.

Born into a patrician South American family in Santiago de Chile in 1893, Vicente García Huidobro Fernández, heir to the title *Marqués de Casa Real*, was earmarked for a life of leisure. For a number of reasons, which we will explore in this book, Huidobro broke out of this comfortable, albeit confining mould, and used his privileged position in a rather unorthodox way: to foment change. At first he was content to push for a change in aesthetic sensibility; later he became more militant, and as a Communist he agitated for social and political revolution as well. Eventually, disappointed with mass movements, he came to espouse a total revolution of the individual. Naturally, he was considered to be something of a traitor: first to his class; then to the party; and finally, even to his poetry. From the beginning he was a figure of controversy. A real 'character', according to an early biographical sketch:*

This young artist is a character. When others of his age, with his social position and his millions, give themselves over to the sterility of a life of

---

* In order to make my sources as accessible as possible to the reader I have directly translated all prose quotations. Reference to the original published source is given in the notes. When quoting from unpublished material, the pertinent portion of the original text is given in the notes. Poetry is always given in the original language, followed by my own plain-prose translation into English.

bland leisure and secret passions, he raises up his pen like a standard of
luminous ideals; he lays down his class prejudices and writes books that
are like a revolt against his birthright . . .

He is quite temperamental: answering only to himself he fears nothing
and allows nothing to interfere . . .[1]

This independence of spirit was to be his hallmark, in life as
well as art.

As a young man in Chile, he studied, along with others of his
position, in the most exclusive school of the time, the *Colegio
San Ignacio*, run by the Jesuits. With them occurs the first of
many scandals. In 1914, with characteristic immodesty, he
places an autobiographical sketch, 'Yo', at the head of *Pasando
y pasando*, a collection of polemical writings on art and literature.
The book is printed and bound in the Imprenta Chile, an enterprise also run by the Jesuits. In spite of this, or perhaps because
of it, Huidobro leads off in the following uninhibited way:

I was born the 10th of January, 1893. An old woman, part witch and
quite wise, predicted that I would be a big thief or a great man. Which of
these options should I take? To be a thief is unquestionably very artistic.
Crime must have its delightful compensations. To be a great man? That
depends. If I am to be a great poet, a man of letters; yes. But to be a great
Congressman, Senator, or Cabinet member, that seems to me most un-
aesthetic.

After passing through some of those quaint schools in which a Doña
Mariquita or Doña Carmelita instructs us and doctors us in the alphabet
and buttons our pants every time we leave the room, I moved on to the
school of the Jesuits.

There I had my first disillusionment. I had actually come to believe
that priests were kind people, always gentle and caring, who give out
gumdrops, holy pictures and relics, since I had always seen them that way
at my house, suave and affable, stuffed with holiday lamb. I found instead
priests who were cranky, strict, easily angered and eager to punish. Before
my eyes, the sheepskin fell away, leaving exposed something black and
severe . . .

The priests did not have to read much further, for the edition
was summarily banned and burned. Only a few copies survived;
enough though to cause a minor scandal at the time.

Later, in Europe, he takes on another sacred cow, the British
Empire, advocating the cause of Irish Independence in *Finis
Britannia* (1923). For this he is reportedly kidnapped. Back in
Chile in 1925, he is beaten and his house is bombed as he makes
a yellow-press bid for the Presidency, accusing the establishment

of all sorts of crimes against the nation. A decade later, we find him in Madrid, championing the Republican cause during the Spanish Civil War. And, with the outbreak of the Second World War, ever anxious to be in the centre of things, he is again in Europe, as a War Correspondent with the Allies.

In literature, he was no less involved, and equally militant. Having mastered the subtleties of Hispanic Modernism in Chile, he goes off to Europe in 1916 to join ranks with Cubism and Dada. Amid stunning successes in Paris and Madrid there are bitter polemics, culminating in 1925 with *Manifestes*, an attack on Breton's Surrealism. In fact, at one time or another Huidobro seems to have quarrelled with every major writer of his generation. Most, however, continued to admire his work. Such was the case, for example, with Pablo Neruda, who, years after Huidobro's death dismissed the 'guerrilla literaria' (literary war) that separated them in life:

I consider Huidobro to be one of the classic poets of our language . . . While most of his prose is flawed by his person, his prankish personalism, his poetry is a mirror in which are reflected images of pure delight along with the game of his personal struggle. It seems to me that Huidobro was consumed in his own game and in his own flame. In spite of the fact that his poetic intelligence is the master key to his brilliance, he had such a predilection to forge himself a legend that in the end the legend consumed him, masking his work and burying him. Fortunately, his poetry will rescue his remembrance, a remembrance that will continue to grow and spread.[2]

The legend however, like the polemics, is an integral part of Huidobro's literary presence. What distinguishes him and his work is not only what he did, but how he did it. And the fact is that he did everything quite spectacularly. Thus, when he arrives in Europe, in his early twenties, with a wife, children, and servants, it is not to sit alone and brood in a café, according to the existential pattern of the expatriate. Instead, he is absorbed, almost instantly, into the artistic life of Spain and France, founding a journal with Reverdy and Max Jacob, befriending Juan Gris, Picasso, and Lipchitz, stimulating the creation of Ultraism . . . What made all this possible? Not his 'millions', which were always more imaginary than real, but something else which money cannot buy: talent. Huidobro was endowed with an extraordinary creative drive, and an equally extraordinary ability to anticipate the new, to be always in the front line. And so he was.

Even in death he was precocious. His end came, in 1948, just
before turning fifty-five. The immediate cause was a stroke,
complicated by shrapnel wounds from the war. He left behind
fifteen volumes of poetry, six novels, two plays, five volumes of
essays, and countless articles marking the ins and outs of his
many careers.

The only constant element in Huidobro's complicated life
and works is not his much touted Creationism, at best a banner
of the 1920s, his personal label for literary Cubism, but rather
change and the ferocity with which he defended the integrality
of his thinking as it evolved. He was a tireless theorist, one who
not only enjoyed explaining his point of view, but endeavoured
to persuade everyone to think just like himself. The problem of
course is that the goals and purposes of his work changed so
often that even the most ardent disciple would have difficulty
in keeping the faith. Few did. What is more, Huidobro was
implacable with others, with those who did not accept his
dictates. Juan Larrea, a Spanish poet and contemporary of
Huidobro — and one of his lifelong friends — once casually
remarked that he was a 'caudillo de la poesia', a strong man of
literature. That remark, or rather that concept, is, I believe, a
useful key to the mystery of the man and his work, for it
permits us to recognize his greatness without being confused
by his shortcomings, the inevitable excesses of an authentic
caudillo.

Huidobro was a caudillo in that he was always placing himself
at the head of something. Nowhere is this more evident than in
his many little magazines. In Santiago, for example, when he
was just nineteen, we find him directing *Musa Joven*. And this
was only the beginning, for over the next quarter century he
would start up at least six others: *Azul*, *Création*, *Acción*, *Total*,
Ombligo, *Vital*. And when he wasn't founding a new journal, he
was encouraging someone else to do so. Reverdy with *Nord-
Sud*, Paul Dermée with *L'Esprit nouveau*, Juan Larrea with
Favorables-Paris-Poema. Here is his rapidly penned advice to
Larrea in a letter of 1922:

It seems to me that you two [Juan Larrea and Gerardo Diego] ought to
found that review you are thinking of doing. It will do you both a lot of
good and make you respected. Make it small, four pages or eight at the
most, but very selective, very élite. Be very tough in accepting contributions so that everyone will want to appear in your company, and let it be
like a stamp of approval, like a certificate of honour to have a place in
those pages and so that it doesn't give you too much work make it monthly

and of a small format. An article in prose, two at the most, and the rest poetry. I think that if you carry this idea through you ought to use as a title something that could be like our banner for Spain and Spanish America and that is related with what we most esteem in this world. A beautiful title would be CREAR, or something like that . . .³

Huidobro was forever organizing little groups around himself, or trying to. By his own account this is what he attempted to do when he first went to Spain: 'I came to Madrid in 1916 and I went to see Rafael Cansinos-Asséns in order to try to form a group. Cansinos told me it was impossible. We talked about it for a few days and then I went on to Paris.'⁴ Lamentable, of course, is that even when he succeeded in forming a group, he could not keep it together for very long.

It was that way from the outset. Among the founders of *Azul* (1913) we find Hernán Díaz Arrieta and Carlos Díaz Loyola, later to become powerhouses of Chilean literature under the pen-names of Alone and Pablo de Rokha. Both spent much of their lives writing against Huidobro and finding fault with his work. Although for different reasons: for one he was too avant-garde; for the other not enough.

How does one get a grasp on such a figure? To study him just as a man of letters is to distort his lively involvement in other activities. To focus on his public posturing is to slight his literary importance. A book-by-book study obliges us to deal with too much writing that is merely occasional; while a chrono-logical approach has the drawback of too many uneventful years. Nor is a theoretical tack fruitful, for his activities are far too varied to expect them all to relate to something as short-lived as Creationism.

For this reason, I propose to deal only with what is major; but in order not to separate the man from his work, it will be necessary to leapfrog between art and life, touching now on an important moment, now on an important work. In this way it should be possible to highlight Huidobro's major activities and the fervour with which he pursued them: his somewhat eccentric formation as a Modernist in Chile; his seminal role in the avant-garde in France and Spain; his passion for polemics throughout his career; visual writing and the lighter side of his post-Cubist poetry; his work with film and the filmic novel; partisan politics; and, of course, his long poems, *Altazor* and *Temblor de cielo*. These are clearly distinguishable facets of a rich and varied life in art.

It will therefore be useful to begin this study with an examination of the spin-offs of change: the little magazines that Huidobro founded, and abandoned. It is in these ephemeral documents that the dynamics of a moment are most candidly revealed.

I
The Little Magazines

What kind of a journal do you prefer? Forty pages for 'other uses', or four pages worth reading?   1925

Huidobro's major moments are marked off by the little magazines he founded and directed: *Musa Joven* and *Azul* during his formative years in Chile; *Nord-Sud* and *Création* during the heyday of the European avant-garde; *Vital*, *Ombligo*, and *Total* during the hectic and eclectic 1930s; *Acción* and *Actual* at the start and finish of his political involvement in 1925 and 1944. In the pages of these publications are recorded his various campaigns for ascendancy, literary, political, and otherwise.

MUSA JOVEN *and* AZUL *(1912–1913)*

These early reviews are the least innovative, reflecting the Modernist sensibility of their time. Rubén Darío inspires both of them: *Musa Joven* dedicates an entire number to him in anticipation of his visit to Chile, and in *Azul* the homage is continued in the title. As for content, both are similar, given over to verses for delicate sensibilities, whispered conversations in abandoned parks, and concern for the perceived decline of art in a bourgeois society — the clichés of Modernism. Herein lies their interest and strength: sincerity and conviction. Huidobro and the writers of his generation lived these ideals; they took from Modernism what was fresh, rejecting or ridiculing what they judged *passé*. In the process they moved toward a new literary sensibility. The Darío that Huidobro exalts in 1912 is not the decadent of *Prosas profanas* but the innovator of *Cantos de vida y esperanza*, the poet of the future: 'The one whose poetry contains everything, from the nightingale's song to the lion's roar; the one who broke the chains of rhetoric, the iron links of metrics; the one who taught us how to fly by ourselves.'[1] This freedom so much admired in Darío did not really impact on Huidobro's work until much later, when he was in Paris.

NORD-SUD *(1917)*

With the outbreak of the First World War, European intellectual life was isolated in distant capitals; and in Paris, because of the

wartime control on paper, there were no literary reviews. Art
was not central to the war effort. In 1916, *SIC*, the brain-child
of Pierre Albert-Birot, was one of the first to obtain authoriza-
tion to be printed. Oriented toward Futurism, it combined
patriotism and the arts in an innovative typographic package.
The following year, Pierre Reverdy and his friends were moved
to start up a rival publication with a more disciplined approach
to the arts. Their goal was to unite the old and the new, tradition and the avant-garde. Hence the symbolic choice of title:
Nord-Sud, the name of the subway line connecting Montmartre
and Montparnasse. Huidobro arrived in Paris when all this was in
the planning stages and quickly became a part of the enterprise.
A consciousness of the historical moment, an aesthetic parting
of the ways, is revealed in the journal's lead article, laying
Symbolism to rest ('Quand le Symbolisme fut mort'). The culture hero for younger poets was no longer to be Verlaine or
Darío, but Apollinaire: 'Before, young poets sought out Verlaine
. . . It is not strange therefore that we should now decide the
moment has arrived to group ourselves around Apollinaire.
More than anyone else alive today, he has laid out new paths,
opened up new horizons. He merits our fervour, our allegiance.'[2]

This allegiance, and the aesthetic unity it implied, fell apart a
year later, following the death of Apollinaire. Poets everywhere
then scrambled to proclaim their own originality. What Huidobro
called Creationism was a part of this struggle.

CREACIÓN *(1921-1924)*

After *Nord-Sud*, Huidobro is involved with several other reviews
(*La Bataille littéraire*, *L'Action*, *La Vie des lettres*, *Le Cœur à
Barbe*, *Dada*), although identifying most closely with Paul
Dermée in *L'Esprit nouveau*. Outside of France, he is instru-
mental in getting Spanish Ultraism under way, as well as Agú,
an offshoot of Dada in Chile. Huidobro, in the early 1920s, saw
himself as something of a promoter of the new, a 'travelling
salesman' of the avant-garde, according to one critic.[3]

In the Spring of 1921, we find him putting together the first
issue of *Creación: Revista Internacional de Arte*, a Madrid-based
magazine whose stated purpose was to show the broad spread of
the avant-garde. There is a striking diversity in language and
kind: articles and poems in French, Spanish, English, Italian,
and German are complemented with music by Schoenberg and
illustrations of paintings and sculpture by Braque, Gleizes,
Gris, Lipchitz, and Picasso. A diversity whose underlying unity

is Cubism, a term then being extended to music and literature as well as the plastic arts. The opening manifesto, probably by Huidobro, is significantly left unsigned and stresses the epochal nature of the artistic moment:

> The period of destruction is over; now we are entering an era of creation. We call upon all constructors and we offer them our pages.
>
> It is necessary to demonstrate to people everywhere that we are involved in the greatest artistic renaissance that history has ever seen.
>
> It is necessary to demonstrate that this enormous break that we have made between yesterday and today had to occur and was pregnant with new life.
>
> This is the cycle of creators and of men whose hands are filled with seeds.
>
> There is no middle ground: Onward or under.

The language is typically militant. With new isms springing up all over Europe and the New World, with Breton working to consolidate the movement for France through the *Congrès de Paris*, Huidobro tries to claim a leading role for Creationism. This was not to pass. Cubism was already the preferred term and Huidobro, despite his efforts to bring together a Creationist group, was himself a rather divisive presence. In this first issue of *Creación*, for example, he inserts a haughty 'Respuesta', a response to an unasked question concerning his uniqueness which must surely have offended the other artists who shared these pages: 'To all those who do not know my work and are constantly asking what is the difference between me and other poets, I now respond: Other poets are instruments of nature and I make nature my instrument.'

As though to prove the principle, he inserts a poem of his own, 'Clocher', a French version of 'Campanario', originally published in *Poemas árticos* (1918):

> A chaque son des cloches
>   Un oiseau s'envole
> Oiseaux de métal
>   Qui meurent dans les ardoises
> OÙ DONC EST TOMBÉE LA PREMIÈRE CHANSON
> Tous les soirs
>   Ce feu de joie
> Le cœur palpite dans chaque feuille
> Et une étoile s'allume à chaque pas
>   Les yeux gardent quelque chose
>   Qui tremble dans ta voix

Là-haut dans la pointe du Zénith
Il y a une horloge qui se vide

(At each sound of the bell / A bird takes flight / Metallic birds / Who die out on the rooftiles / Where the first song has fallen / Every evening / This clamour / The heart throbs in each leaf / And a star lights up at every step / The eyes hide something that trembles in your voice / Up there at the Zenith / There is a clock emptying itself out)

A simple subject, the tolling of church bells at a certain hour, is the point of departure for an imagistic sequence that shifts back and forth between what can easily take place in reality and what can only take place in the imagination. This is what Huidobro refers to when he says that he makes nature his instrument. The procedure is simple, although the effect is subtle. Juxtaposition and synthesis. The linking element in this poem is the sound which is emitted by the bells and the birds who take flight. Both rise up and settle down over the roof-tops with a rhythmic regularity. What is the common denominator between birds and bells? None need be made explicit, for this kind of poetry, like Cubism, is based on joining the dissimilar. In fact, a glance at the Spanish original reveals that in this case the linking element is purely visual:

A cada son de la campana
         un pájaro volaba
Pájaros de ala inversa
         que mueren entre las tejas . . .

(At each sound of the bell / a bird takes flight / birds of inverted wing / who die out on the roof-tiles . . .)

The chimes of the bell are musical notes, birds of inverted wing when graphically annotated; in the French version there is a further synthesis: 'oiseaux de |métal'. Huidobro's writing here adheres pretty closely to the principles of Creationism as first expressed in *Horizon carré* (1917):

Create a poem taking the motifs from real life and transforming them in order to give them a new and independent existence.
No anecdotes nor description. The emotion should arise from the creative force.
Make a POEM like nature makes a tree.

At this time, he was seeking support for the cause with

conferences and lectures. For example, in December 1921, he is in Spain to speak at the Ateneo of Madrid. As Larrea remembers this event it was marked by opposition.[4] This is certainly the attitude which emerges in *Ultra*'s review of the lecture:

Vicente Huidobro spoke first about art in its three successive stages: reproductive art, inferior to the medium; art which adapts itself to the medium; and art which is superior to the medium, in other words that which corresponds to his Creationist modality.

For the most part, the essential elements of Huidobro's postulates are the patrimony of all new art since Apollinaire and Reverdy, right on up to the latest aesthetic experiments. On this point everyone seems to agree, and we cannot understand why Huidobro attributes to himself what is a general characteristic and a common aspiration.[5]

Sensitive to criticism, and failing to form an international movement with any real sense of cohesion, Huidobro falls back to a more tenable position in the second issue of the review, published now in France, and as *Création*. Even the subtitle, 'Revue d'Art', is less ambitious, no longer international. In fact, the whole issue is francophone (Morand, Roche, Radiguet, Tzara, Éluard, Cocteau, Beauduin, Ozenfant and Jeanneret). Again though, a bid is made for Creationism, with a manifesto of sorts, 'Époque de Création', this time signed by Huidobro. Its tone is all-embracing:

We must create.

Man no longer imitates, he invents, he adds to those things created in the womb of nature, other things created in his head: a poem, a painting, a statue, a steamship, an airplane.

We must create.

Such is the sign of our time.

The man of today has broken the shell of appearances and discovered what was within.

Poetry must not imitate the surface aspect of things but carry out the constructive laws that are their essence.

To invent, is to make two things parallel in space contiguous in time or vice versa, presenting through their conjunction something totally new . . .

In this way, Creationism is generalized; it is not touted as the exclusive patrimony of Huidobro but as a characteristic of the time. All modern artists are creators. And, as though to stress this concept, prominent space is given over to 'Intégrer', an essay by Ozenfant and Jeanneret [Le Corbusier] which distinguishes, in a terminology similar to that of Huidobro,[6] between the old and

the new, between copying and creating. Again, he includes only
one poem of his own, 'Ombre' (Shadow), another translation
from *Poemas árticos*:

> L'ombre est un morceau qui s'éloigne
> Vers d'autres plages.
>
> Dans ma mémoire un rossignol se plaint
>   Rossignol des batailles
>   Qui chante parmi les balles
>   Quand ne saignera-t-on plus la vie.
>   Même la lune blessée
>   A une seule aile
>   Le cœur a fait son nid
>   Au milieu du vide
> Cependant
>   Au bord du monde fleurissent les amandiers
>   Et le Printemps vient sur les hirondelles.

(The shadow is a fragment that goes away / Towards other beaches. / In
my memory a nightingale complains / Nightingale of battles / Who sings
amidst the bullets / When will life stop bleeding. / Even the wounded
moon / Has only one wing / The heart has made its nest / In the midst of
emptyness / Nevertheless / at the edge of the world the almond trees
blossom / And Spring flies in with the swallows.)

The poem, like 'Clocher', represents Creationism at its purest.
Even the typographical tricks of *Poemas árticos* are left behind.
Huidobro retains only the use of blank spaces to modulate the
reading, to assure its discontinuity, and to achieve the layered
effect of juxtaposition. As proclaimed in the manifesto, the
poem brings two dissimilar things together, creating in the
process something new. Here it is war and peace, with the
nightingale singing over the sound of the bullets; and the in-
exorable march of time, from the short days of winter to the
full blossom of spring. The final line brings it all together: 'Et
le Printemps vient sur les hirondelles.' Something impossible,
but easily understood in the context of the poem.

Huidobro, despite all his posturing over avant-garde principles
and practice was fundamentally a lyric poet. Both these poems,
which he selected to show his Creationism at its best, are lyric
in inspiration. The truth of the matter is that Creationism, as
such, was relatively short-lived. The review does not appear
again until 1924, and by then it retains only the name and not
the spirit or splendour of its former self. Of a reduced format, it

contains fewer contributions. Besides Huidobro, only Satie, Larrea, Tzara, and Crevel. The opening statement, 'Manifeste peut-être' (Manifesto Perhaps), is a tongue-in-cheek rehash of Creationist principles. It is variously interpreted. *Die Stijl*, for example, was enthusiastic and glossed its main points, while the critic for *Comœdia* was sardonic:

> This review, which has remained inactive for a long time, reappears with a manifesto by its founder, Vicente Huidobro, who tirelessly preaches the virtues of the creative force and considers that 'the greatest enemy of the poem is poesy'. Huidobro is just the opposite of a materialist, since he believes with the firmness of a nail that he drives into the head of his readers in the self-creation of the poem. Thus he imagines he can remake the world with the force of his lyric fancy.[7]

Creationism had run its course, and Huidobro knew it. The poster-like declaration on the back cover is perhaps the most succinct indicator of this recognition 'POETS ARE JUST AS (little) INDEPENDENT AS PAINTERS'. Creationism henceforth would live on only in the minds of its critics, and while Huidobro would be aroused on occasion to defend its uniqueness, even its lineage, he would not insist on it as an aesthetic standard for the time. The times were changing, as were his interests.

ACCIÓN *(1925)*

He was becoming interested in politics. In 1924 there was a flap in Paris over *Finis Britannia*; and, in 1925 he returned to Chile. What brought him back was politics, revolutionary politics, and the fantasy that he could remake, if not the world, his country.

On 23 January 1925 a reformist junta in Chile restores Arturo Alessandri to the presidency (only four months before another military junta had removed him from office). A few weeks later, Huidobro, after delivering an anti-Surrealist lecture at the Sorbonne, embarks for Chile.[8] When he arrives in April, the political situation is still turbulent. He quickly becomes involved. On 17 June he secures a clearance from the Chilean Patent Office to publish a daily newspaper under the title *Acción*. The first issue appears on 5 August, announcing itself in the mast-head as a 'Diario de Purificación Nacional', a Journal of National Purification. The purpose of *Acción* was purely political, although its rhetoric at first seemed like an echo of the early Creationist manifestos, heralding the dawn of a new era: 'The Chile of yesterday is dead or ought to be, today the new Chile begins to live.'

Huidobro saw himself as a Chilean Atatürk, rallying young people to save the nation in its hour of need:

A wave of fatigue and despair is passing over the country. It is said that no one believes that things can be changed. For this reason, we want to demonstrate that there is a group of young people ready to sacrifice their lives, if necessary, to create a new and greater Chile. A group of young Chileans, similar to the young Turks of Mustafa Kemal, intent on saving the country at any cost.

Acción was to be the voice of this group. In order to get the message across, Huidobro transfers to the newspaper format many of the techniques of the literary magazines. For example, the centre column of the whole front page is given over to a manifesto-like statement of purpose in large bold-face type:

Let this newspaper be the banner under which all the sensible men of the country can gather together.

We call on all young Chileans from Tacna to Punta Arenas, on all young people of enthusiasm, still uncontaminated by politics.

Let us unite our forces to purify the country, to burn what must be burned, to destroy what must be destroyed in order to create a new Chile that will be a surprise and example to the civilized world.

Let our hands be tireless at the hour of destruction so that they can be equally tireless at the hour of construction.

The man who as a poet wanted to be a creator now saw himself as a constructor. In fact, this was the term Angel Cruchaga would use several months later (*Acción*, 19 November 1925), to describe Huidobro as a tough-minded politico: 'An independent spirit that of Vicente Huidobro, a fighting spirit. Like the Cid, he could also claim "mi descanso es el pelear" (fighting, for me is relaxation). He has always fought for the right causes, be they aesthetic or social . . . In Vicente Huidobro we can point to the Constructor.' What had happened was that Huidobro had become a candidate for the Presidency. Not really a front runner, but not one to be ignored either.

In the third issue of *Acción*, he publishes a confidential report commissioned by the military and later suppressed because it was too sensitive. The unscrupulous activities of dozens of business men and public officials are detailed in the document: 'Gestores administrativos y políticos peligrosos: Informe reservado del Tribunal de Conciencia' (Dangerous

Lobbyists and Politicians: Classified Report of the Tribunal of Conscience). On the following day, 8 August, Huidobro is attacked by thugs and severely beaten on the doorstep of his home. Interestingly enough, among those who protested against this brutal act is Marmaduque Grove, a reform-minded Air Force offier who later came to power in 1932, in a short-lived military *coup* to set up a Socialist Republic. In his letter of protest to *La Nación* (11 August 1925), then Santiago's principal newspaper, he echoes the rhetoric of *Acción*, exalting Huidobro and the younger generation who want 'action' for a better Chile: 'a new era in which social justice will be a reality and in which Chile will be for Chileans'. It would seem that Grove was one of the 'Young Turks' backing Huidobro.

The attack seems to have spurred the poet–politician on, for *Acción* heightens the intensity of its campaign of accusations at the same time as it begins to outline a nationalist programme of social justice for the new Chile. Prominent among the many issues raised in the campaign is the perennial question of the ownership of the mines, prompted at this time by the attempt of a Chilean–British consortium, Anglo-Lautaro, to get an exclusive concession for the nitrate fields. Naturally, the author of *Finis Britannia* is against foreign involvement in the exploitation of Chile's natural resources.

Acción and its political campaign lasted only a few months; the last issue appears on 21 November 1925 on the eve of elections. Huidobro lost, thus putting an end to his brief career as a candidate for public office. His passion for national politics was not extinguished however. At least one more occasional publication appears in Santiago before he returns to Europe. On 22 April 1926, to denounce the US Ambassador's complicity with certain prominent Chileans regarding another perennial problem, the border question with Bolivia, Huidobro has posted on the walls of the capital, a broadside, 'Yo acuso' (I Accuse), pointing an accusing finger at those who were supposedly working against Chile's better interests.

In the summer of 1926, having failed in his nationalist bid to change Chile and its politics, Huidobro returns to Europe, to resume his literary activities, and to begin a serious study of Marxism, before eventually joining the Communist Party in the early 1930s.

'Vital/Ombligo' (1934–1935)

When Huidobro returns to Chile in 1933, he is a hard-liner. In an interview of the time he has this to say: 'As far as I am concerned, anybody under sixty who is not a Communist sympathizer is mediocre and out of touch with reality; and anybody under forty who is not already in the party is an idiot.'[9] In 1934, he founds another review, *Ombligo/וₒₚₗₗΛ*, a curious pastiche of eight pages. One half is printed from top to bottom, the other half from bottom to top. Like Siamese twins, only one survives. In January of 1935, the second number of *Vital* appears; a testy 'Revista de Higiene Social' (Review of Social Hygiene), it declares itself against cadavers, reptiles, rumour-mongers, venemous people, and microbes. It is really against Pablo Neruda, who is then doing his best to stir up animosity against Huidobro.

In the third number, the target is César Moro, a Peruvian Surrealist (whose friends reply in kind with a nasty pamphlet of their own: *Vicente Huidobro, o el obispo embotellado*). These literary pranks made little sense in a world being menaced by Fascism; and, with the outbreak of the Spanish Civil War, Huidobro puts an end to the frivolity. *Vital* and its sardonic campaign of 'social hygiene' is dropped to make way for *Total*, a grimly serious review with a mission.

TOTAL *(1936-1938)*

On 18 July 1936, Francisco Franco led his troops in rebellion against the Spanish Republic, thus beginning a civil war that was but a prelude to the Second World War. At about the same time a Popular Front government was beginning to emerge as a real possibility for Chile. *Total* was a response to the new situation, its dangers and opportunities. The announced purpose of the review was to make a 'contribution toward a new culture'. Its pages were dotted with slogans supporting the Republican cause and the new social order it then seemed possible to create. The review's opening manifesto, 'Total', affirms the need to create a new art for a new time, a time of populism and popular culture. The poet is now to be the voice of the people: 'A voice that is big and calm, strong and without vanity. The voice of a new civilization on the rise, the voice of mankind and not of classes. The poet's voice belongs to all men and not just to a certain clan. As a specialist, the poet's first specialty is to be human, totally human . . .' Huidobro, of course, saw himself in this new 'totalitarian' role. And sincerely so. During the 1930s his work had changed considerably as he reached out for a wider public. For the second issue of *Total*,[10] Huidobro prepares a long discursive essay, 'Nuestra barricada' (Our

Barricade), in which he attempts to reconcile his personal aesthetic position with the programmatic demands of social realism:

No true Marxist can deny that art has its own field of investigation and realization.

The problem of revolutionary art, of proletarian art, of the art of propaganda, has been poorly presented and we must remedy the errors of perspective and of substance that hamper a proper presentation.

Since the artist is one who is especially sensitive and intuitive it is quite logical that he should feel more strongly than others the problems of his time. And when these problems present themselves in ways so urgent and so vital as they do now, the poet will see himself obliged to abandon his purely aesthetic concerns, his experiments in the development of his art. He will have to leave his work in order to join his energies with those of his brothers who are fighting for the revolution on another front. Later, when the moment of battle is less urgent, when the proletarian order has triumphed, he can resume his task, which is cultural development, creating new forms and new meanings in order to broaden the spirit. And he will then return to his work enriched by the human contact in the common battle against darkness.

Huidobro believed this, for in 1937 he went off to Spain to join the troops of Lister in the defence of Madrid.[11] After returning to Chile, he brought out the second issue of *Total*, in July of 1938, to commemorate the second year of fighting in Spain. But in the interim everything had changed. Human conduct and political reality had an effect on his thinking, and while his goals were the same, his faith in their attainability had been severely shaken. The opening essay of *Total 2*, 'Panorama optimista' (Optimist Panorama), is anything but optimistic. Instead it is a gloomy account of the losing struggle to impose a new order on a bourgeois-oriented world. In spite of this, the literary quality of the journal was on the upswing with contributions by a new generation of writers in Chile (Braulio Arenas, Enrique Gómez), as well as Huidobro's European friends (Arp, Breton, Dali, Éluard, Larrea, Picasso). Two new literary projects were announced: a homage to Rosamel del Valle, and a special number dedicated to the short story. The failure of the Popular Front government in Chile, the defeat of the Republic in Spain, and the fall of France changed all this. *Total* does not reappear. In fact, Huidobro would not be moved to start up another journal until 1944, after the Second World War had begun to turn in favour of the Allies.

ACTUAL *(1944)*

This, the last of Huidobro's occasional publications, is a curious item. More political than literary, of minimal circulation, it seems to have been conceived as an intellectual calling-card. In October 1944, Huidobro arranges to return to France as a War Correspondent with the Allied troops. *Actual* (September 1944), reprints articles by Pedro Barros, Pierre Delisle, and Larrea, along with several items by Huidobro: 'Cartas al Tío Sam', 'América para la humanidad' (Letters to Uncle Sam, America for Humanity). An Americanist sentiment, a faith in the possibilities of the New World as a democratic and cultural saviour for war-torn Europe, is the common theme of these various writings. They show too the poet's willingness at this point in his career to recognize that art is the product of an entire culture and not of nations or individuals: 'Who today could parcel out the major advances of art and science to one country or another? Who would dare to isolate one link of the long chain of culture and say: This is mine, only mine and without essence or precedence before me. No, no one could pretend to do such a thing; in thought there is no single spontaneous source.'

On his way to Europe, he passes through Buenos Aires and Montevideo where he lectures on poetry and most especially on his own poetic practice. It is in the transcript of one of these talks that we have a most eloquent testimony of the poet's personal struggle to create, of Huidobro's repeated dissatisfaction with his own accomplishments, and of his constant urge to begin anew:

He [Huidobro] went on to talk about the doubts that plague all authentic poets. The difficult quest for the right imagery with which one forges the poem and the terrible time period of its elaboration. The poet's subsequent disinterest for the finished product and the disappointment that follows in the wake of what is left in the poem and what has been pruned out, what is actually said and what could have been said . . . and the doubts, turmoil and fear that precede the birth of a poem; the anguish of knowing that something always remains hidden in some obscure aspect of the expression, something that perhaps ought to be brought out.[12]

This discontent with the finished product, confessed to a handful of people in Montevideo in 1944, goes a long way now toward helping to understand Huidobro's many transformations, his constant need to renew himself, in poetry as well as real life.

The goals and purpose of poetry changed considerably over the three decades of Huidobro's ascendancy, moving from Modernism to the avant-garde, and eventually to a writing of social commitment. Huidobro participated in each of these major developments in various capacities: as poet, polemicist, politico, and impresario. The occasional publications he started up along the way are accurate, but necessarily pale reflectors marking off the circuit of his careers.

II
Modernism

I detest routine, cliché and rhetoric. I love whatever is original.   1914

In the 1920s, originality was defined by the European avant-garde. Before then, in the Hispanic world, the parameters of originality were those of Modernism. It was in Chile, during the heyday of this movement, that Huidobro chose the first of his careers, that of a poet. At the Colegio San Ignacio in Santiago he was schooled in metrics and versification with assigned compositions on noble and patriotic themes. *Ecos del alma* (Echoes of the Soul), echoing Campoamor (*Ayes del alma*), was published in 1911, when he was just eighteen, and contains some of these schoolboy exercises: dutiful sentiments regarding Christ, Columbus, Captain Prat, and the Virgin Mary. Huidobro never attributed any importance to this book. Nor should we; except perhaps to note a certain mastery of the techniques of rhyme and metre and an acceptance of conventional sentimentality. One poem, 'Una lágrima' (A Tear), ought to suffice as an example:

> Una tarde sentados en el parque
>   Hablábamos los dos,
> Hablábamos los dos cosas muy tristes
>   De un desgraciado amor.
> Rodó por tus mejillas una lágrima
>   Que a nuestros pies cayó;
> Volví a aquel mismo sitio al otro día
>   Temblando de dolor,
> Y vi maravillado que del suelo
>   Creciendo iba una flor.

(One afternoon seated in the park / We two talked, / We two talked of sad things / Of an unfortunate love. / A tear rolled down your cheek / And fell at our feet; / I went back to the same place the next day / Trembling with sorrow, / And I saw amazed that from the ground / Was growing a flower.)

Huidobro published *Ecos del alma* as a kind of tribute to his fiancée, Manuela Portales Bello, to whom it was dedicated ('A.M.P.B.'), and to whom the last lines were also addressed:

Como un ruiseñor alado
Va volando mi canción.
Dale un refugio sagrado,
Manuela en tu corazón.

(Like a winged nightingale / My song goes flying. / Give it a sacred refuge, /
Manuela, in your heart.)

They were married in 1912. And, soon afterwards, Huidobro
himself would recognize the limitations of this youthful book,
condemning it as 'too romantic, rhetorical and hollow'.[1]
Having decided to be a poet, he took his vocation seriously,
studying the writers who were proscribed by the Jesuits while
subscribing to the most advanced reviews of the time: *Mundial*,
Les Soirées de Paris, and *Vers et Prose*. In the pages of his own
magazines, *Musa Joven* and *Azul*, can be plotted at least one
stage of his evolution in 1912–13: from Bécquer to Darío. The
next stage is not apparent until the end of 1913, when two
books of his verses appear, almost simultaneously. One volume,
Canciones en la noche (Songs in the Night), picks up most of
the poems from *Musa Joven* (1912); while the other, *La gruta
del silencio* (The Grotto of Silence), contains those from *Azul*
(1913), plus many new compositions. Since the first volume
was delayed at the printer, it appeared after the second; this
circumstance prompted Huidobro to add the following explana-
tory note to *Canciones en la noche*: 'With the exception of a
few compositions, I don't have any great love for this book. I
publish it now as a sample of my evolution between that first
romantic book of mine, *Ecos del alma*, and *La gruta del silencio*,
a book that I do esteem and with which I am quite satisfied.'
The difference between the two books of 1913, although not
extraordinary, is significant. One is archly Modernist, and the
other makes a serious attempt to go beyond Modernism.

Since Huidobro's early poetry has been treated almost
exclusively by his critics as a kind of testing ground for Creationism, it has yet to be studied intrinsically. It should be. This
work is interesting in itself, for it shows us a creative writer
struggling with and within the aesthetic conventions of his time
and place.

Canciones en la noche, the earlier book of 1913, is the most
conventional: a showy array of different strophic and metric
combinations, an exotic lexicon, and a tortured syntax certify
the author as an 'artífice de la lengua', an artisan of the language.
Even the subject-matter is self-referentially artistic, as in the

following sonnet — decasyllabic, of course — 'Como un Cirano de Bergerac' (Like a Cyrano de Bergerac):

> Salió a su labio tierna sonrisa
> Mezcla de alegre con algo trágico,
> Una sonrisa de Monna Lisa,
> La que soñara Leonardo el mágico.
>
> Me quedé solo, sumido en honda,
> Profunda angustia. Yo meditaba,
> Mirando a aquella nueva Gioconda
> Que con su risa me apuñalaba.
>
> Me fui temblando, transido el pecho
> De un dolor fiero llegué a mi lecho;
> Dormí tranquilo; sin alma ya,
>
> Tal como el niño duerme en su cuna,
> Y soñé un raro viaje a la luna
> Como Cirano de Bergerac.

(A tender smile came to her lips / A mixture of joy with something tragic, / A smile of Monna Lisa, / The one that the magic Leonardo dreamed. / I was left alone, inmersed in deep, / Profound anguish. / I was meditating, / looking at that new Gioconda / Who was piercing me with her smile. / I left trembling, my chest run through / By a sharp pain I reached my bed; / I slept tranquilly; soulless now, / Just like a child sleeps in its bed / And I dreamt of a strange trip to the moon / Like Cyrano de Bergerac.)

The speaker of the poem is inserted in a ready-made artistic environment.

In some compositions this is carried to an extreme. The procedure in 'Ensoñación' (Dream), for example is accumulative:

> Entre las notas del triste piano,
> Entre las notas sueña Chopin,
> Y arranca arpegios la blanca mano
> Que el alma lleva hacia un Edén.
>
> En la floresta, bajo las flores,
> Byron modula su arpa genial;
> Musset solloza muertos amores
> Entre las rosas de albo rosal . . .

(Among the notes of the sad piano, / Among the notes Chopin is dreaming, / And the white hand draws out arpeggios / That the soul carries off to an Eden. // In the grove, amidst the flowers, / Byron tunes his genial harp / Musset sobs for dead loves / Among the roses of the white rose-bush.)

The naming of the famous goes on like this for half a dozen stanzas. In this and most of the other poems in *Canciones en la noche*, Huidobro seems to have been paying lip-service to one of the dominant aspects of Modernism, equating poetry with the sonorous and the ornamental. That he was dissatisfied with this kind of artistic writing becomes evident in a few compositions, where he can be found making an attempt at something new and different: in some he experiments with form, trying out various graphic presentations; and in others he is concerned with theme, ridiculing the commonplace. Hence, the disparate nature of the book, containing conventionally Modernist poems alongside others which are either anti-Modernist or ultra-Modernist.

While parody is perhaps only implicit and functions on the level of allusion in 'Como un Cirano de Bergerac', where the enamoured speaker is likened to Rostand's caricature of the Romantic lover, it is made quite explicit and direct in 'La obsesión de los dientes' (The Obsession with Teeth). By the turn of the century Modernism had transformed the pearly teeth of Renaissance poetry into keyboards of harmonic smiles. Huidobro takes this conventional topic, the hyperbolic description of the visage of the beloved, and, midway through the poem, combines it with another, the forget-me-not, for a comical result:

> Tenía los dientes tan finos y delgados
> Como las hojas de una margarita,
> Y al reir con los labios despegados,
> Al abrir su boquita,
> Me venía el deseo importuno,
> Sentía la obsesión malvada
> De arrancárselos uno a uno
> Jugando al 'me quiere, mucho, poquito, nada'.

(Her teeth were as fine and as slender / As the petals of a daisy, / And upon laughing with her lips parted, / On opening her mouth, / I was taken by a strange desire, / I felt the wicked obsession / Of plucking them out one by one / Playing 'she loves me, a lot, a little, not at all'.)

An unusual combination of end-rhyme and free verse is used here to modulate the line, to hold the reader in suspense, thus enhancing the shocking effect of the finale.

At the same time as he began to deride certain aspects of the system, he was hard at work perfecting others. Most conspicuous in this sense are the 'Japonerías de estío' (Japaneseries of Summer), a series of four graphic compositions. The first one, 'Triángulo armónico' (Harmonic Triangle), originally appeared in *Musa Joven* in October of 1912, around the time of Darío's proposed visit to Chile. It would seem that Huidobro was trying to impress the master, giving a new form to the Modernist fascination with things oriental:

Thesa

La   bella

Gentil   princesa

Es una blanca estrella

Es   una   estrella   japonesa.

Thesa es la más divina flor de Kioto

Y cuando pasa triunfante en su palanquín

Parece un tierno lirio, parece un pálido loto

Arrancado una tarde de estío del imperial jardín.

Todos la adoran como a una diosa, todos hasta el Mikado

Pero ella cruza por entre todos indiferente

De nadie se sabe que haya su amor logrado

Y siempre está risueña, está sonriente.

Es   una   Ofelia   japonesa

Que a las flores amante

Loca y traviesa

Triunfante

Beşa.

(Thesa / The beautiful / Genteel princess / Is a white star / She is a Japanese star. / Thesa is the most divine flower of Kioto / And when she passes triumphantly in her palanquin / She looks like a tender lily, she looks like

This poem's unusual graphic presentation served as the inspirational basis for other geometric variations on the triangle motif; and, ultimately, for a full-fledged *calligramme*, a poem whose lettristic arrangement is a visual extension of its content, 'La capilla aldeana' (The Country Chapel) (*see over, p. 26*).

Rhyme is retained in these graphic poems, and indeed a new discipline is imposed on the poetic line, shortening or lengthening it to create the appropriate visual effect. In the chapel poem there is evident a certain reciprocity in the creative process as some of the imagery seems to be a result of the visualization of the scene:

> La capilla está ante la paz de la montaña
> Como una limosnera está ante una capilla.
> ....
> La capilla es como una vieja acurrucada.

Years later, in Paris, and in another career capacity, Huidobro would further elaborate this visual writing, eventually adding colour to create what he called a *poème-peint*, a painted poem. In Chile though, these are his only experiments of this nature. Difficulties with the typesetters seem to have been a dissuasive factor. Huidobro implied as much in a statement of 1914, in *Pasando y pasando*, when he was again trying to call attention to the difference between his early books:

> *La gruta del silencio* should have appeared after *Canciones en la noche* which contains verses of 1912 that have nothing to do with my current way of writing, except for a few.
> *La gruta del silencio* came out first because of problems with the printing [of *Canciones en la noche*].

Huidobro was evidently satisfied, for the moment at least, with one of these books. *La gruta del silencio*, his second book of 1913, contains an interesting outcome of the previous experiments with visual presentation. Not a calligrammatic writing, whose ultimate purpose is pictorial, but an attempt to modulate

---

a pallid lotus flower / Plucked one summer afternoon from the imperial garden. // Everyone adores her like a goddess, everyone even the Mikado / But she walks among everyone with indifference / No one is known to have ever won her love / And she is always happy, always smiling. / She is a Japanese Ophelia / Lover of the flowers / That wild and daring / Triumphantly / She kisses.)

```
                    A v e
                    canta
                    suave
          que tu canto encanta
          sobre el campo inerte
                    sones
                    vierte
                    y ora-
                    ciones
                    llora.
                    Desde
                  la cruz santa
          el triunfo del sol canta
        y bajo el palio azul del cielo
      deshoja tus cantares sobre el suelo.
```

Une tus notas a las de la campana
Que ya se despereza ebria de mañana
Evangelizando la gran quietud aldeana.
Es un amanecer en que una bondad brilla
La capilla está ante la paz de la montaña
Como una limosnera está ante una capilla.
Se esparce en el paisaje el aire de una extraña
Santidad, algo bíblico, algo de piel de oveja
Algo como un rocío lleno de bendiciones
Cual si el campo rezara una idílica queja
Llena de sus caricias y de sus emociones.
La capilla es como una viejita acurrucada
Y al pie de la montaña parece un cuento de hada.
Junto a ella como una bandada de mendigos
Se agrupan y se acercan unos cuantos castaños
Que se asoman curiosos por todos los postigos
Con la malevolencia de los viejos huraños.
Y en el cuadrito lleno de ambiente y de frescura
En el paisaje alegre con castidad de lino
Pinta un brochazo negro la sotana del cura.
Cuando ya la tarde alarga su sombra sobre el camino
Parece que se metiera al fondo de la capilla
Y la luz de la gran lámpara con su brillo mortecino
Pinta en la muralla blanca, como una raya amarilla.
Las tablas viejas roncan, crujen, cuando entra el viento oliendo a rosas
Rezonga triste en un murmullo el eco santo del rosario
La oscuridad va amalgamando y confundiendo así las cosas
Y vuela un "Angelus" lloroso con lentitud del campanario.

(Bird / sing / softly / for your song charms / over the still countryside / it
pours out sounds / and weeps / pra- / yers. / From / the holy cross / sing to
the triumph of the sun / and under the blue mantel of the sky / let your
songs fall one by one to the ground. / Unite your notes to those of the

the reading of the text through its distribution on the printed page. In this experimental vein, 'El dolor del paisaje nocturno' (Pain at the Night Scene) relies on a kind of strophic reduction. Five stanzas, of progressively shorter length, serve to concentrate the poem's closure, a closure that the reader is made to anticipate at first glance, before even beginning the lexical reading of the text:

> Voy gozando el paisaje por los blancos caminos,
> El dolor de Belleza es una pena lejana . . .
> El campo está dormido con una paz de anciana,
> Y la luna se asoma entre la hilera de pinos
> Como una enferma tras los hierros de una ventana.
>
> En el suelo escarchado por la luz de la luna
> Se retuercen las sombras de las ramas chuecas;
> Como una idea negra se esconde la laguna
> Y en la cumbre de un cerro una fogata hace muecas.
>
> Los perros viejos raspan con roncos aullidos,
> Una lechuza vuela, envuelta en sus chillidos,
> Del campanario blanco a los pinos dormidos.
>
> Hieren la noche ruidos de reglamento atávico:
> De las ranas el frío canto monosilábico.
>
> Y luego silban rudo los sapos en agudo.

bell / That is just stretching itself awake drunk with morning / Evangelizing the hamlet's grand repose. / It is a morning radiant with kindness / The chapel is outlined against the stillness of the mountain / like an almswoman in front of a chapel. / There is sprinkled throughout the landscape the air of a strange / Sanctity, something biblical, something of lambswool / Something like a dew laced with blessings / As though the countryside were praying an idyllic lament / Containing caresses and emotions. / The chapel is like an old woman hunched over / At the foot of the mountain it seems out of a fairy tale. / Next to it like a bunch of beggars / Grouped and huddled together are some chestnut trees / That peer out curiously through all the arches / With the malevolence of the aged scurrying away. / And in the little picture filled with freshness and charm / In the scene happy with the chasteness of linen / The priest's cassock paints a black brushstroke. / When the afternoon stretches its shadow over the road / It seems as though it were going into the chapel / And the light of the chandelier with its dying brightness / Paints on the white walls, like a yellow streak. / The old boards creak, groan, when the wind comes in smelling of roses / The saintly echo of the rosary grumbles sadly in a low murmur / The darkness goes on amalgamating and blending things together / And a sad *Angelus* floats out with the lento of the belltower.)

(I go along the white roads enjoying the countryside, / The pain of Beauty is a distant pain . . . / The country is asleep with the peace of an old woman, / And the moon makes its appearance among the rows of pine trees / like someone infirm behind the bars of a window. // On the ground frosted by the moonlight / The shadows of the branches are twisted; / The lake is hidden like a dark idea / And on the top of a hill a fire makes faces. / The old dogs grate with their hoarse howling. / An owl takes flight, wrapped in its cries, / From the white bell-tower to the sleeping pines. // Noises of an atavistic order pierce the night: / From the frogs a cold monosyllabic song. // And then the toads' rough whistling on a sharp note.)

The final impact of the strophic progression is enhanced by other, more traditional rhetorical devices: the alternate rhyme at the outset becoming monorhyme toward the end, where the alexandrine, a bi-membered verse, is split so that internal rhyme can stress even further the poem's unusual closing: 'Y luego silban r*udo* — los sapos en ag*udo*'. Rhyme and rhythm organized in this showy way have a predictable effect, forcing the reader to register with a greater intensity what is being so heavily stressed. Huidobro is drawing attention to the fact that Modernist poetry is not normally peopled with frogs and toads, for upon rereading the poem, as the special effects prompt us to, it is quite apparent what the poet was up to. He has taken a traditional Modernist topic, the nocturne, and rather than ridicule it burlesquely, as in the poem about teeth, he has given it a more realistic treatment, chiefly by shifting around the levels of discourse. Although the poem opens in a typical turn-of-the-century fashion, with a lyric reverie (in alexandrines), the predictable is dropped after just two lines: 'Voy gozando el paisaje por los blancos caminos, / el dolor de Belleza es una pena lejana . . .'. The ellipsis at line's end is a way of drawing attention to the fact that what is being cut short is the predictable cliché: a poet's pensive quest for truth and Beauty (with a large 'B') along life's byroads. Accordingly, it is in the next lines that another sort of discourse comes into play. The tone of the poem changes completely: the lyric 'I' is suppressed and there begins a succession of rather uncommon, indeed bizarre images:

> El campo está dormido con una paz de anciana,
> Y la luna se asoma entre la hilera de pinos
> Como una enferma tras los hierros de una ventana.

A simile such as this (of the moon rising amidst the pine trees like a pallid recluse at the bars of a hospital window) has little precedent in the Modernist writing of the time, except perhaps for Herrera y Reissig. More images of this type, based on the most extraordinary associations, continue to accumulate, with a result that is not the usual animistic landscape of turn-of-the-century poetry, where the pensive artist is enraptured by the subtle correspondences of nature; this is rather a landscape shot through by reality: an eerie night scene with dogs barking on the horizon, an owl shrieking in the distance, and toads and frogs croaking near at hand. The purpose of the poem is not to communicate to us the poet's special sensitivity, nor any conventional notion of beauty, but rather to shock our sensibility, presenting us with something unexpected.

The unexpected was original, and this apparently is what Huidobro was after. In fact, one measure of his success is to be found in the negative reaction to *La gruta del silencio*. The Chilean press of the time contains article after article dealing with the unorthodox aspects of this book (Juan Rojas Segovia, 'Al margen de *La gruta del silencio*'; Ronquillo, 'Un volumen decadente'; Ramón Cabezas, '*La gruta del silencio*'; E.M., 'A propósito de una estrofa decadente'; Nadir, '*La gruta del silencio*'). All this attention, mostly negative, must have pleased the young author very much, for the articles are neatly cut out and pasted in a scrapbook. One poem in particular, 'La llanura de noche' (The Flatlands at Night), seems to have drawn the most fire. It began thus:

> En el estanque azogado
> Que está de estrellas florido,
> Una rana masca neuces
> Y un sapito raspa vidrios.

(In the tinned pool / That is flowered with stars, / A frog chews nuts / And a toad grinds glass.)

What most disturbed the critics of course, besides the unseemly presence of frogs and toads, was the fact that instead of having them croak or hiss, Huidobro gives an idea of the noises they produce; and not by naming them with the appropriate verb, as in 'El dolor del paisaje nocturno', but by describing what they supposedly sound like: the chewing of nuts and the scratching of glass. This was simply too much. One critic had this to say:

Decadentism makes those who practice it pass from sense to nonsense. Now we are in the middle of the Grotto. In the most tenebrous part. Everything reeks of humidity and one can even sense the ripples on a nearby lake. The poet then says: 'En el estanque azogado / que está de estrellas florido, / una rana masca nueces / y un sapito raspa vidrios.'

A frog chewing nuts has about the same effect on us as an oyster picking its teeth. If we weren't in the Grotto of Silence we would laugh out loud.[2]

Years later, in *Manifestes* (1925), Huidobro would point out how useful this sort of negative criticism was to his development, helping him to identify what was new in his work:

What most convinced me about my theories was the violent criticism, the burlesque commentaries on my poems, most especially those of *La gruta del silencio*, published in 1913. All the critics had a nervous crisis, without even knowing why, over the verses that pleased me the most.

No one will ever guess just how much this insignificant circumstance made me think. Unintentionally, these critics helped me a lot in my work by cutting out with a sharp scissor verses and images such as these: 'Dans mon cerveau il y a quelqu'un qui vient de loin' (In my head there is someone who comes from afar); 'Les heures qui tombent en silence comme des gouttes d'eau sur une vitre' (The hours that fall silently like drops of water on a window-pane); 'La chambre s'est endormie dans le miroir' (The room went to sleep in the mirror); 'L'étang étamé' (The tinned pool).

At the time, in 1914, in an essay prepared especially for *Pasando y pasando*, and rather quaintly titled 'El arte del sugeri-miento' (The Art of Suggestion), the young poet justified his obsessive pursuit of new imagery in this assertive way:

Let's put behind us once and for all what is old. Down with clichés.

Let there be no more humble ladies in poetry who hide like violets in the grass. Let there be no more careless butterflies fluttering toward the flame.

My God! When will it stop?

That if a soul is mentioned, it should not be *pure and white*. Anything but.

That if there is a mountain, it should not be a high and mighty peak. It is preferable that it be a mountain that chats with the sun or tries to deflower the moon. Anything but high and mighty . . .

Unless something new is to be said, there is no right to waste the reader's time.

In the more daring poems of *La gruta del silencio* Huidobro put these ideas to work and managed to say something new and unusual through a process of literalization, by taking a standard scene and describing it realistically: writing down what is actually seen and heard, rather than what literary tradition calls for. This is the principle at work in 'El dolor del paisaje nocturno', where the night is not the silent moment of meditation, permitting a sensitive soul to perceive nature's hidden harmonies, but a cacophonous assault on the ears by unseen dogs, owls, frogs, and toads. Another step along this process of literalization would take Huidobro completely beyond realism, moving him toward the unreal, the fantastic: from a frog chewing nuts to the deflowering of the moon, the mental distance for a poet is minimal.

A striking example of the new expressive possibilities such literalization affords is 'Tríptico galante de jarrón de Sèvres' (Gallant Triptych on a Sèvres vase), a three-part poem in *La gruta del silencio* based on a favourite device of literary Modernism: the word-picture. Frequently, the Modernist poet would describe an art object, trying to imitate in words what the plastic artist had done with form and colour. For this seemingly routine exercise in artistic synthesis, Huidobro followed the fashion, choosing a painted porcelain vase and proceeding to describe the gallant scenes it portrays. At first, the text alludes to its supposed literary models, Verlaine and Darío, even alternating French and Spanish in an ornamental way:

> Un carnaval veneciano,
> Con algo de 'Fêtes Galantes',
> Con algo muy verleniano,
> Avec plusieurs des amantes.
> Una góndola un cisne mitológico miente . . .

(A Venetian carnival, / With something of 'Fêtes Galantes', / With something very Verlainian, with lots of lovers. / A gondola made to look like a mythological swan . . .

The static tableau however becomes strangely animated as the poet goes on to describe not just what is painted on the vase, but what can be imagined to be there if the scene were interpreted literally:

> Resbala por encima del barco que navega
> Una paloma blanca que mancha el horizonte . . .
>
> En los canales anchos donde la luna llueve
> El barco se desliza cual patinando en nieve,
> Se escapan de su fondo chanzonetas amargas
> Y va estelando el agua con dos ojeras largas.

(There slides over the boat that is sailing / A white dove that stains the horizon . . . // In the wide canals where the moon rains / The boat glides along as though skating on snow, / Distressing chansons escape from below / And it makes a wake in the water with two extended eye-cups [sails].)

In this way, a hackneyed Modernist theme is raised to a new expressive level. Again the process is one of literalization: the vase painting of a gallant scene is taken for reality and described in a way that makes it seem real, for a moment at least, in the reader's imagination. The result is similar to that of 'La llanura de noche', which so upset the critics. In fact, at poem's end, Huidobro's 'tinned' lake makes a reappearance while the scythe-shaped new moon cuts its way through the sky:

> El lago azogado de cisnes se nieva,
> El aire se inflama de viejas querellas,
> Y pasa la guadaña de la luna nueva,
> Pasa rasgando nubes y segando estrellas.

(The tinned lake is snowed over with swans, / The air lights up with old complaints, / And the scythe of the new moon, / Passes by scratching clouds and reaping stars.)

The best poems of *La gruta del silencio* are informed by this same ultra-Modernist sensibility and show the young poet's extraordinary imaginative and expressive capacities hamstrung by a jaded thematic repertory. Huidobro was still searching for something different. His reaction to Futurism was conditioned by Darío, and to Cubism by Apollinaire. In fact, it was in *Les Soirées de Paris* (to which Huidobro was a subscriber), that he may have come across the notion about the artist no longer being a slave to Nature. In the very first issue (February 1912), there is an essay by Apollinaire ('Du Sujet dans la peinture moderne'), in which it is stated: 'Painters, although they still observe nature, need no longer copy from it.' Not long after-wards, Huidobro reformulates the principle in a belligerent address to the Ateneo of Santiago, *Non serviam*:

We have accepted without much reflection the notion that there can be no other realities except those which are all around us, and it never occurred to us that we too could create new realities in a world of our own making, in a world that would need its own flora and fauna. A flora and fauna that only the poet can create, using that special power that Mother Nature gave to him and him alone.

Non serviam. I don't have to be your slave, Mother Nature; I shall be your master . . .

I'll have my own trees that won't be like yours; I'll have my own mountains. I'll have my rivers and seas, I'll have my sky and my stars.

And you won't be able to say to me: 'This tree is not very good, I don't like that sky; mine are better.'

I would reply that my skies are of my own making and not yours, and that there is no reason at all why they have to look alike.

The echo of Apollinaire is apparent. The Apollinaire of *Meditations Esthétiques* (1913), who justified the Cubist painters' alteration of reality by stressing the need for all artists to free themselves from their enslavement to nature:

Far too many artists still revere plants, stones, the sea and people.

One becomes accustomed to the enslavement of the marvellous. And servitude ends up creating its own satisfactions.

We give the workers free rein and it turns out that gardeners are less awed by nature than artists.

It is time that we became the masters.

Such theoretical similarities notwithstanding, what is interesting is Huidobro's development, and the fact that after *La gruta del silencio* his poetry moved in several new directions, culminating in 1916 with two dissimilar books, *Adán* (Adam) and *El espejo de agua* (The Mirror of Water). The first is a free-verse meditation typical of later Modernism; the second is a more concentrated kind of writing which brought him close to the European avant-garde.

Huidobro's transition from 1913 to 1916 has not been an easy one for scholars to explain, principally because he brought out no books of poetry in the interim. Searching through the periodical literature of the time, I have turned up just one published poem: 'Vaguedad subconsciente' (Subconscious Vagary), from 1915. Huidobro evidently had not given up writing poetry during these years, for on several occasions he announced new collections, variously titled *El canto imperceptible* and *Los espejos sonámbulos* (The Imperceptible Song, The Sonambulant Mirrors). Neither was ever published.

Among his papers there is a draft of what was to have been a table of contents for *El canto imperceptible*. Of the twenty-six poems listed there, three were published: 'Refinamiento espiritual' (Spiritual Refinement) and 'El paisaje sencillo' (Simple Landscape), surfaced in the *Selva lírica* anthology, when it finally appeared in 1917 (and are now included in the Hugo Montes edition of the *Obras completas*); the third is 'Vaguedad subconsciente', found in the July 1915 issue of *Ideales*, and is

prefaced with some unusual observations, probably supplied by
Huidobro himself:

Vicente Huidobro is not, as one might think, a Modernist; what he is, is
a 'rare' poet, thoroughly original . . .
His deep and intense feeling pushes him, in his conceptualizations, to an
absolute abandonment of form . . .
This poet manages to produce just an emotion, quite free of literary
artifice, or, as he is wont to say, to give just the pure sensation.

The poem that follows, 'Vaguedad subconsciente', was then
indicated to be from his work in progress, *El canto imperceptible*:

Pienso en las caras amadas que se han muerto,
Caras que mis ojos no verán ya nunca . . .
¿Quién entra por las puertas que se abren solas?
¿Quién hace crugir los muebles y cambia las posturas?

Amigos: contadme todas vuestras quimeras muertas,
decidme de las tardes que llevan al silencio,
habladme de las frentes que llegan más allá;
del fondo del espejo que es Clepsidra del Tiempo . . .
Yo pensaré en los versos que no haré jamás.

Vuestros brazos huelen a mujeres desnudas,
tenéis en los ojos el paganismo heleno,
vuestro cansancio duerme en las ojeras lívidas,
y lleváis en los labios un recuerdo obsceno.

Amigos: ¿Nunca en la noche habéis sentido
al ser que quiere tomar vida
y se desliza azorado como un niño perdido?
Yo amo mucho a los hijos que no he tenido . . .
¿Por qué pasé el umbral que trae a la desdicha?

Tengo una vaga obsesión subconsciente,
me siento entrar en los Misterios de repente
el Silencio se puebla de una voz insonora
el instante se duerme en el espejo
que se hace camino para llevarme lejos
y me siento nadando en una gran luz incolora.

Yo buscaré las sombras para hablar conmigo
y el Silencio se cuajará de caras olvidadas . . .
Oh, cuántos ojos muertos mirarán
el dolor de mis sauces en el alma!

Más allá de la vida, más allá del abismo
se besan los poetas muertos y los que no han nacido.
Poetas: adorad complacientes al Misterio . . .
¿Quién entra por las puertas que abre el viento?

(I think about the loved faces of those who have died, / faces that my eyes shall never seen again . . . / Who comes in through the doors that open by themselves? / Who makes the furniture creak and changes its position? // Friends: tell me all your death chimeras, / speak to me of afternoons that lead on to silence, / talk to me of visages that reach the beyond; / from the bottom of the mirror that is a Clepsydra of Time . . . / I will think of the verses that I will never make. // Your arms smell like nude women, / you have in your eyes a Hellene paganism, / your weariness sleeps in your livid cupped eyes, / and you carry on your lips an obscene remembrance. // Friends: Have you ever felt in the night / the being who wants to come to life / and who slips away frightened like a lost child? / I love the children I never had . . . / Why have I passed the threshold that leads to misfortune? // I have a vague subconscious obsession, / I feel myself passing into Mysteries quite suddenly / the silence is peopled by a voice without sound / the instant goes to sleep in the mirror / that becomes a road to carry me far away / and I feel myself swimming in a big colourless light. // I will search for shadows to talk with me / and the Silence will take the form of forgotten faces . . . / Oh, how many dead eyes will look upon / the pain of willow trees in my soul! // Beyond life, beyond the abyss, / the dead poets and those not yet born embrace. / Poets: adore complacently the Mysterious . . . / Who comes in through the doors that are opened by the wind?)

This is certainly a different type of writing from that of *La gruta del silencio*. What is most striking is not any so-called 'absolute abandonment of form', but rather a new form of organization based on abrupt transitions and unanswered rhetorical questions. The poem reads like an early attempt at oneiric writing, where the unknown is made to seem pregnant with meaning.

The system of discontinuous discourse around which this poem is organized derives directly from the ideas set forth in 'El arte del sugerimiento', a theoretical essay of 1914. Then, to illustrate what he meant by art based on suggestion, he outlined the following principles of composition:

The art of suggestion is very helpful for concision, since it can give an ondulation to the phrase, grace and precision, along with certain pleasing and unexpected turns.

Suggestion eliminates the need for linking elements between one idea and another, links which are really unnecessary, since the reader instinctively supplies what is missing with his imagination (. . .).

For this reason, the perception of this poetry, vague and remote, poetry that we could term 'of the horizon', the perception of this poetry that drifts by, that is ethereal, that moves on, is in direct relation to the reader's sensibility.

Perhaps so, but these principles of composition and the concomitant abstrusity of 'Vaguedad subconsciente' were not well received in Chile at the time. Thus, when Huidobro was interviewed in *Ideales* a few months later (October 1915), he was treated with mocking irreverence:

Externally, Huidobro is like any other mortal we come across in our prosaic march from life to death. He is also a regular at the aristocratic Café Olimpia, where he can usually be seen taking discreet cognacs or orangeades, as the occasion demands. There in the presence of select geniuses, he talks of art . . .

The transcendental affirmations, the subtle and complex paradoxes, the light and graceful irony, the deep meditations, all this has its natural place in a select assembly of intellectuals who there gather to examine the most ardent aesthetic problems to the vibrant sounds of a tango . . .

Huidobro detests with a passion all that is old. But don't get the idea that he detests what is old because he finds fault with it; rather he detests it for a much simpler reason, because it is old . . .

Huidobro is a poet, or at least he takes himself for one. In any case, this fellow actually believes that the day is not far off when Science will move Poetry out of the realm of sentiment. From the laboratories of Science is to come the formula that changes Art for all time. Such nonsense shows that Huidobro is neither a poet nor a scientist . . .

That Huidobro was looking for a magic formula is not surprising; and that he should hope to find it in science might seem quaint today, but really shows the extent of his awareness then that the Modernist system was something of an anachronism. That he did not yet possess the formula, but was getting closer to its realization, is evident in the poems he turned over to *Selva lírica*. In 'Refinamiento espiritual', also announced for *El canto imperceptible*, he is working with what was later to become a procedure of avant-garde writing, chaotic enumeration, suppressing the linking elements of discourse:

> El ruido más sutil, el roce más prudente:
> calofrío en el musgo, figura que resbala,
> la sombra que se escurre, el ala más lejana
> lo que nadie adivina, lo que nadie presiente
> en mi espíritu toma vibración de campanas.

(The most subtle noise, the most prudent touch: / trembling in the moss, a figure that slips by, / the shadow that hurries on, the farthest wing, / what no one can divine, what no one can feel beforehand / in my spirit takes on the vibration of bells.)

Huidobro was evidently on to something. But he was still not able to give it adequate form and substance. Part of the problem is clear in the verses above: he had not yet abandoned the outmoded role model of the poet as *voyant*. Although he did abandon the projected edition of *El canto imperceptible*, reducing the book to just one of its parts, *Les espejos sonámbulos* (The Somnambulent Mirrors), which was announced as a separate item in *Adán* (1916).

A few of the poems that were to have made up this volume have been conserved in manuscript form ('Mi espejo', 'Caridad de espejo', 'Ocaso en el espejo' — My Mirror, The Mirror's Gift, Sunset in the Mirror). None, to my knowledge, was ever published. They are all rather long and show a certain laboured mirror imagery, of the sort already seen in 'Vaguedad subconsciente', where the mirror was abstracted into 'Clepsidra del Tiempo', water-clock of time. The closing strophes from 'Ocaso en el espejo' should suffice as an example:

> En el jardin y en el espejo
> Caen las hojas de los árboles
> En el jardín y en el espejo
> Se van las horas por la tarde
>
> El jardín se sabe duplicado
> Por el divino mago
> Y aumenta sus encantos
>
> Por el espejo y por el Ocaso
> Ha cruzado un párajo
>
> Y este mago cristal
> Se me hace un arroyuelo
> Y se alarga indefinidamente
> Para dar a mis pies atracciones de sendero
>
> En el espejo acuoso muriendo va la tarde
> En una despedida interminable

(In the garden and in the mirror / The leaves fall from the trees / In the garden and in the mirror / The afternoon hours drift away // The garden knows it is being duplicated / By the divine magician / And it augments its enchantments // In the mirror and in the Sunset / A bird has crossed //

And this magic crystal / Seems to me like a stream / And it gets indefinitely longer / Giving my feet the temptation of a path // In the watery mirror the afternoon goes on dying / In an interminable goodbye)

Huidobro was not satisfied with these verses and he withheld them from publication. While *Los espejos sonámbulos* did not become *El espejo de agua*, much of the mirror imagery was carried over from one project to the other, as is evident in the piece that gave its title to the volume:

> Mi espejo, corriente por las noches,
> Se hace arroyo y se aleja de mi cuarto.
>
> Mi espejo, más profundo que el orbe
> Donde todos los cisnes se ahogaron.
>
> Es un estanque verde en la muralla
> Y en medio duerme tu desnudez anclada.

(My mirror, fluid at night / Becomes a stream and leaves my room. / My mirror, deeper than the orb / Where all the swans are drowned. / It is a green tank on the wall / And in the middle sleeps your nudity anchored.)

These verses from 'El espejo de agua', more concise and less sentimental, show the process of stylization at work. The twice-repeated noun subject ('mi espejo'), conspicuously absent from the third strophe, makes the idea gain in power, for the verb which is in its place obliges us to supply a subject: '[mi espejo] *es* un estanque', The image is stronger because it is of our making. As Huidobro had said in his 1914 essay on the power of suggestion: 'the reader instinctively supplies what is missing with his imagination'.

There is always a gap between theory and practice. A gap accentuated in this case by the outbreak of the First World War. Apollinaire's journal, *Les Soirées de Paris*, like other literary magazines in Europe, ceased publication in 1914. Huidobro was left to fend for himself. By the middle of 1916 he had begun to bridge the gap. Hence his excitement when he spoke at the Ateneo Hispanoamericano about his own poetry. This was in Argentina, in July of 1916. He had apparently been invited there by Fernán Félix de Amador, the young poet to whom *El espejo de agua* is dedicated. While in Buenos Aires, he spoke at the Ateneo and was a guest at a literary dinner offered by *Nosotros*, the same Modernist magazine that was later to open its pages to Ultraism. There is mention of the speech in *Mundo*

Argentino (26 July 1916), a weekly news-magazine. Unfortunately, there is no published record of what was said. However, among Huidobro's papers there is the rough draft of a text which begins in this exultant way:

> I have tried out all the schools. I have composed poems that were classic, romantic, decadent, symbolist, pantheist (the dumbest of all), modernist, unanimist, simultaneist, etc. etc. All the isms imaginable.
> And this, even though any imbecile might interpret it otherwise, is the proof of my absolute sincerity.
> Besides, imagine the *métier*, the *savoir-faire* that such practice has given me and the cumulus of knowledge that I have acquired.
> I am one of the few poets of today who has behind him an authentic and enormous artistic labour.
> I challenge anyone to have fathomed Art more than I have and to consider himself an initiate in the divine mysteries of Poetry.
> When you have penetrated the temple of the initiated, when you know all the rules of the exceptionals and you know with mathematical precision just how the old masters worked, what a laugh you get reading the studies of that pack of imbeciles that in the outside world are called critics.
> How does one penetrate into the Mystery of the Initiates? When one doesn't call on them, when one does what they do, in other words, by creating something new.

Huidobro goes on to explain in his characteristically Olympian way just what is meant by 'creating something new':

> Just imagine the pleasure that would have been felt if someone were able to contemplate the moment in which God made the world and its creatures. The pleasure that would have been felt is what I would someday like to give to my readers, the only difference being that the pleasure I would like to give would not be like that, basically dynamic, but rather purely poetic: The poet must be a little God.

The point of reference echoes the concluding maxim of 'Arte poética' in *El espejo de agua*:

> Por que cantáis la rosa, ¡oh Poetas!
> Hacedla florecer en el poema;
>
> Sólo para nosotros
> Viven todas las cosas bajo el Sol.
>
> El poeta es un pequeño Dios.

(Oh Poets, why do you sing to the rose! / Make it flower in your poem; / For us alone / Everything under the Sun is alive. / The poet is a little God.)

Huidobro felt he had come a long way, and in this text he details, somewhat wide-eyed, the path he had travelled:

> This is what the poet ought to do, make something that is neither an imitation nor an exaggeration of reality.
> Make a poem that is nothing other than a Poem. With no extraneous elements, something completely pure, absolutely separate from everything: A poem is a page in the sky.
> After realizing this came the problem of putting it into practice. The fact: On wanting to carry out what was the fruit of long studies and much meditation, on making the first such poem that could be called pure, after struggling so that each verse would be something created entirely by myself, I ran into enormous difficulty.
> I had made a poem; but it didn't please me. I made two, three, four, at least ten, but there was something wrong. None satisfied me.
> I thought I was mistaken and wanted to retreat and drop everything, but it was useless. I tried making poems like before, but I felt such an enormous repugnance for that ordinary poetry. Fortunately, I felt in my soul a kind of interior voice that said: Keep at it!
> And after terrible days of great depression, without knowing how, one night, going over the latest poems I had written, it came to me like a flash of light. I realized what was wrong.
> The reason was simple. As happens with any new thing, I had been exaggerating and had fallen into an extreme. To create everything, to distance myself from reality, I had gone over to pure fantasy, the fantastic, as repugnant and dangerous as realism, and generally grotesque.
> Then I saw that I had to dance between these two traps: the Fantastic and the Real, without falling into either.
> And the principal problem was resolved.[3]

The allusion is clearly to the more concise writing style of *El espejo de agua*. This book, printed perhaps in Buenos Aires as Huidobro was embarking for Europe in November 1916, was stillborn. In Paris the avant-garde had already coalesced around principles quite similar to those Huidobro had worked out for himself in South America. Thus, it was not the book, but the thinking which informed it, which placed Huidobro *au courant* with the Cubist group. Max Jacob, 'the Mallarmé of Cubism',[4] acknowledged as much when he put the following inscription in *Le Cornet à dés* (1917): 'To the poet Vincent Huidobro who has invented modern poetry without knowing the outcome of the European effort and whose place among us was pre-ordained.'[5]

III
The Avant-Garde (Cubism)

Make a poem like nature makes a tree.   1917

Huidobro did not evolve in a vacuum. Nor did Apollinaire. However, it is one thing to follow the emergence of the new on a subscription basis and quite another to be a direct participant. And in Europe, rather than the derision of his contemporaries, Huidobro was to enjoy their support and advice. In this sense, no one was more helpful than Juan Gris, a Spanish painter established in France with whom Huidobro found instant rapport.

In fact, what little we know of his route of access is Hispanic. He even went over on a Spanish ship, the Infanta Isabel de Borbón. Pencilled on his ship's programme for 12 November 1916 are some random notes: the name of Picasso and directions for Adrienne Monnier's bookstore, a rendezvous for the avant-garde on the rue de l'Odéon. Evidently anxious to get on to France, Huidobro stayed only briefly in Spain, where he saw Cansinos-Asséns and Alfonso Reyes.[1] Fernán Felix de Amador had already put him in contact with Ventura García Calderón and Alejandro Sux, long-time residents of France. A letter from Sux fixes Huidobro's arrival in Paris in December of 1916:

Paris, December 26, 1916

Dear Sir: Just today, back from a trip, I passed by *La Prensa*, and I hasten to write you so that we can have a long and friendly chat. Being a friend of Amador I consider you as my friend. I am at home: 38, rue Eugène-Carrière, Nord–Sud, Lamarck, all day today, Tuesday, until midnight. Tomorrow I leave for Verdun and, believe me, you would give me a great pleasure coming today to the house of your friend,

Alejandro Sux.[2]

García Calderón was no less cordial, inviting Huidobro to prepare a selection of Chilean poetry for a series he was then directing for Maucci, a Barcelona publisher.[3]

Paris (1917)

But Huidobro had not come to Paris to be ghettoized; once settled in he wasted no time in seeking out the most advanced group, the group of writers and artists then becoming known in

Paris as Cubists (Apollinaire, Max Jacob, Picasso, Blaise Cendrars, Juan Gris, Pierre Reverdy). In fact, it was at a recital of Reverdy poems, in January of 1917, that the two poets first made contact. Pierre Albert-Birot, then editor of *SIC*, has recalled the event: 'where, in a studio on rue Huyghens, around 1917, the extraordinary Greta Prozor [reading from Reverdy] lit up all those who were present, a veritable flash for Huidobro'.[4] Reporting the same event to Cansinos-Asséns, Huidobro claimed to have been so moved by what he heard that 'he spontaneously went up and embraced Reverdy'.[5]

He had turned up at a good moment. The war was going better for France and literary activities were perking up. There was talk of reviving Apollinaire's *Soirées de Paris*, while Reverdy and others thought the moment propitious for bringing out an entirely new avant-garde review. Max Jacob's correspondence with Jacques Doucet in the early months of 1917 permits us to reconstruct Huidobro's role in this venture. In a letter of 6 February, Jacob mentions 'talk of a new review'; and, a month later, on 7 March, he goes into detail:

> You ask me what is new in the group. A new review in the genre of *Soirées de Paris*, but with greater homogenity. *391*, which used to appear in New York, reappears now in Barcelona in conditions that do not please us at all. There is also a review, *SIC*, that tries to vulgarize (for 4 sous), our tendencies. It is a cut-rate *L'Élan*. None of this goes well with us. Reverdy is in touch with a Brazilian.[6]

The new review he talks about is of course *Nord-Sud*, and the 'Brazilian' must surely be Huidobro, who, back in Chile in 1919, referred to his role as a co-founder:

> When I arrived in Paris I came to know various literary groups. Some young poets, trying to escape from Symbolism, had fallen into something much worse: Futurism. These people were publishing SIC, whose director was Pierre Albert-Birot, and among whose collaborators were Pierre Reverdy, Jean Cocteau and, occasionally, Apollinaire. Birot, although he thought himself a Futurist, was just a Symbolist . . .
>
> After long conversations and a continuous exchange of ideas with the most interesting of these younger poets, Pierre Reverdy, I founded with him the review *Nord-Sud*, in March of 1917. In this review a new tendency took shape, the most serious and profound development since Symbolism.[7]

The development is literary Cubism (although Huidobro was then calling it Creationism), and its spiritual mentor was Apollinaire.

Huidobro's first contribution to *Nord–Sud* was 'L'Homme triste' (The Sad Man), a translation of one of the poems from *El espejo de agua*. His French was only rudimentary at this point, and Reverdy helped him to translate. Later it was Juan Gris.[8] Indeed, among the poet's papers there is some material in the handwriting of both Gris and Huidobro, attesting to a close collaboration between them. The translation of 'L'Homme triste' though seems to have been Reverdy's doing, for the page proofs of *Nord–Sud* (in the Jacques Doucet Library, Paris), which show him tinkering with almost everyone's final versions, including those of Apollinaire, are remarkably clean with regard to this poem, the only difference from Huidobro's manuscript being the addition of the author's name (Frenchified to 'Vincent' Huidobro), and the clarification 'Traduit de l'Espagnol' (translated from the Spanish). The translation of this poem for the April issue of *Nord–Sud* must have been the occasion for Reverdy's dedicatory testimony to Huidobro underlining the similarity of their work:[9] 'A mon cher ami, le poète Vicente Huidobro, nos efforts parallèles se sont rencontrés, Pierre Reverdy, Avril 1917'.*

Huidobro's second contribution to *Nord–Sud*, 'Automne' (Autumn), translated for the May issue begins with an obvious Hispanism ('Je garde *en* mes yeux', *Nord–Sud* < 'Guardo *en* mis ojos', *Espejo* — I retain in my eyes), that was not remedied until afterwards, when Gris and Huidobro were going over these poems for inclusion in *Horizon carré* (Paris: Birault, 1917). Then it is the painter who corrects the homophonic error, changing *en* for *dans*.

As Huidobro attempts to write original poems in French, toward the middle of 1917, one can see his dependence on Spanish and appreciate the quality and extent of Juan Gris's assistance. The manuscripts for 'Aveugle' (Blind), for example, reveal a process of composition in which Huidobro prepared a rough text in French and Spanish; Gris revised it, and Huidobro, profiting from these revisions, gave the poem its final form. The opening lines of an early draft, transcribed below, show an easy flow from one language into another:

> Más allá de la última ventana
> Les cloches du Sacre Coeur
> Font tomber les feuilles

---

* To my dear friend, the poet Vicente Huidobro, our parallel efforts have finally come together, Pierre Reverdy, April 1917.

(Beyond the last window / the bells of Sacré-Cœur / cause the leaves
to fall)

Gris then translated the first line to read: 'Au dela de la derniere
fenettre' [*sic*]. He had not been schooled in French, and the
conventions of spelling and accents were always elusive for him.
And for Huidobro as well; only when this poem was set to type
was his own curiously circumflexed *fenêttre* finally corrected to
fenêtre. But these are minor flaws which do not detract from
the extraordinary nature of this collaborative endeavour bringing together the unique approaches to imagery of a painter and
a poet.

Manuscripts of other *Horizon carré* poems are entirely in
Gris's hand, suggesting the possibility of a rewrite so extensive
that Huidobro's original was abandoned. Gris evidently enjoyed
this project, for in preparing translations of poems whose
rhetoric was outmoded, he took considerable liberty with the
original. This is the case with 'Arte poética', the opening text
for *El espejo de agua* (reproduced below for the purpose of
comparison):

> Que el verso sea como una llave
> Que abra mil puertas.
> Una hoja cae; algo pasa volando;
> Cuanto miren los ojos creado sea,
> Y el alma del oyente quede temblando.
>
> Inventa mundos nuevos y cuida tu palabra;
> El adjetivo, cuando no da vida, mata.
>
> Estamos en el ciclo de los nervios.
> El músculo cuelga,
> Como recuerdo, en los museos;
> Mas no por eso tenemos menos fuerza:
> El vigor verdadero
> Reside en la cabeza.
>
> Por qué cantáis la rosa, ¡oh Poetas!
> Hacedla florecer en el poema;
>
> Sólo para nosotros
> Viven todas las cosas bajo el Sol.
>
> El poeta es un pequeño Dios.

(Let the verse be like a key / That opens a thousand doors. / A leaf falls;
something flies by; / Let whatever the eyes see be created, / And the soul

of the listener will remain trembling. / Invent new worlds and cultivate your vocabulary; / The adjective, when it doesn't give life, kills. / We are in the cycle of nerves. / The muscle hangs, / like a memento, in the museums; / But not for this reason are we less strong: / True vigour / is in the head. / Oh Poets, why do you sing to the rose! / Make it flower in your poem; / For us alone / Everything under the Sun is alive. / The poet is a little God.)

The translation departed substantially from the original. So much so that the end result is an almost completely different poem. The following text, mostly in Gris's hand, bears eloquent testimony to the fact that the painter was a poet as well:

> Que le vers soit comme une clef
> qui ouvre mille portes.
> Quelque chose passe dans l'air, quelque chose tombe.
> Quand les yeux cherchent sans rien voir
> et l'âme cependant
> reste tremblante.
> Un bouton
> un léger coup
> et toutes les chambres s'éclairent.
> La parole juste
> est plus belle si elle est nue.
> L'adjectif
> un rideau, cacher [*sic*] de beauté.
> L'épée de Musée
> trop lourde.
> Siècle du nerf.
> On ne connaît pas les muscles.
> Rien d'étranger au poème.
> Toute concession au public
> amoindrit et mêle
> un élément impur.
> Le sujet attache à la terre.
> On ouvre la tête
> comme une fenêtre.
> Tous les arômes et les vents.

(Let the verse be like a key / that opens a thousand doors. / Something passes by in the air, something falls. / When the eyes look without seeing anything / and the soul meanwhile keeps on trembling. / A button / a light flick / and all the rooms light up. / The right word / is more beautiful if it is naked. / The adjective / a screen, hider? of beauty. / The Museum sword / too heavy. / Century of nerve. / Muscles are not known now. / Nothing extraneous to the poem. / Any concession to the public / cheapens and mixes in / an impure element. / The subject ties to the earth. / One can open one's head / like a window. / All the aromas and winds.)

The closing simile, with its innocent quasi-rhyme, has an arresting quality; especially when followed, as in this case, by an incomplete statement, a kind of newsflash evoking the possibilities opened up by the new aesthetic attitude: 'On ouvre la tête / comme une fenêtre. / Tous les arômes et les vents.' Gris has 'interpreted' the *ars poetica* well, demonstrating in his own way what was meant by Huidobro's plea that the poet should invent new worlds, singing not to the rose, but making it blossom in the poem.

And too, the much quoted declaration of aesthetic principles placed at the beginning of *Horizon carré*, calling on the poet to make a poem like nature makes a tree, owes something to Gris. Various rewrites of this idea in both Spanish and French are among Huidobro's papers: all point to a determination to synthesize the principles of *Nord–Sud* and Cubism into a kind of maxim. The revising went on until the very last moment, for in the printer-ready copy of *Horizon carré* there is pinned over Huidobro's final draft Gris's rewrite of a portion.[10] The text ultimately published was a synthesis of the two: 'Create a poem taking its motifs from real life, but transforming them so as to give them a new and independent existence. No anecdotes nor description. Emotion should arise only from the creative force itself. Make a POEM like nature makes a tree.'

To attempt to sort out one man's contribution from another is virtually impossible. The collaboration between Gris and Huidobro during the course of 1917 was so close, and so intense, that it is tempting to consider the two men working together as one. But collaboration seems to have been the norm in the halcyon days of the Cubist group, when, confident of individual worth, poets, painters, and musicians were all working together and learning from one another. This extraordinary ambiance of co-operation and mutual esteem is evoked by Huidobro in an unusual anecdotal aside to one of his manifestos:

I remember how, one afternoon in 1917, in Juan Gris's studio, we amused ourselves, along with several other friends, by composing poems in which each one of us would write down a verse on a piece of paper that we would then fold over and pass on so that the next person could write his verse without reading the others . . .
Picasso, who was among us, amused by the game, began to talk about a machine that you could fill up with words and phrases clipped out of the

newspapers, and with which anybody could have a chance at a poem, by putting in a few coins, as with a slot machine . . .

Another day, in my house, after dinner, Max Jacob and I composed a poem together (a poem I still have), each of us taking turns writing down verses with the first thing that came to mind.[11]

This close rapport with the Cubist group explains in part the rapidity of Huidobro's evolution during his first year in Paris.

So close was the link between writers and artists that critics of the time began to talk of Cubist poetry and, with regard to the painters, of 'plastic metaphors'.[12] Picasso was working on 'sculpted houses' and Huidobro on the 'painted poem'. For a time at least, a real fusion of the arts seemed possible and a unifying term was needed. Cubism seemed the most practical one to describe what was going on in France. Although Reverdy was against the term at first, posterity has assigned it to him.[13] However, when Huidobro went off to Spain in 1918, he reported confusion regarding its usage there. Gris was irked by this, and in a letter to Huidobro, then in Madrid, he commented: 'What you tell me seems quite comical: that people who have never worked on this, and who never even approved our effort nor defended it, should now claim for themselves the denomination *cubistes*, and pretend to know our aesthetic better than we ourselves.'[14] Was it because of this, that Huidobro came up with a new term, Creationism, falling back, perhaps, on 'Création', Reverdy's October 1917 *Nord–Sud* article? To no avail though, for the Spaniards responded with yet another, Ultraism.

Everyone in the avant-garde wanted to be original and yet belong to a movement. To be a part of the future without rejecting the present, or the past. Huidobro's *Horizon carré*, for example, was really two books of poetry sandwiched into one. It was even printed that way, divided into two sections: the first, containing for the most part, his *Nord–Sud* poems and others translated from *El espejo de agua*, is dedicated to his mother; the second section, containing his later, more original compositions, is dedicated to Juan Gris.

The book as a whole though, was packaged as something more than a collection of his work during the course of 1917. Of a grand art-book format (25 cm. × 36 cm.), it begins with 'Nouvelle Chanson' (New Song) and closes with 'Fin' (The End), framing in this way its contents. Both poems make the same point about a new kind of poetry, a poetry to be read silently, not declaimed. For this reason, so much importance was given to the visual aspect of the text, its typographical presentation.

FIN

La neige qui tombe
A blanchi quelques barbes
           Les yeux à moitié ouverts
           Sont des morceaux de verre
           Mais il reste encore
           Un peu de feu
                 S
En arrivant   I
        la mort   L
Coupe la dernière syllabe   E
Et tous ceux qui pleuraient   N
Allèrent se dispersant   C
                 E
Au long du chemin
           Il y a des étoiles effeuillées
Et les feux follets
           Qui s'éloignent entre les branches
Laissent une odeur de cigare
        S I L E N C E

(The snow that falls / has whitened some beards / Eyes half-opened / are
pieces of glass / but there still remains / a bit of fire / On arriving / death /
cuts off the last syllable / and all those who were crying / went wandering
away / SILENCE / Along the road / there are some plucked stars / and the
swamp lights / that go off among the branches / leave a cigar smell /
SILENCE)

This is Cubist poetry. As such, and like Cubist painting, it shares
several characteristics with the avant-garde in general, while
others are unique.

Common to the time is the lack of punctuation and displaced
margins, as well as the use of different type and isolated words,
what the Futurists called 'words in liberty'. These liberties, so
scandalous to tradition-minded critics, were often used in traditional ways. Here, for example, the poetic line, although freed
of measure, has the length of logical syntactic units, the natural
pause at line's end serving to modulate the reading; and the
displaced margins function much the same as strophes, blocking
out groups of verses. Nor is typography arbitrary. In this poem,
large type is used to call attention to certain words: the title
('FIN'), and the final 'SILENCE', reinforcing the idea of silence
laid flat, the silence of death, the silence of endings (the end of
life, the end of the poem, the end of the book).

What is unique to literary Cubism is the disciplined use of the printed page, the idea of constructing a poem, as Max Jacob said of Reverdy in 1917, 'like a painting'.[15] One of the hallmarks of Cubist painting in this early experimental period was its concern with shape and form, with the problem of presenting three-dimensional space on the flat surface of a canvas. To overcome the limitations of the medium solid objects were broken down and studied from a variety of perspectives, their various surfaces being presented side by side. Cubism was thus an art of juxtaposition, the juxtaposition of the seemingly unlike, creating in the process a new likeness. A hill and a guitar, say, in the Juan Gris illustration gracing the original edition of *Horizon carré*; the slope of one and the curve of the other are brought together so as to make apparent their similarity of shape. Transferring this idea to poetry, otherwise unrelated ideas were juxtaposed in an analogous way. In both arts, the resultant collision of the dissimilar created metaphor, a plastic metaphor for the painters, a lyric metaphor for the poets.

Returning to 'Fin', it is apparent that this poem is based on a series of such juxtapositions. In the first lines, the unifying element is colour, the whiteness of snow and a graying beard (winter and death). Then it is a flickering crystalline quality that is common to half-shut eyes, broken glass, and a dying fire. Finally, the idea of light, or rather a waning light, permits the juxtaposition of a cigar glowing in the middle of the night with stars and a will-o'-the-wisp. The catalyst for these various strophic units appears toward the end of the poem in a joltingly incongruous line referring to the odour of a cigar. It is this jolt, however, that brings together all these various images, linking death with a snuffed-out life. In this context, the silence at poem's end and the vertically printed silence cutting short the central strophe are also interrelated, not as typographical adornments, but as a spatial and ideational frame for the reality constituted by the poem itself. The end referred to in the poem's title is death, and it is silence that marks the ritual dispersal of the living when the death-watch is over:

<pre>
                                        S
        En arrivant   I
              la mort   L
        Coupe la dernière syllabe   E
        Et tous ceux qui pleuraient   N
        Allèrent se dispersant   C
                                        E
</pre>

The formula for this kind of writing was to take something from reality and transform it in the poem so that it takes on a new and independent existence. Like Juan Gris's guitar painting, this is not a poetry about a given subject, but rather a creative exercise in the imaginative possibilities presented by the subject. This parallel with Cubist painting is especially apparent in Huidobro's poem on the same motif:

GUITARE

Sur ses genoux
            Il y avait quelques notes
Une femme petite dormait
Et six cordes chantent
                        dans son ventre
    Le vent
            a effacé les contours
                        Et un oiseau
                        becquète les cordes
    Le silence   Chacun croit
    se cachait   vivre en
    au fond de   dehors de
    l'armoire   soi-même
    Quand l'homme
                        cessa de jouer
    Deux ailes tremblotantes
                        tombèrent de ses mains

(Across his knees there were some notes / A small woman was sleeping / And six strings [chords] sing / in her tummy / The wind / has effaced the contours / And a bird / picks at the strings [chords] / Silence went into hiding in the depths of the armoire / Everyone thinks he is living outside of himself / When the man / stopped playing / Two trembling wings / fell from his hands)

Again, a series of cross-overs occur. The curvature of the guitar is that of a woman, its wooden body an armoire, the plucking of its strings is the pecking of a songbird, the hands of the guitarist hanging loose after playing are a bird's folded wings. One image generates another. None are arbitrary in the surrealist manner of free association; all are interrelated in a tightly structured whole. Most interesting in this respect is the use of space to create an impression of simultaneity. The two parallel columns of verse in this poem generate a kind of tension between inside and outside, between a silence filled by music and the alienating effect of that music:

Le silence	Chacun croit
se cachait	vivre en
au fond de	dehors de
l'armoire	soi-même

Space is also used to create a gap between images. Instead of the traditional connectives of simile likening one thing to another, Huidobro makes a sudden transition, forcing the reader to bridge the gap in his imagination. In this way, the unreal is momentarily made real. The final lines, for example, do not say that the guitarist's hands are *like* folded wings. The reader jumps to this conclusion, or rather is pushed into it, by the abrupt way the verse is cut: 'Deux ailes tremblotantes / *tombèrent* de ses mains'. The verb is the element that vitalizes the metaphor, syntactically joining the dissimilar (e.g. 'Et six cordes *chantent* / dans son ventre'; 'Et un oiseau / *becquète* les cordes'). Here, the absence of punctuation is important. The unpunctuated verses, appropriately cut, create both the pause and the run-on effect necessary for the total comprehension of the image.

Huidobro's experiments with typography would ultimately distance him from Reverdy. As a former printer's assistant, Reverdy had some pretty fixed ideas about the format of the printed page. The sober presentation of *Nord-Sud* vis-à-vis other reviews of the avant-garde is evidence enough. Were more needed, there is his article on 'Ponctuation' (*Nord-Sud*, October 1917), and a revealing comment by Max Jacob regarding Reverdy's determination to steer away from any 'typographic fantasies' in *Nord-Sud*.[16] With regard to Huidobro, there is the case of 'Moi Flamfolle' (My Flashfool), a poem prepared for the October issue of *Nord-Sud*. The page proofs of the review in the Doucet Library show that Huidobro was dissatisfied with the straightforward way this text was printed and indicated a series of changes to be made in the disposition of the verses (adding space between lines, displacing margins, etc.). Reverdy evidently annulled these instructions to the printer, since the poem appeared in *Nord-Sud* unchanged. Later, when Huidobro revised it for inclusion in *Horizon carré*, he had his own way, as these whimsical lines from the end make apparent.

Les marionnettes qui pendent
Aux rayons des étoiles
Sont des araignées
DANSE
     VIEUX TAM
          DANSE
Au milieu des sept enfants de la montagne
Dans la main prends
Celui qui joue de la flûte
TA
   TETE
      PEND
         DE LA
           FUMEE
              DE TON
                CIGARE

(The puppets that hang / from the rays of the stars / are spiders / DANCE / OLD TAM / DANCE / Amidst the seven children of the mountain / take in your hand / the one who plays the flute / YOUR / HEAD / HANGS / FROM THE / SMOKE / OF YOUR / CIGAR)

Then there is the matter of the book's title. Huidobro, in his quarrelsome days, made much of the fact that he squared the horizon, whereas Reverdy merely rounded a skylight.[17] One of the typographically innovative poems in *Horizon carré*, 'Matin' (Morning), may be the text which prompted the assertion:

                    SOLEIL
Qui réveille Paris

SOLEIL   *Le plus haut peuplier de la rive*   Sur la Tour Eiffel
                           Un coq à trois couleurs   SOLEIL
                           Chante en battant des ailes
                           Et quelques plumes en tombent

En recommençant sa course
La Seine cherche entre les ponts
La vieille route

          Et l'Obélisque
          Qui a oublié les mots égyptiens
          N'a pas fleuri cette année
              SOLEIL

(SUN / That wakes up Paris / SUN / The tallest poplar on the riverside /
On top of the Eiffel Tower / A tri-coloured cock / Crows fluttering its
wings / And some feathers fall / SUN / Taking up its course once again /
The Seine searches out among the bridges / Its old route / And the Obelisk /
That has forgotten its Egyptian words / Has not flowered this year / SUN)

Such a 'squaring' of the horizon surely owes much to Gris
and the Cubist concern with collage. This is a postcard view of
Paris from a variety of perspectives. In Huidobro's landscape the
Eiffel Tower is a big tree and the Obelisk is a tall flowerless
shoot; the Seine is a snake searching out a path under the bridges,
and the French flag atop the tower is a rooster stretching its
wings at dawn. The fanciful nature of the collage is enhanced by
the typographic arrangement of the verses, bringing together
what is geographically separate.

Huidobro's experiments along these lines represent a revival
of his earlier interest in graphic writing (as manifest in the
chapel poem of *La gruta del silencio*, 1913). Now, however,
there is a new dynamism. The text is not simply a graphic illustration of the poem's content, but a more complete aesthetic
event, an event which takes on its fullest meaning in the process
of being read and seen at the same time. The four corners of
Paris in 'Matin', or the more elaborate scene in 'Paysage' (*see
over, p. 54*).

All Reverdy's principles of composition are violated in this
poem, where Huidobro gives free reign to his fancy and bends
his writing to create a visual landscape. To enhance the total
artistic effect, and involve the reader more, the poem is even
printed sideways, as a two-page centrefold in the already over-
sized *Horizon carré*.

This composition, oddly enough, ends Huidobro's experiments with the pictorial possibilities of the printed page. He
would later develop the *poème-peint* of course, and even have
an exposition of his own hand-painted poetry in 1922 (which
would include a reworked 'Paysage'), but in his printed work of
the Cubist period he would return to a linear use of space to
modulate the reading of the text. Reverdy was right. Poetry,
after all, was literature, and relied on the printed page as a
medium of diffusion. The Cubist poem, for all its painterly
qualities, was ultimately a text to be read as well as seen, and in
the reading process certain visual conventions were to prevail.
Top to bottom, left to right. What really counted was not the
visual image, but the mental image created by bringing together
different ideas. Poetry was metaphor, not metamorphosis.

LE SOIR ON SE PROMENERA SUR DES ROUTES PARALLÈLES

La lune
où
qui
te regarde

L'ARBRE
ÉTAIT
PLUS
HAUT
QUE LA
MONTAGNE

MAIS LA

MONTAGNE

ETAIT SI LARGE

QU'ELLE DEPASSAIT

LES EXTREMITES

DE LA TERRE

LE
FLEUVE
QUI
COULE
NE
PORTE
PAS
DE
POISSONS

ATTENTION A NE PAS

JOUER SUR L'HERBE

FRAICHEMENT PEINTE

UNE CHANSON CONDUIT LES BREBIS VERS L'ETABLE

(In the evening we'll stroll along parallel paths / The moon in which you can look at yourself / The tree was higher than the mountain / But the mountain was so wide that it went beyond the ends of the earth / The river that flows has no fish / Careful not to play on the grass freshly painted / A song leads the sheep toward the stable)

Horizon carré constituted Huidobro's official début as a poet in France. The book, although printed in December of 1917 by Paul Birault, then Paris' favoured publisher of the avant-garde, was not put into circulation until the Spring of 1918, when Huidobro, Gris, and Lipchitz were all off together on holiday with their families in Beaulieu-près-Loches. Coinciding with the first published reviews is a note from Cocteau, punning on the title:

April 3, 1918
My dear Huidobro: Thanks for the horizon that reposes the eye — I would
like to see you. Write soon.

Cocteau.[18]

Such subtleties were beyond the newspaper critics of the time,
who, still relatively unfamiliar with avant-garde writing, did not
comment at all on the painterly aspect of any of the poems;
although they were concerned with Huidobro's peculiar use of
language. For some, he was just an upstart, a 'foreigner', who
dared to write in a language not his own: 'The Spaniard Huidobro doesn't manage to be as original as he would like in his
Horizon carré. He is simply bizarre (. . .). I always distrust these
foreigners who want to renovate our aesthetics.'[19] Naturally,
such a chauvinist view did not go unchallenged for very long:

In *Horizon carré* Vicente Huidobro demonstrates a talent already quite
developed. The circumstance of his being Spanish American and the fact
that he has chosen the path of modern poetry have caused it to be said
that the new theories make it possible to be a French poet without knowing French. Where have we heard that before? That was said of the Parnassians (. . .). The fact that José-Maria de Heredia was a Spanish American
didn't prevent him from carrying that school to its ideal perfection.[20]

By analogy, Huidobro would do the same for 'modern poetry';
although modernity for these reviewers seems to have been little
more than an updated Symbolism: 'Huidobro's *Horizon carré*
is the book of a real poet, spiritually akin to Laforgue, Verlaine,
and Rimbaud, but in which 'joie' is now the dominant note'.[21]
In all fairness, it must be said that most of these critics, however
naïve, did make an effort to understand the book on their own
terms, sorting out what they liked and disliked:

Horizon carré? It is a way of seeing, and it is just as defensible as the
notion of space in *n* dimensions. What counts is to be a poet and not a
slave to procedure. Huidobro, who used to write in Spanish and who now
brings out his first book in French, is such a poet. He is capable, we
believe, of deep poetry. Although in this book (. . .) there are too many
fleeting impressions that are hardly the makings of great poetry: false
images (planes going to the moon), sometimes as unreal as opium, and
often amusingly futile (a man's head hanging from the smoke of his
cigar).[22]

Basically, the first part of the book, containing the *Espejo de
agua* poems, was cited to support the belief that this was the

work of a real poet; while what was really new in *Horizon carré* was either ignored or derided.

Much the same happened in Chile, where the most traditional compositions were singled out for praise, while Cubism as such was roundly rejected. Omer Emeth, for example, after ridiculing the new aesthetic, found some saving grace in 'Automne', an *Espejo de agua* poem: 'Nevertheless, it cannot be denied; that piece (with or without Cubism, with or without solidarity), leaves an impression of melancholy on the soul of the one who reads it and, therefore, it is poetic, it is real poetry.'[23]

Serious criticism did not come from the newspapers, but from within the avant-garde. Most of it went unpublished. The best of what was published appeared around 1920, when Huidobro's position in France was consolidated and Cubist poetry had earned its place in literary history. Nicolas Beauduin's article ('La Poésie nouvelle et Vincent Huidobro', *La Bataille littéraire*, June 1920), is perhaps classic, as is Jean Cassou's study ('Cubisme et poésie', *La Vie des lettres*, October 1920). For Cassou, an art historian, Cubism was a major moment in Western art, the moment which established the autonomy of the created object, be it a poem or a painting:

Every civilization will always vacillate between these two poles: subject and object. Cubism brings us the triumph of the object. Everything for the object, everything for the work of art. A painting is a painted canvas. A painting must therefore be made from scratch. Huidobro, at the head of one of his books, has written: 'Make a poem like nature makes a tree.'

The artist, like God, was to be a creator. Interestingly enough, while few subscribed to Huidobro's Creationism, practically everyone accepted as a succinct definition of literary Cubism, the maxim prefacing *Horizon carré*. And no wonder, for this definition grew out of both arts, a unique example of the fruitful collaboration of poets and painters in the Paris of 1917.

Madrid (1918)

A collaboration that was continued in Madrid, where the Huidobros went in the middle of 1918 to escape the noise of the war.[24] There they came in contact with the Delaunays, who were in Spain for similar reasons. Huidobro's collaboration with Juan Gris was, in a sense, continued with Robert Delaunay. In fact, they brought out together *Tour Eiffel* (Eiffel Tower), an expanded version of Huidobro's *Nord–Sud* poem (August 1917) of the same title. Printed on heavy composition paper in an assortment of colours (green, gray, pink . . .), it is illustrated by a screen-painting of a tree-like Eiffel tower by Delaunay. Other collaborative projects were envisaged, the most ambitious being a ballet, along the lines of Cocteau's *Parade* for the Ballets Russes. Tentatively titled *Football*, it was to have music by Stravinsky, set design by Delaunay, and story by Huidobro. But the poet did not stay in Europe long enough to carry the project through.[25] In fact, by the end of 1918, he is back in Chile.[26]

But more important than his comings and goings, than what he didn't do, is what he did do during his short stay in the Spanish capital where, in 1918, he published four volumes of poetry: *Tour Eiffel*, *Poemas árticos*, *Hallali*, and *Ecuatorial*. *Poemas árticos* (Arctic Poems), like *Tour Eiffel*, was a continuation of his Parisian writing: individual compositions presented as discrete exercises in the imagistic possibilities of given themes, both Cubist and classical. *Ecuatorial* and *Hallali*, like the earlier *Adán* (1916), are books organized around a single theme, in this case, war.

Poemas árticos is the earliest example of avant-garde writing in Spanish and, containing short poems, was the volume most accessible to readers unfamiliar with the new aesthetic. Its poems were read and reread, studied, and imitated by a whole generation of young Spaniards ready for something new. Those who could not acquire the book itself, hand-copied its content. Some of these early enthusiasts, like Antonio Machado, were eventually disturbed by Huidobro's extravagant imagery; while others, like Gerardo Diego, saw new possibilities for lyric poetry.[27] Juan Larrea was an instant convert. He recalls how Gerardo Diego, returning from Madrid in May of 1919, passed through Bilbao, 'bringing with him three Huidobro poems that he had copied by hand from *Poemas árticos*'. For Larrea, these poems were decisive: 'Their novelty impressed me in such a way that from that day on I began to feel that I was a completely different person.'[28] One of the poems was 'Luna' (Moon):

> Estábamos tan lejos de la vida
> Que el viento nos hacía suspirar
>
> LA LUNA SUENA COMO UN RELOJ
>
> Inútilmente hemos huido
> El invierno cayó en nuestro camino
> Y el pasado lleno de hojas secas
> Pierde el sendero de la floresta

Tanto fumamos bajo los árboles
Que los almendros huelen a tabaco

Medianoche

Sobre la vida lejana
alguien llora
Y la luna olvidó dar la hora

(We were so far from life / that the wind would make us sigh / THE
MOON SOUNDS OFF LIKE A CLOCK / Uselessly have we fled / The
winter fell across our route / And the past filled with dry leaves / Loses the
trail in the grove / We smoked so much under the arbour / That the almond trees smell of tobacco / Midnight / Over the distant life / someone
cries / And the moon forgot to give the time)

What impressed Larrea was the poem's otherworldly atmosphere,
particularly the intriguing quality of the false simile around
which everything seems to be organized: 'LA LUNA SUENA
COMO UN RELOJ'. It is only after thinking about the poem,
and analysing the mechanism of its imagery, that one is able to
decode the comparison: the disk of the full moon is taken for
the illuminated face of a church clock; as night falls the moon-
clock fails to give the time. For an acute reader such as Larrea,
the poem is only momentarily disorienting, and that is its
charm. A less acute reader could however be left outside the
poem, completely excluded from its private system of associations.

This is the sort of thing that Juan Gris was concerned about
in *Poemas árticos*, its occasional hermeticism and the forced
quality of some of its imagery. In a letter of October 1918, he
raises the point with Huidobro:

Regarding your books I ought to tell you first the great pleasure your
dedication gives me ['To Juan Gris and Jacques Lipchitz, remembering our
evening chats in that corner of France', in *Poemas árticos*] and then the
great poetic emotion that I had in reading them, especially *Poemas árticos*.
In these books something is given off that does not exist for example in
the book of Juan Ramón [Jiménez] that you sent me: a lyricism and a
poetry that it is quite rare to find and that is the only thing that interests me.
    And now since I am your friend and since on repeated occasions you
have asked me to do it, I proceed to make a critique of your books.
    I consider *Poemas árticos* to be superior to *Ecuatorial* or at least I
understand it better, being more familiar. The other book is too grandiose
for me and I haven't yet managed to penetrate it. The two of them are

certainly better than *Horizon carré*, but . . . since then I have reflected a lot about certain things and if before I could accept certain literary procedures that you use now I don't accept them. I will explain myself better. There is in your productions a certain itch for imagery that is exaggerated and that takes some force away from your poems and from the true emotive image. Thus, when you write cotton clouds you make an image that is clever but arid and not poetic, but when you write the clouds passed by sailing toward the Orient you give an emotion, while an elevator like a diver has no other basis than your own cleverness. Notice how all the powerful images in your book have in common a solid base. The winter comes, etc. (cold cemetery). Tied to a ship etc. (tied to destiny), and nothing more vulgar than a handkerchief drying in the sun to which you add in the moon. Surely, a good adjective is worth more than a clever non-emotive image, and even some of Mallarmé's *touffe* is better than an image that is forced.[29]

Huidobro was fortunate in having the candid criticism of a mind as sharp as that of Gris. But art was moving away from the cerebral kind of synthetic Cubism preferred by the painter, and Dada, with its penchant for striking metaphor 'found' by chance, was in the air. Especially in Spain, where Picabia had returned to bring out *391*. Huidobro would eventually move in this direction, although only briefly; but for now, his books of 1918 must be considered within the framework of literary Cubism. A somewhat heterodox Cubism to be sure, as Gris's critique makes apparent, but one in which the imagery, however bizarre, was not the result of mere chance, but of the poet's mental inventiveness. Actually, what was happening in Huidobro's poetry, and what Gris did not completely grasp, was that as the author abandoned the idea of the picture-poem in the manner of 'Paysage' for its essentially static quality, he began to cultivate a new kind of textual dynamism, based on the principle that a poem is read through from beginning to end. Rather than a collage of words, a poem is really a verbal sequence. Similarly, a book is a sequence of texts. And in *Poemas árticos* one text often generates another. Not in a rigidly structured pattern, but in a loose intertextual way. A poem like 'Luna', for example, is related to another, earlier poem in the book, 'Luna o reloj' (Moon or Clock), where a night scene is evoked: 'Después en el valle sin sol / un mismo ruido / la luna y el reloj' (Later in the valley without sun / one same noise / the moon and the clock).

There are many such images in *Poemas árticos*, images that through the force of repetition lose their hermeticism and acquire their fullest significance only in the larger context of

the book. Cigarettes glowing in the dark, for example, generate
a whole family of luminescent associations, usually serving to
make near what is far, or vice versa. And too, something as
elusive as time is often made tangible; in one case through an
implicit relation to the oval shape of an hourglass: 'Los frutos
que caen son ovalados / y las horas también' (The fruits that fall
are oval / and the hours also). These lines from 'Donjon' (Turret) can be made to reflect back on other poems and, ultimately,
to clarify the closing image of 'Horas' (Hours), the book's first
poem:

> El villorrio
> Un tren detenido sobre el llano
>
> En cada charco
> > > duermen estrellas sordas
> Y el agua tiembla
> Cortinaje al viento
>
> > > > La noche cuelga en la arboleda
>
> En el campanario florecido
>
> Una gotera viva
> > > desangra las estrellas
>
> > De cuando en cuando
> > Las horas maduras
> > > > caen sobre la vida

(The scrub town / A train stopped on the prairie / In every puddle / deaf
stars sleep / And the water trembles / Curtains to the wind / The night
hangs in the grove / In the flowered bell turret / A heavy leak / bleeds the
stars / From time to time / The ripe hours / fall down on life)

Here, ripeness (*madura*) is the idea that triggers the association
with fruit and time. In a similar way, some lines from 'Cigarro'
(Cigar), can be summoned to illumine the enigmatic central
image of the night hanging in the grove ('La noche cuelga en la
arboleda'): 'Aquello que cae de los árboles es la noche' (That
which is falling from the trees is the night). Language is being
stretched throughout *Poemas árticos* to make possible in the
reader's imagination what does not exist in reality.

In 'Horas' we have a static sequence. Verbs are used to arrest
action or, alternately, to give the idea of a perpetual, almost
frozen-in-time stasis to the scene: a train stopped in a prairie

town in the dead of night. A sense of stability is created by the unusual vocabulary: collective nouns (*cortinaje*, *arboleda*), presenting as a single mass what plurals would otherwise break down into separate components (*cortinas*, *árboles*). The inanimate is made animate, albeit statically: 'deaf' stars, light years away, brought to earth by their reflection in a puddle, being bled to death by time. An ordinary night scence is thus transformed, turned inside out in the poet's mind, and given a new and independent existence. In this way, time, an otherwise abstract concept, is rendered concrete. Time does not merely 'hang heavy', as in the popular expression; in this poem it is made to fall.

This is a more intense application of the principle of artistic transformation of reality outlined in *Horizon carré*. Eventually, in the manifesto to *Création* (November 1921), Huidobro would spell out the formula for this particular kind of 'creationism': 'To invent is to make two things parallel in space come together in time, or vice versa, thus presenting in their conjunction something new. The ensemble of diverse new realities united by a common *esprit* is what constitutes the created work.' Juan Gris was then saying much the same thing about his own work, when, defining his art as one of 'synthesis', he specified: 'I try to make concrete what is abstract; I proceed from the general to the particular in order to arrive at something new.'[30] The difference between them is not one of method but of means, and of temperament. Gris, like Reverdy, was disciplined and analytic; Huidobro was lyrical and fanciful.

The poet's transformation of just one of the painter's images is sufficient to appreciate this difference: when Gris was translating 'Arte poética' from *El espejo de agua*, he added in these lines, entirely of his own invention:

> Un bouton
> un léger coup
> et toutes les chambres s'éclairent.

Electricity as the symbol of the modern age. Huidobro, in *Poemas árticos*, putting Gris's genial inspiration into Spanish, raised it to a higher level of fantasy. In 'Nadador' (Swimmer), a flick of the switch doesn't merely light up the house, but the universe:

> Apretando un botón
> Todos los astros se iluminan

> (Pushing a button / all the stars light up)

It was this aspect of Huidobro's work that then attracted
Dada, a movement in which he was somehow absorbed. The
fact is that when Tzara included 'Cow Boy', a poem from
Horizon carré in *Dada 3* (December 1918), one critic of the
time based his review of the movement on it, finding this poem
not only 'representative', but capable of 'enchanting everyone
with any lyric sensibility'.[31] Not everyone. The poem contains
a variant of that elevator image Gris found so gratuitous in
Poemas árticos: in 'Llueve' one went down like a diver ('Des-
ciende el ascensor mejor que un buzo'); in 'Cow Boy' they are
rising up like thermometers: 'Les ascenseurs montent comme
des thermomètres'. Huidobro, like the avant-garde movement of
which he is an integral part, was moving in several different
directions at the same time in his personal quest for modernity.

Only fleetingly in his work does one encounter the trappings
of modernity of the sort which so enthralled the Futurists: airplanes, race-cars, skyscrapers, etc. When they do appear though,
they are thoroughly, often whimsically transformed in the
poet's imagination; man's inventions are made more man-sized,
brought to the level of the ordinary, as in the elevator example.
In 'Universo' (Universe), an airplane, the symbol of the age, is
but a moth:

> Junto al arco voltaico
> Un aeroplano daba vueltas

(Next to the electric light / an airplane was fluttering about)

The *Nord-Sud* group, put off by the more superficial aspects
of the modern, thought of themselves as charged with restoring a
kind of order to the avant-garde. Paul Dermée, on several occasions in the review, raised the idea of a new classicism, most
especially in 'Quand le Symbolisme fut mort' (March 1917) and
'Intelligence et Création' (August–September 1917). Huidobro
in Spain, and later in Chile, spoke of the group's effort in these
same terms, prompting Cansinos-Asséns to write in 1919: 'they
are like new Parnassians, the Thermidorean reaction to the revolution; they have even proclaimed themselves classicists.'[32]

This classicism could be, and was, interpreted in various ways.
On a theoretical basis, to write like the classics meant to imitate
them in their inventive capacity; and much was then made of
the fact that poet (*poietes*) in Greek, means inventor, creator.
On a practical basis, classicism also meant updating the classics,
'translating' the great works of the past into the modern idiom

of the avant-garde. Huidobro did this with 'Egloga' (Eclogue), a
modern version of Saint John of the Cross' 'Noche oscura del
alma' (Dark Night of the Soul). This masterwork was described
by the Spanish mystic as a poem 'in which the soul sings of the
fortunate adventure that it had in passing through the dark
night of faith (. . .) to union with the Beloved'. The setting is
pastoral:

> Quedéme, y olvidéme
> el rostro recliné sobre el Amado,
> cesó todo, y dejéme,
> dejando mi cuidado
> entre las azucenas olvidado.

(I stayed, and lost myself completely / I layed my head on the Loved
One, / everything came to a standstill, and I let myself go, / setting aside
my cares / losing them among the lilies.)

Huidobro, in an attempt at what today would be called
réécriture, reworked this Renaissance poem, putting it into the
language of his *Poemas árticos*:

> Sol muriente
>
> Hay una panne en el motor
>
> Y un olor primaveral
> Deja en el aire al pasar
>
> En algún sitio
>   una canción
>
> EN DONDE ESTAS
>
> Una tarde como ésta
>   te busqué en vano
> Sobre la niebla de todos los caminos
> Me encontraba a mí mismo
>
> Y en el humo de mi cigarro
> Había un pájaro perdido
>
> Nadie respondía
>
>   Los últimos pastores se ahogaron
>
> Y los corderos equivocados
> Comían flores y no daban miel

El viento que pasaba
Amontona sus lanas
                Entre las nubes
                Mojadas de mis lágrimas

A qué otra vez llorar
                lo ya llorado

Y pues que las ovejas comen flores
Señal que ya has pasado

(Dying sun / There is a breakdown in the motor / And a springlike aroma /
Remains in the air on passing / Some place / a song / WHERE ARE YOU /
One evening like this / I looked for you in vain / Over the mist of all the
roads / I kept on running into myself / And in the smoke of my cigar /
There was a lost bird / No one would answer / The last shepherds had
drowned / And the confused sheep / Were eating flowers and giving no
honey / The wind that was passing by / Piles up the wool / Among the
clouds / Wet from my tears / Why cry again / over the already lamented /
And since the sheep are eating flowers / Sign that you have just passed by)

Huidobro himself has explicated this poem, or at least tried to.
When he was in Chile in 1919, spreading the word about the
new aesthetic, he was taken for an iconoclast. Seeking to
correct this misinterpretation, he visited Hernán Díaz Arrieta,
his conservative-minded friend from the days of *Musa Joven* and
Azul, and then critic for the influential weekly *Zig-Zag*. As evidence of his classicism, he pointed out 'Egloga' and tried to
explain its imagery. The critic, although unconvinced, has fortunately left us a record of the attempt:

After a long conversation with the author [of 'Egloga'], we have arrived
at the following conclusions. The dying sun offers no difficulty; it could
be creationist, just as well as classicist, or even romantic. It is the same old
sun that dies out every afternoon. The breakdown in the motor? I first
took that to mean that the poet had gone on a trip and that his car had
broken down. But no; the breakdown is suffered by the sun and it is for
this reason that it is dying. That's what Huidobro says. Alright. At bottom,
it is not really an important issue. Continuing along in the poem, one hears
a lost song, someone is looking for something, remembers, feels alone. All
this is stated in a rather extravagant manner; but when have poets ever
expressed themselves like the rest of us? Suddenly, 'in the smoke of my
cigar a lost bird'. And this? What is it? No one replies; the last shepherds
are drowned, in other words they are silenced. Someone, then goes on
calling out for someone else. One comes across some sheep strangely

confused. Up above, the clouds pile up like mountains of wool. A reflection of contentment. And the explanation for the sheep eating flowers: someone special had just been there . . .
— Do you understand now?
— Very little.
— But this is a translation of an eclogue of San Juan de la Cruz!
— It doesn't surprise me; if you had translated it into Chinese I wouldn't have understood it either.[33]

It was the patently whimsical nature of this sort of inventiveness that astonished the readers of *Poemas árticos*, exasperating some and enchanting others.

But Huidobro was cultivating two types of poetry in 1918: the playful and the serious. In *Poemas árticos* he put together an assortment of compositions, some forty-four in all, that were more or less intertextually related, although in an unsystematic way. A systematic sequence involves a trajectory: a beginning, a middle, and an end. Images then do not merely reflect back upon one another, but fold into one another to generate a total meaning for the text. *Hallali* and *Ecuatorial* are, in this sense, systematic. Although one is in French and the other in Spanish, both deal with the same theme: war and its aftermath. Both are intensely lyrical, songs of love inspired by the country that had become the author's second homeland. Neither, however, received the attention of *Poemas árticos* and *Horizon carré* by readers of the time. Perhaps they were, as Juan Gris said, 'demasiado grandioso'. Perhaps; although some sixty years and several wars later they seem somewhat less so. Actually, both point toward a kind of poetry that was to become very important in Spain and Spanish America: the long metaphysical poem on the order of Neruda's *Tentativa del hombre infinito* (1926) and Alberti's *Sobre los ángeles* (1929), not to overlook Huidobro's own *Altazor* (1931).

Hallali, subtitled 'Poème de guerre' (War Poem), merits our attention at this point. It was printed in Madrid in October of 1918, before the war was over. Organized in five separate cantos, it presents the trajectory of the war from its beginning to its hoped-for conclusion: '1914', 'Les Villes', 'La Tranchée', 'Le Cimetière des soldats', 'Le Jour de la victoire' (1914, The Cities, The Trench, Military Graveyard, Victory Day). The book's title, *Hallali*, an onomatopoeia for the sound of a hunting horn, is itself a generative image.

1914

Nuages sur le jet d'eau d'été

    La nuit
                Toutes les tours de l'Europe se parlaient en secret

Tout d'un coup un œil s'ouvre
La corne de la lune crie

Hallali
                                                                Hallali
Les tours sont des clairons pendus

AOÛT 1914
                        C'est la vendange des frontières

Derrière l'horizon il se passe quelque chose

            Au gibet de l'Aurore toutes les villes sont pendues
            Les villes qui fument comme des pipes

Hallali
                                                                Hallali
Et ce n'est pas une chanson
                        Les hommes s'en vont

(Clouds over the spray of summer's fountain / The night / All the towers
of Europe were talking in secret / Suddenly an eye is opened / The horn of
the moon cries out / Hallali / Hallali / The towers are pendant trumpets /
AUGUST 1914 / It is the harvest time of borders / Behind the horizon
something is going on / On the gibbet of Aurora all the cities hang / Cities
that are smoking like pipes / Hallali / Hallali / And this is no song / Men
are going off)

The canto is extraordinarily rich in imagery of a generative
nature. With one image, for example, the horn of 'hallali', there
is a repeated cross-over between sound and shape which forces
together in a kind of metaphor-cluster things as dissimilar as the
cornet of the moon and the clarinet towers of Europe's warring
capitals (London, Paris, Berlin, Saint Petersburg). At a given
moment in August 1914, as though on cue, all make the same
clarion call to action, 'hallali' (from four corners of the page).
Just what this action might be comprises yet another mixed
cluster: a hunt, a harvest, a letting of blood. Several sets of
interrelated ideas are thus alternated like links in a chain. Moreover, there is a generative order to the enchainment. As in a film
sequence, one frame leads into another: dark clouds > night >

moon > cornet > hallali > hunting > reaping > hanging. At this point, midway through the canto, there is an implicit multiple metaphor of considerable force: war as a ritual, a seasonal hunt. The text is thus charged for the trigger image, contained here in the poem's only explicit comparison: 'Les villes fument comme des pipes'. Hunters lighting up their pipes, factories stoking up for war.

In the next canto, this kind of imagistic cross-over, no longer novel, is explicitly tagged. A plane on a bomb-run passes out of sight:

> Il s'était égaré dans la fumée des cigares
> Nuées des usines   Nuées du ciel
> C'est un trompe-l'œil

(It got lost in cigar smoke / Factory clouds / Storm clouds / It's an illusion)

Returning to '1914', it is through such a trompe l'œil that the city skylines are transformed from conspiratorial towers at night to game hanging on the gibbet at dawn ('Au gibet de l'Aurore toutes les villes sont pendues'). These two lines of imagery, war and the hunt, are repeatedly crossed. At the end of the sequence, to reinforce the closure, there is a change in tone, an authorial aside to the final 'hallali'. A rhetorical conjunction is then used to slip in this jarring plain-prose commentary: 'Et ce n'est pas une chanson'. Indeed. Men are being called to war, to hunt one another down ('Les hommes s'en vont').

Huidobro's writing has evolved: from a kind of Cubist collage in 1917 to an almost filmic sequence the following year, from the static 'tableaux' of *Horizon carré* to the 'tableau vivant' of *Hallali*. Movement is paramount in this poematic newsreel of the war's development. And, in subsequent cantos, the focus shifts from the cities to the trenches as the whole world gets pulled into the conflict: 'La tranchée / fait le tour de la Terre' (The trench encircles the Earth). There is a strange, almost magic quality to images such as these, where the syntactic flow of the sentence allows an idea to drift from one dimension to another, moving the reader's mind back and forth between the cosmic and the human. The earth is but a sphere with a trench cut around its middle; the quarter moon a hunting horn. In 'La Tranchée' there is a full moon, reduced to a target on the shooting-range of World War I. In this way, the opening metaphor of war as a hunting party is functional throughout *Hallali*:

dogs bay at the moon; cannons bark out their fire; the sky is a target shot through with holes; and, the moon is a bull's-eye:

C'est une belle cible la lune

L'ombre d'un soldat
Etait tombée dans un trou

On voit par terre sanglant
L'aviateur qui se cogna la tête contre une étoile éteinte

Et mieux qu'un chien
Le canon surveille

Quelquefois
Il aboie

LA LUNE

Toutes les étoiles sont des trous d'obus

(It's a pretty target the moon / The shadow of a soldier / had fallen into a hole / On the bloody earth you can see / The pilot who bumped his head on a dead star / And better than a dog / The cannon keeps watch / Sometimes / it barks / THE MOON / All the stars are holes from artillery fire)

Through the book, and from canto to canto, certain core images like that of the moon, are cycled in and out, generating numerous variations on themselves. Variations that ultimately create an impression of unity, giving a fluid integrality to this kaleidoscopic view of the war. The end is thus a variation on the beginning. The last canto, 'Le jour de la victoire', a visionary song to victory, revives an image from the first, the 'jets d'eaux'. As the festive fountains are turned on again, the dark clouds of war are gone, replaced by hats tossed into the air: 'Et les chapeaux monteront dans l'air / mieux que les boules dans les jets d'eaux' (And hats will rise up in the air / better than balls in the jet of a fountain).

Huidobro has constructed a text that works on the reader's imagination, causing him to link ideas, to make the connections that spark metaphor. Much of the imagery in *Hallali* is intratextual, generated from within the poem. But the stuff of literature is always literature, and this volume is also a kind of homage to the wounded Apollinaire: 'Le premier tué a été un poète' ('Les Villes' — The first victim was a poet). Accordingly, at poem's end, when planes fly over the cemetery, dipping their wings in salute, it is an image from 'Zone' that informs Huidobro's own:

LES AEROPLANES

De quel cimetière de héros
Sont envolées ces croix
Chanter la gloire de leurs morts

(AIRPLANES / From which cemetery of heroes / did these crosses take flight / to sing the glory of their dead)

Each plane's silhouette as a cross in the sky.
  And, at the very end of the book, a final transformation. When the speaker at last inserts himself, he assumes a cosmic dimension for his closing epilogue:

Et après
Tout en haut de la Tour Eiffel
J'allume mon cigare
              Pour les astres en danger

Là-bas
        Sur la borne du monde
Quelqu'un chante un hymne de triomphe

(And afterwards / At the very top of the Eiffel Tower / I light up my cigar / For the stars in danger [of falling with the fireworks] / Way down there / Along the edge of the world / Someone is chanting a hymn of triumph)

This is the selfsame oracular tone Huidobro adopted in *Ecuatorial*, a longer and more ambitious metaphysical poem dealing with the aftermath of war. In fact, the ending of one and the beginning of the other seem interrelated. Where *Hallali* leaves off, *Ecuatorial* begins:

Era el tiempo en que se abrieron mis párpados sin alas
Y empecé a cantar sobre las lejanías desatadas

(It was the time in which my eyelids were opened without wings / And I began to sing along remote parts set loose)

And this poem, envisaged in the grand manner of a cosmic trip through space and time would generate yet another, *Altazor*.
  In November of 1919, passing through Spain on his way back to France, Huidobro announced his next big project to Cansinos-Asséns.

Vicente Huidobro returns at an opportune moment, when the desire for renovation stimulated by his last books has generated a following, contributing by his example and contrast to the innovative movement which has sprung up among us with the indeterminate name of Ultra (. . .). The poet who repeats the miracle of Darío, goes beyond the lyric daring of his own *Poemas árticos* and *Ecuatorial*, carrying with him a new book, *Voyage en parachute*, in which difficult aesthetic problems are confronted and resolved.[34]

The subject of this poem is poetry, and the author's own experience with the limitations of avant-garde writing. Although fragments in both French and Spanish were to appear sporadically over the next decade, it would not be published in its entirety until 1931, and then in Madrid under the title *Altazor: o el viaje en paracaídas* (Altazor: or the Voyage in a Parachute).

Many other things would draw Huidobro's attention in the interim, not the least of which was a heated polemic over the new aesthetic.

IV
Polemics

I have complete faith in myself. I am so sure of what I am doing, that if D'Annunzio himself were to attack me, I would feel sorry for him.   1914

Huidobro always envisaged himself as a fighter, a champion of his own originality. Long before he was important enough to interest anyone in literary battle, he put up a determined effort to show his readiness. Hence the toughness toward D'Annunzio.

And toward Marinetti. For no apparent reason, other than pure belligerency, Huidobro in 1914 comes out with an attack on Futurism, the earliest development of the avant-garde. In 'El Futurismo' (*Pasando y pasando*, 1914), he lashes out at the movement for being both frivolous and old-fashioned at the same time. Huidobro's sallies are made from the same conservative corner as Rubén Darío's 1911 piece on Marinetti. He even calls on Darío for support:

All this business of singing to temerity, courage, audacity, gymnastics, boxing, is just too old. Let Marinetti go and read the *Odyssey* and the *Iliad*, the *Aeneid*, or any of Pindar's odes to the winner at the Olympics and he'll find there all his so-called novelty.

As for declaring war on women, besides being a cowardice unworthy of men as virile as the Futurists, it is simply ridiculous. As Rubén Darío has said so well, which is more beautiful, a nude woman or a storm? A lily or a cannon shot?

Yet Marinetti prefers an automobile to the pagan nudity of a woman. This is the preference of a little kid. The toy train first. Goo-goo Marinetti.

A decade later, in Paris, and from his own corner of the avant-garde, Huidobro would again come out swinging; his rhetorical tactic in 'Futurisme et Machinisme' (*Manifestes*, 1925), was much the same: 'To sing to war, boxers, violence, athletes, is something that goes back to Pindar.' But this public hostility to the movement did not prevent him from having a cordial relationship with its founder, as Marinetti's dedication to *Zang-Tumb-Tuuum* makes apparent: 'A Vincente Huidobro, vivissima simpatia futurista . . .'.

In Huidobro's view, controversy was an integral part of literature — its dynamic component. A public airing of conflicting ideas was an artistic event calling for a certain measure of showmanship; a full-fledged polemic an occasion to advertise for oneself. It is in this competitive spirit that he fought, and sought, his many literary battles.

His first contenders were local. Old friends in fact. Armando Donoso, for example, who had prefaced *La gruta del silencio* in 1913, came under fire in 1916 for a comment in *Zig-Zag*, in which he supposedly slighted Huidobro's uniqueness, comparing him to a Spanish writer, Rafael Cansinos-Asséns. The poet, ever contentious, responded with an open letter detailing Donoso's failings, as a critic and as a friend.[1] The issue is less important at this point than Huidobro's eagerness to respond, and to couch his response within a larger literary tradition. In closing, he olympically dismisses Donoso and other would-be detractors with an oblique allusion to Aristophanes (when, in *The Frogs*, Dionysus crosses the Acheronian river in search of a new dramatist to replace the dead Euripides): 'I can assure you that I will continue on my way, inperturbed by the wailing all around me that reminds me of those frogs in Aristophanes: brekekekex, coax, coax.' As in the earlier piece on Futurism, there is the same childlike urge to pick a fight, the same jeering rhetoric.

And as with children, Huidobro's sensitivity having been exposed, others were quick to join in taunting him with all sorts of accusations touching on his originality. Ernesto Guzmán, reviewing *Adán* for *Los Diez* (September 1916), accused him of imitating Pedro Prado, raising in the process the spectre of Cansinos-Asséns. This, on the eve of Huidobro's departure for Europe, was actually a handy pretext for writing to the Spaniard, whom he then went to visit in Madrid.[2] Ernesto Guzmán, the accuser, was handled much later, from Paris, in a long letter published in Santiago's *Aliados* in March of 1917. Typically, his reaction was an overkill; turning the same charge back on Guzmán, he accused him of plagiarizing Prado, practising what he called 'literary vampirism'. Such charges and countercharges were all in the nature of the game, at least as Huidobro played it. However, as the stakes got higher prudence was called for. Huidobro was forever brash.

Therefore, it is surprising to note that in France, during the course of 1917, he had no public quarrels. His uncertainty with the language was perhaps a tempering factor, as was the initial cohesion of the Cubist group. In Spain, however, things went quite differently. Besides spreading the word there in 1918 about the new aesthetic, he also sowed the seeds of discord. Ultraism was, in a sense, a reaction against Huidobro's dictatorial impulse to organize the Spanish avant-garde in his own image.

His first public dispute in Spain though was with a Chilean, Joaquín Edwards Bello. This was soon followed by one with Gómez Carrillo; and finally, he met his match with Guillermo de Torre, the promoter of Ultraism. The quarrel with Edwards was truly trivial, concerning who had introduced whom to Apollinaire and whether or not they were second cousins. A biographical note in *Grecia*, accompanying a poem by Edwards, was what aroused Huidobro's fighting instinct. Accordingly, he felt impelled to set the record straight with a characteristically pugnacious open letter. Isaac del Vando Villar, director of *Grecia*, moved by Huidobro's concern, innocently wrote to him in Paris:

Seville, January 31, 1920

Dear poet:
Your letter has surprised me, since, in truth, I never thought that the vanity of Edwards could attain such a ridiculous extreme. In number 39 of *Grecia*, under today's date, I am publishing your letter in a conspicuous place, along with an introductory note in which I point out that the person who supplied the biographical data on Edwards was none other than that hapless Lasso de la Vega.[3]

And so it went. Naturally, Edwards replied in kind (*Grecia*, February 1920); and Lasso de la Vega, not to be left out, eventually came up with a cutting piece against Huidobro in *Cosmópolis* ('La sección de oro', December 1920).

This was the sort of attention Huidobro was looking for. Or so it might seem. However, as in Chile, once his testiness was known, others were eager to provoke him. Gomez Carrillo picked up the gauntlet in June with an article on Cubism in which he had Reverdy accuse Huidobro not only of imitating him, but also of falsifying the publication of one of his books, *El espejo de agua*.[4] To this Huidobro penned a most vigorous reply, an eleven-page 'Respuesta a Gómez Carrillo', in which he lashed out at practically everyone, including Reverdy. In a postscript, he even broached the question of a duel: 'As I am signing this piece a friend comes up to warn me that I had better be careful since Carrillo is an accomplished duellist. I am not, but if that is what Carrillo wants he ought to know that my address is 41, rue Victor Massé.'[5] This time he had gone too far; his text was so defamatory that no one was willing to publish it. A note in the September issue of *Grecia* indicates that he even travelled to Spain to see about getting it into print:

A few days ago the American poet Vicente Huidobro was in Madrid.

According to what he told us, the purpose of his trip was to refute Gómez Carrillo's article in which the paternity of Creationism was attributed to Reverdy. In a plaintive attitude, Huidobro went from office to office of the principal papers trying to publish some pages in which he replied to Gómez Carrillo in a most violent manner and with an ambiguous syntax.

No one would print it, not even *Grecia*. Thus, the most serious charge against him went unchallenged. Guillermo de Torre quickly picked it up and went on to repeat it in so many variations that it has continued to haunt Huidobro criticism ever since.

What is remarkable about the controversy is that Huidobro himself brought it on, perhaps intentionally, perhaps inadvertently. Its origins go back to 1918, when Reverdy published in Paris a second edition of his 1916 *La Lucarne ovale*; Huidobro, then in Madrid, did the same with *El espejo de agua*. Reverdy updated his second edition, dropping the punctuation; Huidobro left his unchanged. If they were really rivals then — which I doubt — they were most cordial about it, for in Chile in 1919 Huidobro was still speaking of their twin efforts. Although he did, quite naturally, insist on his own originality:

There is a spiritual analogy in our work, and in fact the first day we met in Paris we were able to note this by reading poems to one another in which there was a certain shared aesthetic base. Nevertheless, aside from this common base, one need only read our works in order to perceive the absolute difference between us. While Reverdy is an eminently dramatic poet, I believe I am a purely lyrical one.[6]

The question of rivalry in the avant-garde came up after the death of Apollinaire, when it became necessary for someone else to take the lead. Petty differences then began to surface within the Cubist group, but they were kept petty by the arrival on the scene of another giant, Tristan Tzara, and the subsequent development of Dada in Paris. In this way, after the war, Cubism suddenly passed from the front lines of the avant-garde into the back pages of literary history. Huidobro tried to give it a second life by rebaptizing it with the name of Creationism, an all-embracing 'movement' of his own invention with lots of fellow-travellers, but few real followers. No one in Paris objected to this until 1924, when one critic, enthused by Huidobro's work, credited him with inventing literary Cubism; then it was Max Jacob who was offended, and in an interview with yet another critic claimed the honour for himself.[7]

The real objections to Huidobro's Creationism came not from Paris, where individual spin-offs from Cubism and Dada were a regular occurrence, but from Spain and centred on *El espejo de agua*. Huidobro, sensing rumblings about this book, or perhaps causing them, wrote to his friends soliciting testimonials *before* Gómez Carrillo published his supposed interview with Reverdy. In this way he accumulated a documentary defence of *El espejo de agua*, including a letter from the Spanish publisher certifying the second edition to be exactly the same as the first. Just why he did this is not clear, however some idea of his thinking can be gleaned from a letter to a friend in Chile, Angel Cruchaga, a few weeks after the publication of Gómez Carrillo's piece:

You ought to read my reply in the Spanish papers. I have destroyed them [my enemies]. If only you could see how all the people who are worth anything make fun of them. No need to tell you that all the young people in Spain are with me. Soon you'll see the articles coming and going in my defence. Here in Paris the same thing. All the artists of worth are in my favour and this trouble has served me enormously well for its *réclame*.[8]

Had he fabricated this scandal to draw attention to himself with the intention of producing the saving documents at the magic moment? Whatever the plan, it backfired, for when he went to publish his little dossier no one would have it. His 'Respuesta a Gómez Carrillo' went unread. When it finally did appear, years later, it had been thoroughly transformed; toned down and translated into French, only its principal argument remained intact: that Creationism was his own. In this way it was included in *Manifestes* (1925) as 'Le Créationnisme'. In the interim Huidobro's writing had evolved. So much so, that by 1925 he was a Creationist in name only.

Guillermo de Torre would not let the issue rest. From August of 1920, when he first sensationalized it in *Cosmópolis* as 'La poesía creacionista y la pugna entre sus progenitores', until his death in 1971, he was unrelenting, returning to the attack in countless books and articles.[9] But, like Huidobro, he too could be on disarmingly cordial terms with his contender. For example, a copy of *Hélices* dedicated in February 1923, 'senza rencore', was followed a few months later by a new offensive: 'Los verdaderos antecedentes líricos del Creacionismo en Vicente Huidobro'. In this piece, which appeared in *Alfar* (September 1923), the Spaniard has the Chilean stealing his ideas not from Reverdy, but from an Uruguayan, Herrera y Reissig. And when

Huidobro tries to reply he again has difficulty getting into print in Spain. This time though, he refused to be silenced and in February of 1924 he came up with the stratagem of reviving *Création*, dormant since 1921, and inserting in it a Spanish-language supplement: 'Al fin se descubre mi maestro'. Only after this did *Alfar* print his reply, in April 1924; but then merely as a pretext to let Guillermo de Torre have another go at him in the same issue: 'Rasgos polémicos: réplica a Vicente Huidobro'. With Guillermo de Torre, Vicente Huidobro had finally met his match.

He had also learned a lesson. And although his fighting spirit was undiminished, henceforth his tactics would be different. The *ad hominem* attack would be replaced by a more reasoned appeal concerning the issue in dispute. In fact, when Angel Flores rehashed the matter of *El espejo de agua* in the *Herald Tribune* book section (29 November 1931), Huidobro wrote to him in New York suggesting that he go back and read the text in order to see the hollowness of the debate he was giving lip-service to. The result was a cordial reply from Flores (6 June 1932), setting up a future meeting in Paris:

I have followed your work rather faithfully and with considerable admiration. (. . .) I am not therefore the stubborn enemy on your trail that you were supposing, and although we might bare our teeth in the discussion of details I want you to consider me as one of the most humble of your admirers — and one of the most sincere. (. . .) I'll be passing through Paris at the beginning of September on my way to Spain. Let me know if you'll be there so that I can come by and greet you.[10]

In public debate too, Huidobro was more measured after his experience with Guillermo de Torre. In October of 1924, for example, when André Breton published the first Surrealist manifesto, Huidobro came out against it. He was not alone. Noteworthy, however, is the fact that this time he deals with the issue and not with the personalities involved. So complete was his transformation in attitude, that one reviewer of the time, commenting on the sudden explosion of hostility to the new movement, could cite Huidobro as a model of probity: 'They are slugging it out pretty hard again, and it is Surrealism that has started it. (. . .) The outcome? Perhaps Huidobro can give us a clue: "The more one studies poetry, the more one believes in it, and the less one believes in the poets." '[11]

Typically, Huidobro wasted no time in getting into the fray. In early 1925 he brought out *Manifestes*, a volume of theoretical writings in which he set out to refute Surrealism from his personal perspective on the avant-garde. The book contains ten manifesto-like essays, some of which had been published before, and is almost as interesting for what it does not reprint as for what it does. Uncollected, for example, is the 1921 *L'Esprit nouveau* piece on 'La Création pure', which had once served as the basis for his promotional lectures in Madrid and Paris, as well as providing the preface for *Saisons choisies* (Paris: La Cible, 1921), a showcase anthology of his Creationist work. Instead, making the case for himself, we have 'Le Créationnisme', a thoroughly cut-down version of his unpublished reply to Gómez Carrillo, in which he pretty much limits himself to a culling of his earlier writings so as to show that, in his own words: 'Creationism is not a school that I tried to impose on anyone; Creationism is a general aesthetic theory that I first began to work on back in 1912.' Be that as it may, Huidobro makes no claims for the present-day scope of the ism, and is content instead to assert that Reverdy was never a Creationist — a point that the French writer would find little reason to dispute. For Breton he has no rancour; only a reasoned critique that cuts to the core of Surrealism's reason for existence. Examining the 1924 manifesto in the light of other avant-garde proclamations, including his own, Huidobro leads off his critique with 'Manifeste Manifestes':

The first thing to observe is that we all coincide on certain points: a logical overestimation of poetry, and an equally logical contempt for realism. (. . .) Surrealism is unique in advocating dreams and automatic writing. According to Aragon, Surrealism was supposed to have been discovered by Crevel in 1919 and the definition given by Breton is the following: 'Pure psychic automatism by which we propose to let the real thought process be expressed. Dictation of thought without any control by the reasoning faculty.'

For Huidobro, as indeed for much of the literary avant-garde, 'automatic writing' was an unacceptable proposition, since it removed art from the creative control of the artist. The subconscious, freed from the constraints of reason, was to be the new source of imagery. But whose subconscious? And why should the reverie of a dreamer, any dreamer, be more artistic than that of a wakeful creator? What was at issue was not Creationism, but artistic creation itself. And it is no wonder that many of the most creative writers of the time questioned the efficacy of automatism as proposed by Breton. The reactions against the manifesto were inevitable, and in them can be found the various limits of the entire avant-garde enterprise.

Futurism set words free. Cubism took that liberty and disciplined it, advocating the creation of new images by means of the juxtaposition of 'distant realities'. Reverdy's definition for *Nord–Sud* (March 1918), is the most succinct: 'The image is a pure creation of the mind. It does not arise from a comparison but from the bringing together of two more or less distant realities. The greater the distance between the two realities thus confronted, the stronger the image.' Huidobro shared this idea, adding only that there was a hidden element permitting this forced *rapprochement* to work: 'The poet is the one who brings out the hidden relations among the most distant things, the hidden threads that unite things. One must pluck these threads like the strings of a harp, and produce a resonance that sets in motion the two distant realities.'

Dada took this same notion a step further. Recognizing the stunning power of unusual combinations, Tzara advocated the use of chance to bring together the dissimilar. His well-known formula — to clip words and phrases from a newspaper, put them in a hat, and then spill the contents out on a table to see the result — had the effect of reducing the poet's role to that of an arbiter, a judge of what happens to be poetic, or unpoetic. In this way, art was not created but 'found'. Huidobro apparently tried this, for among his papers there is a packet of such clippings labelled 'Frases y recortes'; but even before the emergence of Surrealism, he came out pretty strongly against the idea of chance in 'Manifeste Peut-être' (*Création*, February 1924):

And the fortuitous? Without doubt, something can turn up with the impartiality of an involuntary gesture born of chance, but such a thing is too close to the instinctual, and for that reason it is more animal than human. Chance is fine when a roll of the dice turns up five aces or four queens; but otherwise it ought to be excluded. No poems tossed out by chance; on the poet's table there is no green felt.

Breton was of the opposite view. Broadening the rules of the game, he reduced the artist's role even further: from that of arbiter to medium, vehicle for recording the free-thought flow of the subconscious. The catchwords in the manifesto were 'appareil enregistreur' for the poet, and 'écriture automatique' for the poem. The concept was revolutionary, and for a time at least it captured the imagination of some and aroused the enmity of others. But in the end, it proved difficult, if not impossible, to put into practice; and in 1930, when Breton brought out his second Surrealist manifesto, he expressed regret over the failure of automatic writing to produce the anticipated breakthrough to an unmediated form of artistic expression.

Huidobro was right; automatism carried to its ultimate consequence was unworkable. But so was Creationism. And he himself would deal with this literary fact of life in *Altazor* (1931). But, even before that, he knew he was alone and fighting a losing battle for the total autonomy of the poem: 'the created poem, in which each constituent part, and the whole ensemble, shows something new, independent of the external world, detached from every other reality except its own' ('Le Création-nisme'). This was always more of a goal than a reality, and by 1925 he had fairly well abandoned the goal. In fact, one of the more intriguing texts of *Manifestes* is a kind of poster-page announcement (*see over, p. 80*). A cryptic announcement that can lead to many interpretations, the common denominator of which must be Huidobro's realization that he was alone. Whatever his conception of the avant-garde and his seminal role in its development may once have been, by 1925 he knew he had no followers. Creationism belonged to history.

His passion for polemics was not spent however. The only difference was one of focus. Politics was now of more importance to him than poetics. These battles were waged on two fronts, the public and the private. A dispute with Buñuel in 1931 was carried on exclusively at the private level. Huidobro was a Communist then, and his quarrel with the filmmaker was mostly political. None the less, it does contain an interesting epilogue to his position regarding Surrealism, which he then ridiculed as 'sub-realism':

I just found out that you have mixed my name in affairs of yours in which I am not involved, saying things that are absolutely untrue. You have said that I was going on attacking sub-realism because I wanted to join it and couldn't. That is an outright lie. In the first place I have never wanted to belong to sub-realism; in the second place it is not true that I am attacking it now. I attacked it years ago, and in writing, facing up to what had to be attacked, and so right was I then that they themselves recognize today that automatic writing — precisely what I then attacked — has been a failure (. . .). Thus it is false that I had ever wanted to join in sub-realism and I challenge you to demonstrate the opposite. I have pertained to the most interesting movement of this century — and not simply as one of a crowd, but among the front runners — and I have never tried to use that fact to set myself off. On the contrary, I have preferred to pull back and work in silence. At the moment I am not interested in fanfare, but when I feel like jumping into the fray you'll see then that I know well how to do it and am familiar with the technique.[12]

Je suis arrivé en retard pour prendre le train que j'avais mis en marche.

AVIS
AUX
TOURISTES

J'ai eu le temps de prendre en mouve- ment le dernier wagon et chaque fois que le train allait dérailler je faisais des signes au conducteur lui mon- trant de loin la ma- nœuvre. Dans les wagons de troisième, de seconde et même de première classe, s'étaient faufilé plu- sieurs commis voya- geurs de grandes mai- sons. En arrivant à la gare je m'aperçus que le train avait changé d'itinéraire et de chemin. Je des- cendis et je pris tout seul la route des rêves polaires.

Le motor-man me ressemblait vaguement mais ce n'était pas moi-même.

(NOTICE TO TOURISTS / I arrived too late to catch the train that I had set in motion / I had only enough time to hop on the last car of the moving train and each time it was about to go off the tracks I would sig- nal to the conductor showing him from a distance the manœuvre. In the third-class cars, as well as those of second and even of first class, various travelling salesmen had slipped themselves in. On arriving at the station I realized that the train had changed tracks and itinerary. I got off and I took alone the route of polar dreams / The motorman looked vaguely like me but he wasn't me.)

He soon did jump into the fray again, or was drawn into it back in his native Chile. In the mid-1930s, as Neruda's star began to rise, Huidobro's admirers tried to bring the younger poet down to earth, accusing him of plagiarism, the bugbear of every new writer working out of a literary tradition. Neruda handled himself well. Rather than suffer what one critic has diagnosed as 'the anxiety of influence', he publicly admitted to a paraphrasing of his source and went on to attack Huidobro — the supposed instigator — in a privately circulated poem *Aquí estoy*. Huidobro's response was private too. Writing in code to a friend identified only as 'Poroto' (Chile-bean), he complains of 'Bacalao' (Codfish): 'I see by your letter that the intrigues of the Black Gang and of its chief, poor Bacalao, are following their normal course. I already knew that he had sent out circulars slandering me (. . .). It's enough to make one die laughing. What is behind it all is that I am the only real Communist among all those fake intellectual revolutionaries.'[13] Politics not only separated the two poets, but kept their quarrel almost clandestine. In May of 1937, Tristan Tzara, heading a group of leftist intellectuals, had asked both Huidobro and Neruda to cool things down for the good of the cause — the Civil War in Spain and the Popular Front in Chile.[14]

For this reason, Huidobro's public side is better seen in his polemic with Pablo de Rokha, an old friend from the days of *Musa Joven* and *Azul*, whose jealousy was piqued in 1935 when *Zig-Zag* brought out an important new anthology of Chilean poetry, the *Antología de poesía chilena nueva*. In this anthology, the major figures (in order of importance) were Huidobro, Neruda, and de Rokha. Wishing to see this order reversed, Pablo de Rokha published a long critique in *La Opinion* for four days running ('Marginal a la antología', June 10–13). Huidobro need not have responded; but he did, and this gave rise to an exchange of charges and countercharges, before finally degenerating into simplistic jeers. Huidobro was having fun, and in his sign-off article, 'A Pablo de Rokha para siempre y hasta nunca', he could not resist taking one last poke at his adversary, stuttering a pun on his pen-name: PAPABLO DE ROKAKA.[15] It was on this same prankish level that he publicly scorned César Moro, a Peruvian Surrealist with whom he was then also at odds: 'Don César Quíspez, morito de calcomanía' (*Vital*, June 1935).

Greater energies were reserved for political disputes, in which he occasionally arrived at physical blows. Santiago newspapers report a fist-fight on the steps of the National Library in March of 1936. And in October of the following year Huidobro was

seriously beaten up by some foreign agents for publishing
'Fuera de aquí', a broadside protesting against Mussolini's
having sent some military advisers to South America.[16]

He was always outspoken and self-confident, but at this point
in his life he was particularly buoyant. Convinced of the greatness of his work, he cultivated an especially truculent attitude
toward whatever displeased him. Insight into his comportment
comes from Carlos Morla Lynch, a Chilean diplomat whose
memoirs contain a candid portrait of his compatriot in Spain
just after the publication of *Altazor* in 1931:

> Huidobro turns up in Madrid one day, and is the same as always: on top
> of the world. He tells us that he is going to start up a new magazine, to be
> called *Insult*. A promising title. Impetuous verbosity. When Vicente starts
> to speak he becomes a torrent, but which neither carries along nor per-
> suades. Everything he says and affirms takes on in his mouth the character
> of an irrefutable judgement, a final verdict. An ego that dims the brilliance
> of his enormous talent. All the artists and poets whose names come up in
> our conversations are dismissed by him as 'id-i-ots' (that's the way he
> draws out the word), and their work as absurd and ridiculous. From this
> peremptory judgement, from this hecatomb of his making, only he is left
> standing; he is the only one with any sense. This arrogance is really pitiful,
> a forced 'dadaism' on his part that is not even sincere, for he is fundamen-
> tally a good fellow.[17]

This arrogance, however affected, was a part of his public
posture. As late as 1933, questioning why Neruda and other
younger intellectuals hadn't yet joined the Communist party, he
falls back on the same jeering qualifier, claiming that 'anybody
under forty who is not a party member must be an idiot'.[18]

Actually, this was a new stage in Huidobro's life. Economic
difficulties brought him back to Chile for good in 1932. And it
is in this latter stage that he would be not only aloof, but
generous. Especially with younger writers. Gonzalo Rojas, a
prime mover of the Chilean generation of 1938 which emerged
under the twin shadows of Neruda and Huidobro, has recalled
how the former Creationist was a kind of father-figure for them,
one who took an interest not in moulding writers into his own
image, but in helping them cut through the web of tradition to
arrive at their own originality:

> Huidobro was freedom itself: the one who sowed the deepest. In me,
> and in so many others: in each according to our own measure. A freedom
> that made men out of us: responsible poets, with utopias, with anarchy.
> But without being servile. It's not that he was our only progenitor but,

without him, everything would surely have been different for us. He drank from the living rock of Apollinaire's *esprit nouveau*, and he was truly the great giver: the one who gave us everything without our having to ask, and he asked nothing in return. He loved youth and he knew how to listen to us, always (. . .). He wrote neither praise nor prologues, but he taught us to be what we are; freedom and heresy in the amplest sense: aloofness versus pathos.[19]

Ironically, this generation saw itself as setting in motion a second wave of Surrealism. But no matter, for Huidobro was then serene in his conviction that everything new began with him. In 1940 he could even afford himself the luxury of a peace overture to his arch-enemy Guillermo de Torre, as a letter from the Spaniard makes apparent:

Buenos Aires, August 13, 1940
Dear friend:
Excuse the delay and the brevity with which I am replying to your kind mailing of *Sátiro* and the two pamphlets accompanying it. I too have thought of you on various occasions, inquiring after you among our common friends. Because, forgotten now, at least for me, our differences of yesterday, your name and your figure remain associated in my mind only with the best days of my literary initiation, with that Madrid of 1918, almost a fable now, after what came later . . .
If you come one day to Buenos Aires — I have been projecting a trip to Chile for a long time now, but I don't know when I'll be able to do it — don't fail to let me know. It would give me great pleasure to evoke those distant times with you and to compare our current views.
Meanwhile very cordial greetings from
Guillermo de Torre[20]

The fighter was convinced that he was retiring as a champion. In Neruda's memoirs there is mention of Huidobro's efforts to patch things up between them.[21] And, in 1946, not long before his death, he himself redefined his attitude with regard to polemics. In reply to a question about Neruda, he states: 'Believe me; these little literary battles are without interest. I live far from all that, very far. At the moment literary politics don't interest me at all, nor political literature.'[22] Huidobro's change of attitude is not surprising. Polemics were always for him a way of placing himself in the centre of things. In his mature years, he needed no such artificial limelight.

V
Beyond Cubism

A poem is a poem when it contains the unexpected. As soon as it becomes routine, it neither shocks, nor marvels, nor even disturbs; it is then no longer a poem.   1925

In the early 1920s Huidobro made a grand effort to rally the avant-garde around the idea of Creationism. In 1921 he founded *Creación/Création*, a multilingual review of the arts; in that same year he also put together *Saisons choisies*, a sampling of his own work prefaced by a discursive essay of aesthetic principles, 'La Création pure'. It is in this essay that he diagrammed the role of the artist in the creative process:

System is what controls the selection of things, while technique is what reshapes them into something new. This is an assembly-line concept of art as a product manufactured in the poet's mind. Creationism, thus loosely defined, became for Huidobro a kind of trademark for anything so 'created'. However, even in this simplified scheme of the poetic process, it is not difficult to see that the inspirational input being relatively constant, output can be varied only through a change in technique. As a consequence, in the pursuit of originality, Huidobro was obliged to go beyond Cubism, beyond the technique of studied juxtaposition.

He did so, but not before first trying to generate a movement with himself at its centre. In the Autumn of 1921, he writes to Gerardo Diego, seeking to arrange a forum in Madrid. The Spanish poet in turn wrote to Ciria y Escalante, then on the board of the Ateneo, to see about setting up a lecture there: 'Voilà l'affaire: I just received a letter from Huidobro (in Paris) in which, with his customary optimism, he tells me of his artistic tourneys. He also tells me that he wants to come to

1 Family house, where the poet was born in 1893.

2 As a child, writing.

4 A *calligramme* in the making, 1912.

3 MS of 'Ocaso en el espejo', part of the projected *El canto imperceptible*.

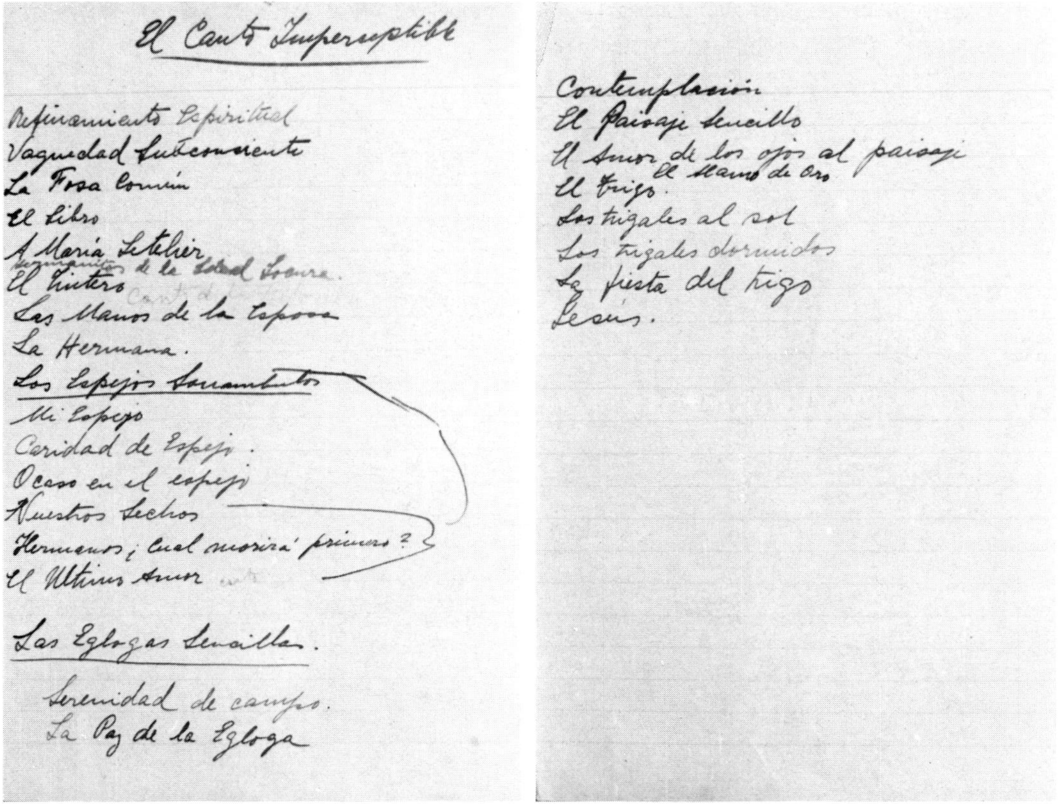
El Canto Imperceptible

Refinamiento Espiritual
Vaguedad Subconsciente
La Prosa Común
El Libro
A María Letelier
El Tintero
Las Manos de la Esposa
La Hermana.
Los Espejos Sonámbulos
Mi Espejo
Caridad de Espejo.
Ocaso en el espejo
Nuestros Lechos
Hermanos ¿Cual morirá primero?
El Último Amor

Las Églogas Sencillas.

Serenidad de campo.
La Paz de la Égloga

Contemplación
El Paisaje sencillo
El Amor de los ojos al paisaje
El Trigo.
Los trigales al sol
Los trigales dormidos
La fiesta del trigo
Jesús.

5 Table of contents for a projected book, 1915.

6 At 17, before getting married.

Sur la table il y avait quelques grains de poudre
ou de café. La guerre ou le repos ; mais pourquoi
tout ensemble ? L'odeur nous guidait le soir plus
que nos yeux et le moulin broyait du noir, dans
nos têtes. Pourquoi les levez-vous en remuant les
lèvres ? Le voisin connaîtra vos pensées.

8

*A mon cher ami
le poète Vicente Huidobro.
Mes efforts parallèles se sont rencontrés*

Pierre Reverdy
Avril 1917

7 Reverdy welcomes Huidobro (on a page-proof of his 'Moulin à café', 1917).

*Je garde dans mes yeux
La chaleur de tes larmes   Les dernières
~~Le dernier~~
Maintenant tu ne pourras pleurer
Jamais plus*

*Par les chemins qui ne finissent pas
l'Automne vient
Des doigts blancs des neige
Arrachent toutes les feuilles*

Quelle fatigue

*Le vent   Le vent
Une pluie d'ailes
Couvre la terre*

8 MS of 'Automne', with corrections by Juan Gris.

9 Travelling to Europe, 1916.

Art Poétique.

Que le vers soit comme une clef
qui ouvre mille portes.
Quelque chose passe dans l'air, quelque chose
quand les yeux cherchent...
Et l'âme...

Un bouton...
Un léger coup
et toutes les chambres s'illuminent.

La parole juste
et plus belle qu'elle est nue.

L'adjectif
un Pielcau ; cachin de beauté
L'épée de Muse
trop lourde.

siècle du nerf.
On ne connaît pas les muscles
Rien d'étranger au poème.
Toute conception au public
Amoindrit et mêle
un élément étranger...
Le sujet attaché à la Terre.
On ouvre la tête
comme une fenêtre
Tous les arbres et les vents.

10 Gris's rewrite of Huidobro's 'Arte poética'.

11   With Gris and Lipchitz in Beaulieu-près-Loches, 1918.

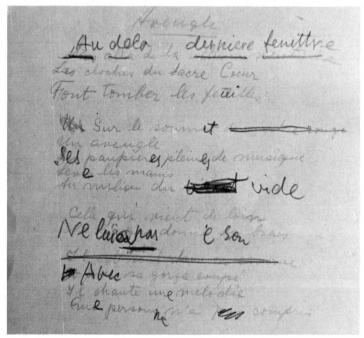

12   MS of 'Aveugle', with corrections by Gris.

14 MS of 'Moi Flamfolle', revised for inclusion in *Horizon carré*.

13 Page-proof of 'Paysage', 1917.

15 In Chile, *en famille*, 1919.

16 With his father in Chile, 1919.

La Galerie G. L. Manuel Frères

47, Rue Dumont-d'Urville, 47

Présente au Théâtre Edouard VII
du 16 Mai au 2 Juin

UNE EXPOSITION DE POÈMES

DE

Vincent HUIDOBRO

Vernissage Mardi 16 Mai, de 3 h. à 5 h.
Ce Catalogue tient lieu d'Invitation.

VINCENT HUIDOBRO, *par Pablo Picasso*

17   Catalogue of the painted-poem exhibition, 1922.

18 Interior of Paris studio, 41 rue Victor Massé, 1922.

19 A Paris banquet, 1924 (with Kahnweiler,Gris, Léger, Diego, Dermée . . .).

20 Trick photo: talking to himself.

21 With Lya de Putti and other starlets, 1927.

VOTE POR

VICENTE HUIDOBRO

Candidato de la Juventud

El único que ha demostrado amar al pueblo, no con palabras sino con hechos, hasta exponer su vida.

Si quiere que el Chile Nuevo sea un hecho
vote por Vicente Huidobro

Si quiere salvar el Salitre
vote por Vicente Huidobro

Si quiere limpiar el país y verlo pronto grande y rico.
vote por Vicente Huidobro

Si quiere el desarollo de la Instrucción
vote por Vicente Huidobro

Si quiere salvar la Raza
vote por Vicente Huidobro

Si quiere que los móviles de la Revolución se cumplan pronto
vote por Vicente Huidobro

El Ex-Director de "ACCIÓN", herido por su valentía, es el único hombre capaz de regenerar nuestra Patria.

Secretaría General: Galería San Carlos, Oficina 9, (Altos).

Imp. Ah'Wan, 11 de Mayo 737

UN CATACLYSME

L'Effondrement de l'Empire Britannique

est proche. – Lisez le livre prophétique de Vincent Huidobro :

"FINIS BRITANNIA"

Prix : 4 fr.

Le XX siècle sera le tombeau de l'Angleterre

ÉDITIONS FIAT LUX
LIBRAIRIE JEAN BUDRY ET Cⁱᵉ

22 Handbill for *Finis Britannia*, 1924.

23 Political flyer, 1925.

SÁBADO 8
AGOSTO · 1925
SAN CIRIACO

Lo que es la Lotería Nacional Argentina y sus beneficios sociales

Los que se quejan del destino deberían mejor quejarse de sí mismos.

Las Últimas Noticias

M. C. —Es propiedad.—Compañía 1314.—Casilla 13-D.

AÑO XXIII — N.o 6.663   SANTIAGO DE CHILE   20 CENTAVOS

EL AUDAZ ATENTADO DE QUE FUE VICTIMA ANOCHE DON VICENTE HUIDOBRO

Angel Cruchaga, primer redactor de "La Acción", habla para nuestro diario.—Recordando el secuestro de Huidobro en París. Otros periodistas que han sido atacados de hecho por emitir opiniones

UN PERIODISTA QUE TUVO MIEDO

"La Acción", un diario de la tarde que ha aparecido recientemente, publicó en una de sus últimas ediciones un informe que un "tribunal de conciencia" había expedido sobre la actuación pública y privada de un numeroso grupo de políticos, cuya participación en el manejo de las cosas del Gobierno fué en otro tiempo muy preponderante.

En este informe aparecen juicios crudos y severos relacionados con actos de orden particular y político de los caballeros que componen la larga lista de los "juzgados".

La aparición de esta publicación, según parece, ha dado origen a un atentado de que ha sido víctima el director del diario mencionado, don Vicente Huidobro.

Según da cuenta la prensa de la mañana, el señor Huidobro al salir de su casa, fué asaltado por uno ó dos individuos, quienes lo golpearon brutalmente, dejándolo en estado bastante grave.

Hasta hoy en la mañana, el enfermo continuaba en estado muy delicado.

DON VICENTE HUIDOBRO FERNANDEZ

La personalidad del director de "La Acción" es bastante conocida dentro y fuera del país. La prestigiosa situación que ha alcanzado la debe principalmente a su interesante labor literaria. Se le considera como el fundador del creacionismo. Sus publicaciones han sido estimadas como un poderoso impulso de renovación, no sólo para la literatura, sino para el arte en general.

El Creacionismo ha sido definido en numerosas ocasiones, no solamente por el señor Huidobro, sino también por diversos escritores europeos y americanos. Sin embargo, es difícil dar en pocas palabras una idea acertada de esta tendencia. La definición que parece hallarse más cerca de los propósitos que persiguen los creacionistas es más ó menos la siguiente, debida a la pluma del mismo señor Huidobro:

"No hay que cantar la rosa, poetas; hay que hacerla florecer en el poema."

HOY VISITAMOS AL ENFERMO

Hoy temprano estuvimos en casa del señor Huidobro para imponernos de su salud y obtener algunas impresiones suyas sobre el ataque de que ha sido víctima.

Recibidos por la señora Huidobro, nos comunicó que, por orden terminante del médico, estaban estrictamente prohibidas las visitas. Según declaraciones de la misma señora, el paciente continuaba algo mejor.

CON EL SEÑOR ANGEL CRUCHAGA

Ante la imposibilidad de conversar con el señor Huidobro, fuimos en busca del señor Cruchaga, quien es primer redactor del diario que publicó el documento que indicamos antes.

Fuimos recibidos muy cortésmente por el señor Cruchaga, quien nos dijo:

—Las primeras noticias del atentado las recibí por los diarios de la mañana, de manera que yo no podré darles mayores detalles de los que aparecen en la prensa. Luego iré a casa del amigo Huidobro y

DON VICENTE GARCIA HUIDOBRO FERNANDEZ, DIRECTOR DE "ACCION", SEGUN NUESTRO DIBUJANTE VAGNILLY

Don Angel Cruchaga Santa María, primer redactor del diario "Acción"

ré modo de conversar con él. Después nos agregó:

—Naturalmente, este ataque ha producido en mí y en todos los colegas de redacción honda impresión, y protestamos de que la fuerza bruta quiera aplastar el espíritu sano y patriota de nuestro director.

—¿Hay presunciones sobre quién pueda ser el causante de este atentado?, preguntamos.

—Ya le he dicho que carezco de noticias. Pero es evidente que ha sido uno de los aludidos el que ha cometido por sí mismo ó ha encargado hacer el salvaje atentado de anoche.

—¿Qué actitud tomará "La Acción" frente a este ataque?

—Conozco mucho el temple y el espíritu tenaz de Huidobro por lo que creo que continuaremos, imperturbables, nuestra campaña de depuración y denunciando todos los malos manejos que merecen reprobación pública. Este haremos mientras no se cierre nuestra imprenta, porque, como ustedes saben, "en Chile no se puede decir todo lo que se quiere".

Nos agregó:

—La persona de Huidobro es una garantía de rectitud para la campaña en que estamos.

lo que le permite formarse un juicio muy independiente de las cosas que suceden, tanto más cuanto que jamás ha pertenecido a un partido político.

EL SECUESTRO DE HUIDOBRO EN PARIS

El señor Huidobro ha vivido durante muchos años en París, donde ha hecho la mayor parte de sus publicaciones. Justamente, a raíz de la aparición de una de ellas se vió envuelto en un incidente que preocupó con mucho interés a la prensa de Europa y de América.

Los hechos pasaron así: El señor Huidobro publicó "Finis Britannia", obra que contenía un ataque para Inglaterra. Apenas apareció el libro, el autor desapareció, asegurándose que había sido secuestrado, suposición que vino casi a confirmarse por un anónimo que recibió la señora del desaparecido que decía:

"Sou mar! est gardé sous sept clefs".

En esta ocasión hubo algunos diarios parisienses que estimaron un ataque para Inglaterra y reclamó del autor del libro, destinada a despertar la curiosidad del público. Se recordó que Pie-

ro Benoit había usado de una estratagema parecida con fines idénticos cuando publicó "L'Atlantide".

Este incidente terminó cordialmente con la vuelta del señor Huidobro a su hogar, quien al ser preguntado, respondió que no recordaba lo que le había sucedido en el tiempo que permaneció fuera de su casa.

RECORDANDO OTROS ATAQUES A PERIODISTAS

El caso sucedido anoche a la persona del señor Huidobro no es el primero que presenciamos.

En una oportunidad, los distinguidos señores Locquentti y Falgar fueron apaleados por publicar una caricatura que se consideró ofensiva para un alto dignatario de la Administración.

Igualmente el redactor de "El Diario Ilustrado", señor Vélela, fué golpeado por hacer publicaciones contrarias a las tendencias de un político de bastante figuración.

Un caso análogo pasó con una publicación del señor Renato Valdés.

Más recientes son los incidentes en que se encuentran mezclados los señores Jenaro Prieto e Ismael Edwards Matte, por emitir opiniones molestas para algunos personajes de la política.

UN ESCRITOR QUE TUVO MIEDO

A propósito de esto mismo, se recuerda, a pesar de los muchos años transcurridos, el incidente en que participó un antiguo y brillante periodista, que, siendo casi un maleante de antecedentes muy tenebrosos.

Al ajustarse el precio de los "trabajos profesionales" del maleante en cuestión, este estuvo contento el periodista que lo solicitaba:

—De precio mejor hablaremos una vez que usted haya visto el "trabajito"...

Fué tanta la impresión que produjeron en el periodista las declaraciones sugestivas del sujeto buscado que desistió de sus propósitos.

CONJETURAS DEL PUBLICO

En todos los círculos se comenta en formas muy variadas el incidente de que damos cuenta, barajándose algunos nombres de los caballeros afectados por la publicación como los autores ó instigadores del ataque al señor Huidobro.

LAS INVESTIGACIONES POLICIALES

La Sección de Seguridad ha tomado medidas para dar con el responsable de este delito. Aun cuando se estima que no es difícil encontrar al autor del atentado, hay bastantes probabilidades de obtener éxito.

Desde luego, hay sospechas muy bien fundadas sobre uno de los aludidos en el informe del "tribunal de conciencia", cuyo temperamento muy fogoso y muy conocido en la masa popular...

Una vez que el médico haya levantado la prohibición que impide hablar al señor Huidobro, es posible que se adelante bastante en el descubrimiento del responsable.

---

24   Assaulted in Santiago, 1925.

25   In the Spanish Civil War (*ABC*, Madrid, 23 June 1937).

26   In France as War Correspondent, 1945.

Spain to give a lecture.'[1] He did lecture at the Ateneo, in December of 1921, but his performance then seems to have backfired, dividing without conquering the Spanish avant-garde. Back in Paris the following month, the newspapers announce him as giving a talk on 'La Création pure en esthétique'; and Huidobro himself has referred to yet other lectures on the same topic in Berlin and Stockholm.[2] For all practical purposes though, this lecture tour marked the end, as well as the beginning, of his abortive campaign on behalf of Creationism. Significantly enough, in 1925, when he brought out *Manifestes*, a collection of essays and critical writings on the avant-garde, 'La Création pure' was *not* included.

Several factors combine to cause this turnabout. Foremost among them certainly, was Huidobro's failure to stimulate any real adhesion to himself. What is more, his own poetic practice was evolving in such a way and at such a pace as to place him outside the theoretic frame of Creationism which, needless to repeat, was essentially that of Cubism. The popular view of Huidobro as a dyed-in-the-wool Creationist ignores this change and in doing so ignores the basic character of the avant-garde: the constant scrambling of its militants for a front-line position. When Huidobro put Creationism behind him, he did not stand still. Indeed, never was he more active than during the five-year span of his second residence in Paris, from 1920 to 1925.

Three important developments occur in Huidobro's work during this short period. In each he goes beyond Cubism, although in different ways. First, his shorter compositions take on an orality and a whimsicality not unlike Dada. These are mostly found in *Automne régulier*. Secondly, his experiments with visual writing resurface and reach something of an apex in 1922 with a public exhibition of his painted poems. And thirdly, in 1925, as Huidobro rejected Breton's rationale for Surrealism, he came up with his own variant of automatic writing in *Tout à coup*. These are distinct, but not unrelated developments. In the interests of clarity it is convenient to examine them separately, relying on a little literary archaeology to pick up the trace of Huidobro's hitherto hidden evolution beyond Cubism.

It is now known that the poet was in Spain in 1918, in Chile in 1919, and that by 1920 he was back in Paris, at the same address in Montmartre, 41 rue Victor Massé. The *Nord–Sud* group, after the death of Apollinaire, had lost its cohesion and Dada was emerging as the new force of the moment. Huidobro, although on good terms with Tzara, has a greater affinity at the

time with the Cubists, some of whom were then trying to hold
the line against Dada with *Action*, a review apparently founded
for this purpose by a group of poets and painters. Albert
Gleizes's article on 'L'affaire Dada' (April 1920), sets the tone,
condemning the new movement as 'the final outcome of the
decadent spiritual values of a fetid bourgeois hierarchy'. The
siege mentality of the whole enterprise is born out by Huidobro's first contribution (October 1920), a translation into
French of 'Bay Rum', a Cubist piece from *Poemas árticos*. It is
not until much later, in May of 1921, that there is something
new by him there, 'Automne régulier'. Significantly enough,
this is the poem that would lead off his 1925 volume of the
same title. In its verses Huidobro speaks with a changed voice.
Rhyme is used for its special resonance, stressing not the
disciplined order of the lines but the absence of any such order
where the linking takes place mainly at the phonic level:

> Je ne sais plus de blonde ou brune
> Laissons la place aux matelots
> Viens regarder dans mes îlots
> La nature morte de clair de lune
> Avec l'assiette au bord de l'eau
> Et la rose s'effeuillant sur l'oiseau qui chante
> A minuit quarante

(I don't know any more about blond or brunette / Let's leave it to the
sailors / Come look in my little islands / at the still life in moonlight /
With the plate on the water's edge / And the rose shedding its petals over
the bird who sings at forty past midnight)

In these lines all that remains of Cubism is the moon/saucer
image, while the end-rhyme is of the nonsense variety which so
delighted Dada: 'la rose s'effeuill*ant* sur l'oiseau qui ch*ante* à
minuit quar*ante*'. *Action* went on with its anti-Dada campaign
until well into 1922, but understandably, without Huidobro.
Things were getting so complicated at the time of the| *Congrès
de Paris* (May 1922), that Juan Gris wrote to Huidobro about a
Picabia petition that he had received. Was it for or against? 'I
received a letter of protest against the Congress signed by Satie
and a few Dadas as well as a printed flyer from Picabia, but I
can't make out if he is for or against the Congress. You know
though, I don't really give a damn.'[3] Nor did Huidobro. Although a signatory to the Congress, he was just then beginning
to pull back from literary politicking[4] to take up real politics.

Before doing so, however, he threw himself completely into his work and in the process came up with some modes of expression as bizarre as they were original.

This is a confused and confusing time period in Huidobro's literary development. Confused mainly because so little scholarly work has been done on his second stay in Paris after the *Nord–Sud* adventure; confusing because of the language problem. Huidobro in the early 1920s was beginning to think of himself as a 'French' writer; Gris then even writes to him in that language. All of *Ecuatorial* was put into French (although not published), and items from *Poemas árticos* were translated for Paris reviews like *Action* and *La Bataille littéraire*. In 1920 however he still can be found doing some original writing in Spanish for *Grecia* and *Cervantes*, Ultraist reviews of the time. One such poem 'Tarde' (*Grecia*, June 1920), was rewritten a few years later for *Automne régulier*. Even the most cursory comparison of both versions is sufficient to highlight the terminal points on Huidobro's trajectory of change between 1920 and 1925:

TARDE

Yo poseo la llave del Otoño
El pecho está lleno de alas amarillas
Y lloraré una tarde todos los arroyos

EL DIA MUERE EN TUS MEJILLAS

Ondula tus cabellos la música del arpa
El mundo viene a dormir bajo estas ramas
Un último recuerdo
Se ha posado en mi dedo

PAJARO VACIO

Todas las canciones cayeron en el río
Y aquello que guardaba en mi garganta
Se alejó sobre el alba

(*EVENING* / I possess the key to Autumn / My chest is full of yellow wings / And one evening I'll weep all the rivulets / THE DAY DIES IN YOUR CHEEKS / The harp music waves your hair / The world comes beneath these branches to sleep / A final thought has perched on my finger / EMPTY BIRD / All the songs fell into the river / And what I was keeping in my throat / Went off upon the dawn)

CLEF DES SAISONS

Je possède la clef de l'automne
De ma poitrine naissent les feuilles jaunes
Et un soir je dois pleurer tous les ruisseaux

A quoi bon suivre l'oiseau du tout d'un coup
Le jour meurt dans tes joues

Ne pense à rien
Entre les feuilles il y a la nuit qui vient
Il y a une heure qui s'enfuit
Et l'horloge est agreste
Il y a la pluie à gauche et l'aéroplane à l'est

Il y a une musique de harpe qui a frisé tes cheveux
Et au fond du ciel un arbre en feu
Pour dormir la terre s'épanche
Cachée à nos regards sous quelques branches

La pensée moins végétale de la journée
Dans mon doigt s'est posée
Pour attendre ensemble l'aube acide
Toutes les chansons tombèrent de la mésange en vol

Séduisons l'oiseau qui se vide
Et qui meuble des chants les ardoises et le sol

(I possess the key to autumn / From my chest yellow leaves are born / And one evening I'll have to weep all the rivulets / What's the use of following the bird of suddenness / The day dies in your cheeks / Don't think of anything / Among the leaves there is the night that is coming / there is an hour that flees / And the clock is rustic / There is the rain to the left and the airplane to the east / There is some harp music that has curled your hair / And in the depths of the sky a tree ablaze / In order to sleep the earth unbosoms itself / Hidden from our sight under some branches / The least vegetable thought of the day / has perched in my finger / In order to await together the acid dawn / All the songs fell from the titmouse in flight / Let's seduce the bird who is emptying himself out / and who furnishes the roof-tops and the ground with song)

The poem has been expanded over the years in its passage from one language to another. Not so much lengthened as broadened. Where at first Huidobro presented an outline sequence of striking images, he later preferred to supply the reader with the thought mechanism behind those images. It is as though he had rewritten the poem so as to restore what had previously been edited out. In the process, he has forced into the background what was formerly most prominent. For example, the typographically featured 'PAJARO VACIO', an arresting combination of seemingly unrelated words is drained of impact in the final version where its conceptualism is detailed: 'l'oiseau qui se vide / et qui meuble des chants les ardoises et le sol'.

Are both poems the same? Obviously not. And it is in their difference that one can best perceive the extent and quality of the transition effected between 1920 and 1925, years of major change for Huidobro and for the avant-garde. Years which witnessed the eclipse of Cubism by Dada and the rise of Surrealism. In this context of changing aesthetic values what helps distinguish one kind of writing from another is the poet's attitude toward his work: the poem as an artefact or as a record of experience. 'Clef des Saisons' is of the latter variety, and its rambling loquacity puts it closer to Surrealism than to Cubism.

Both versions of the poem treat the same hallowed subject — the transitory nature of things — in quite dissimilar ways. The power of the earlier text derives from its sudden transitions, obliging the reader to bridge the gaps, and in so doing to complete the imagery in his own mind. 'Clef des Saisons' functions differently, taking the reader into the thought process. This is done through the addition of conversational locutions, circumlocutions in fact. The first variant of consequence is the transformation of the typographically distinct 'EL DIA MUERE EN TUS MEJILLAS' to the more roundabout 'A quoi bon suivre l'oiseau tout d'un coup / le jour meurt dans tes joues.' A speech-level wordiness characteristic of the next added segment as well: 'Ne pense à rien . . .'. Huidobro's attitude regarding the nature and function of his poetry had changed considerably in the five years separating these two texts, moving away from Cubist concision toward an almost casual word flow.

In 1921, when he brought out *Saisons choisies*, he was vigorously pushing what he then called Creationism and the volume was intended as a kind of showcase of its growth and development. Accordingly, it was arranged in chronological sections headed by the much diffused theoretical piece on 'La Création pure'.[5] Significantly, only one poem was included from *El espejo de agua* (the period piece 'Miroir d'eau'), along with six from *Horizon carré* ('Nouvelle Chanson', 'Téléphone', 'Oiseau', 'Romance', 'Vates', 'Fin'), seven from *Poemas árticos* ('Maison', 'Gare', 'Balandre', 'Fils', 'Lune', 'Cigar', 'Bay Rum'), and five new compositions ultimately destined for *Automne régulier* ('Automne régulier', 'Femme', 'Globe-Trotter', 'Ombres chinoises', 'Océan ou dancing'). These latter poems already contain the seeds of something different. Juan Gris was one of the first to comment on them, expressing his admiration for their newness, most especially 'Ombres chinoises' (Shadow Theatre). It is interesting that the painter should have singled out this piece, for it contains the earliest evidence of the play-fulness that would come to characterize Huidobro's writing over the next few years. Sound in 'Ombres chinoises' seems to be as much of a generative impulse as the visual ramifications of an idea once were for literary Cubism. Simple end-rhyme, once avoided, is now exploited (as is *double entendre*):

> Détaché de moi-même je me regarde en face
> Ce serait ma lune ou bien ma glace
> Et je me dis bonjour
> En ôtant l'abat-jour

(Detached from myself I look myself in the face / This could be my moon or else my looking-glass / And I say good morning to myself / Taking off my sleep mask [tipping my lampshade-hat])

Levity abounds; even when the poem's nuclear image (the moon) reappears in a typically Cubist juxtaposition ('La lune est son banjo'):

> Tu danses
>   Tu chantes
> Le lac du clair de lune est au degré cinquante
>
> Le nègre rit comme un piano
> Il a la bouche
> Pleine de touches
>
> La lune est son banjo
> Et dans la gorge il étrangle un oiseau

(You dance / You sing / The lake of moonlight is at fifty degrees / The negro laughs like a piano / He has a mouthfull / of keys / The moon is his banjo / And in his throat he is strangling a bird)

This is a long way from Rubén Darío's 'risa armónica'; and longer still from Huidobro's desacralization of the image in 'La obsesión de los dientes'. Poetry, a combinatory word-art, is being pushed to a new expressive level. Studied juxtaposition, from which a startling image is to arise, is no longer an end in itself; such imagery is now the basis for the creation of an even greater fantasy. The poem in this way does not relate an experience; it becomes one. And so it is that Huidobro's work begins to take on a performance dimension.

From Cubism he had learned to treat the text as an object to be visually perceived; from Dada he came to realize that perception is largely determined by context (the object-lesson was Duchamp's *pissoir*). As a consequence, Huidobro began to experiment with new contexts for his writing, working in several media almost simultaneously: music, fashion, and painting. For Edgar Varèse, a 'concrete' musician, he excerpted some lines from the core of *Tour Eiffel* to create 'Chanson de là-haut' (Song from on High). Varèse set the piece to music and even directed the première concert in which it was performed in New York in May of 1922:

> La Seine dort sous l'ombre de ses ponts.
> Je vois tourner la terre
> et je sonne mon clairon
> vers toutes les mers.
>
> Sur le chemin de ton parfum
> toutes les abeilles et les paroles s'en vont.
> Reine de l'Aube des Pôles,
> Rose des Vents que fane l'Automne.
> Dans ma tête un oiseau chante toute l'année.[6]

(The Seine sleeps beneath the shadow of its bridges. / I watch the Earth spin / and I sound my bugle / toward all the seas. / Along the path of your perfume / all the bees and the words are going away / Queen of the Polar Dawns. / Rose of the Winds [compass card] that Autumn withers. / In my head a bird sings all year long.)

The text, read straight through in just a few seconds, seems incomplete. And well it should. It is designed to be heard, not read, and to function in another, musical context. Each phrase is sung at a different tempo, completely set apart from the others. In concert it takes several minutes to perform. Ample time for the listener, guided by the music, to let his imagination take over. Huidobro's goal was to create a participatory experience, a divertissement that stimulates the aesthetic sensibility. As he himself said way back in 1914: 'Art (. . .) is not made by plunking down whole ideas, but by hinting at them, *leaving the pleasure of reconstitution to the reader.*'[7]

The pleasure of the text, to borrow a contemporary critical expression, was nowhere more apparent than in Huidobro's collaboration with Sonia Delaunay, also in 1922. Poetry and high fashion then teamed up in a novel way, creating the 'poème-robe',

a text to be worn. A Parisian newspaper contains this account
of a fashion show:

> A certain poet pleases you, Madame? You can embroider on your
> blouse one of your favorite verses by him.
> This fashion, of which we have already spoken in a previous chronicle,
> will not fail to please many women. It is Madame Delaunay, wife of the
> famous painter, who first had the idea of these garments, these blouse-
> poems. She has now carried it to an exquisite perfection, and a charming
> young lady, Mlle Geneviève Domec, has undertaken to launch the first
> model: a blouse on which is embroidered one of Huidobro's verses: 'Petite
> chanson pour abriter le cœur'. The blouse was lovely, the person wearing
> it was no less so . . .
> It was a big hit.[8]

The complete text of the poem turned up only recently, in a
retrospective exhibition on the Delaunays held at the Bibliothèque Nationale in 1977. Among Sonia Delaunay's papers is
the following manuscript by Huidobro, titled 'Corsage':

> Petite chanson pour abriter le cœur
> le jour de froid met l'oiseau de merveille
> sur chaque côté quelques mots de chaleur
> vers et cœur toujours en battement pareils.

(A little song to shield the heart / the cold day clothes the marvellous
bird / on each side a few words of warmth / verse and heart ever in unison
throbbing)

A reading of the poem is only complete in its proper context: a
word-corsage that blooms with meaning on the breast of its
wearer. There is hidden meaning too. Hidden at least to readers
unfamiliar with the stock imagery of Huidobro's Cubist period:
the 'oiseau de merveille' is the heart throbbing in the rib-cage.
    Huidobro's writing is still visually oriented. Only a few
months before the fashion show there was a gallery exhibition
of his poetry at the Théâtre Édouard VII. A fusion of art and
literature that was then called 'poème-peint', a painted poem.
The poem in this view is not merely a text but a word-picture.
Even in its simplest form the effect on the reader–viewer is
subtle since the text creates its context, a context which in turn
influences the reading. One poem, perhaps the most striking,
consists of white letters painted on a black background, creating
the impression of a starry night:

UN ASTRE A PERDU SON CHEMIN

SOIT BOLIDE OU SERPENTINE ELLE EST JOLIE LA FETE VOISINE

LA LUNE ET MON BALLON
SE
DEGONFLENT LENTEMENT

NID OU L'ETOILE
VOICI L'ATOME

ICI C'EST LA VALLÉE DES LARMES ET L'ASTRONOME

(A heavenly body has lost its way / Be it a meteor or a kite tail the neighbouring pageant is beautiful / The moon and my balloon slowly go flat / Nest or atom / Here is the star / This is the valley of tears and the astronomer)

The text comments upon itself, putting before the viewer the words to describe what is being seen: 'Voici l'étoile'. The act of reading is thus made to coincide with seeing.

In another poem of the series, 'Moulin' (Windmill), the process of perceiving is even more controlled with arrows pointing us into a circular reading, the circularity of the mill:

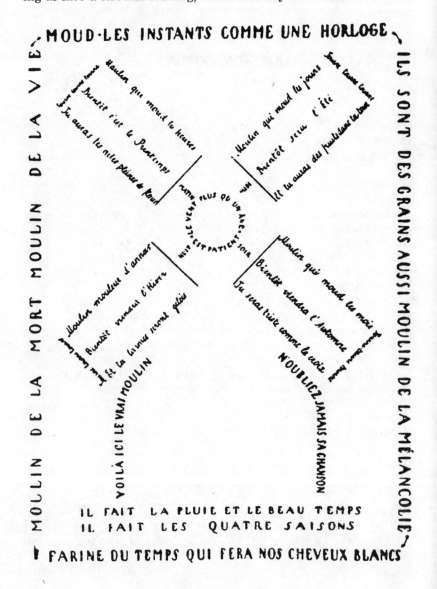

(Windmill of death windmill of life / Mills the instants like a clock / They are grains as well windmill of melancholy / Flour of time that will turn our hair white / Turn turn turn / Windmill that mills the hours / Soon it will be Spring / You will have your vanes full of flowers / Morning / Turn turn turn / Windmill that mills the days / Soon it will be Summer / And you'll have fruits in the tower / Midday / Turn turn turn / Windmill that mills the months / Soon it will be Autumn / You will be as sad as the cross / Evening / Turn turn turn / Windmill miller of years / Soon Winter will come / And your tears will be frozen / Night / The wind more than a mule / is patient / Here is the true windmill / Don't ever forget its song / It makes rain and sunshine / It makes the four seasons / Flour of time that will turn our hair white)

This poem was printed as a flyer to accompany the catalogue invitation to the exhibition. It was evidently designed as a little object lesson in the reading of visual poems, for on one side of the sheet is the graphic rendering of the windmill and on the other is a text that is equivalent, save for its more conventional typographic presentation.

Reading is sequential and is based on a word flow; seeing is instantaneous and contemplative. Both acts function in time, one requiring some eye movement while the other does not. 'Kaléidoscope', another poem from the show, exploits this duality in perception. Bands of coloured paper are used to set off the spatial arrangement and the verses are numbered to indicate the reading sequence (*see over, p. 96*).

The piece functions somewhat like its namesake, kaleidoscope, where shifting sets of relationships always coalesce into a pattern, a pattern whose harmony is here brought out both visually and verbally through complementary colours, sounds, and ideas. Hues of bright orange and conspicuous end-rhyme hold things together in a vaguely complementary way until the reader, completing the numbered sequence, focuses back on the central image: 'COUCHANT / AU BOUT DU NEZ'. In this way all that flickering luminescence of the diagonal segments suddenly coalesces into a pattern: the sunset right in front of the viewer's nose. Huidobro, joining the expressive capabilities of two media, has created what one critic (Waldemar George) aptly called a 'lyric pleonasm'.

Thirteen such compositions are listed in the printed catalogue for the exposition. Only a few have survived.[9] Originally, the plan was to bring out a volume, *Salle 14*, containing the full-colour reproductions. The volume never appeared. Probably because the exhibition was not a real success. Only a few days

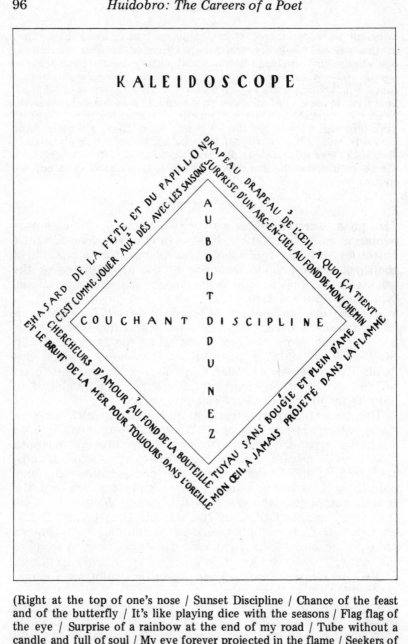

(Right at the top of one's nose / Sunset Discipline / Chance of the feast and of the butterfly / It's like playing dice with the seasons / Flag flag of the eye / Surprise of a rainbow at the end of my road / Tube without a candle and full of soul / My eye forever projected in the flame / Seekers of love at the bottom of the bottle / And the sound of the sea forever in the ear)

after the opening, we find Huidobro writing to Larrea, boasting of the scandal he had caused: 'My exhibition was a big hit on opening night and among the élite, but later the public protested; there was a real battle over it and the management of the theatre had it taken down for being too modern and avantgarde (. . .). There were protests in the papers and they'll soon be obliged to hang my poems again.'[10] Evidently true, for a few months later, on 18 August 1922, when Guillot de Saix reviews it for *Le France*, it is at the Galerie Manuel, headquarters of the sponsor who had originally placed it in the lobby of the elegant Théâtre Édouard VII.

Huidobro is very much a public figure now and he seems to revel in this role, treating his writing like a commodity: something not only to be seen, worn, and performed, but also to be sold — publicly. In February of 1923, he can be found among the organizers of the Bal Travesti Transmental, where one of his poems is actually auctioned off. Simply titled 'Poème', the manuscript is later modified for inclusion in *Automne régulier*, that catch-all of his early 1920s French verse. Huidobro makes irreverent use of traditional religious iconography, a hotel-room lithograph of the Sacred Heart of Jesus:

Colonise l'ennui avec ta voix
Enfant de mer sans soucis alternes
Il dort à l'ombre de ma flûte et de ses doigts

Regarde bien mon cœur est une lanterne
Et mes prières montent comme l'arbre en escalier interne

Tu cherches l'échelle de corde et le violon civil
Ici sous l'églantine
Et la couronne d'épines
Dis-moi toujours que tu adores mes cils

Car si j'étais ruisseau ou bien touriste
Vous m'aimeriez tous comme on aime les artistes
Mais je déteste l'hiver et les draps de l'œil
Et ta petite étoile qui tourne à merveille

Je peux seulement te dire que tu es belle
Comme une chambre d'hôtel

(Colonize tedium with your voice / Child of the sea [mother] with no other cares / He sleeps in the shadow of my flute and its fingers / Look carefully my heart is a lantern / And my prayers go up as in a tree's internal staircase / You look for the rope-ladder [scale] and the public violinist / Here under the wild roses / And the crown of thorns / Keep on

telling me how you adore my eyelashes / Because if I were a stream or else
a tourist / You would all love me the way artists are loved / But I detest
winter and the bed-sheets of the eye / And your little star that turns like a
dream / I can only say to you that you are as lovely as a hotel room)

What these lines show, besides the patently anti-religious sentiment of the author, is an extraordinarily free flow of words and
ideas. The closing simile, appended as if an afterthought, has
the ring of a nursery-rhyme. Its gratuitousness is especially
apparent in the original manuscript, where even spelling errors
are allowed to stand: 'Je peut [*sic*] seulement te dire que tu
est [*sic*] belle / comme une chambre d'hotel [*sic*].' These 'errors'
are an important clue to Huidobro's attitude toward composition
in the mid-1920s, a time in which his writing began to take
on an outward appearance of spontaneity as he shifted his
conceptual base away from Cubism toward what would eventually come to be called the Surreal.

Huidobro's opposition to Surrealism, although well documented, is little understood, for while he was condemning
the movement's credo, his own writing had taken on characteristics not unlike that of the condemned. The fact is that as
Huidobro went beyond Cubism, careful juxtaposition gave way
to generative word-flow as the basis for the creation of new
patterns of meaning. In this process, metaphor often turned out
to be less the result of design than of chance. Or so it would
seem. A glance at the titles for the later poems of *Automne
régulier* reveals many of them to be of the 'found' variety:
'Été en sourdine', 'Relativité de printemps',[1] Honni soit qui mal
y danse', and 'Hiver à boire'. Easily recognized mutations of a
musical term, a scientific theory, a popular maxim, and a café
slogan, they read at first like malapropisms; until we realize
that Breton's *Poisson soluble* and *Clair de terre* are based on the
same principle: a standard locution is modifed in some aspect so
as to give rise to an image that while strange is yet somehow
familiar. It is this duality that identifies Surrealist writing and is
responsible for its disconcerting charm.

Although Huidobro took a strong stand against Breton's
formulation of Surrealist practice, his own writing of the time
can only be understood when inserted in the context of that
movement. In 1925, coinciding with *Automne régulier*, col-
lecting poems written over the previous five years, he published
two totally unanticipated works: *Manifestes* and *Tout à coup*
(Suddenly). This latter volume must have circulated very little,
if at all, for I have found no reviews of it. Nor, to my knowledge,

were any of its thirty-two poems published previously. The book remains something of a loner even today.

What immediately sets it apart for any reader, then as now, is its presentation. Sandwiched between title-page and text is a turn-of-the-century engraving with the following caption: 'Huidobro par Picasso'. This spurious 'portrait', with its self-mocking allusion to other, authentic ones of him by Picasso and the Cubists, helps define the special context in which the book must be read. The incompatibility of word and image is clearly contrived so as to produce in the reader a sense of surprise. Similarly, the poems of *Tout à coup* are all striving for a de-stabilizing effect. Number 31, for example, systematically de-familiarizes that most traditional of images:

> Jésus Jésus
> tes yeux étaient grands comme deux
> soldats
> Tu auras un bouquet de fleurs
> Pour mettre dans ton cœur
> Dans ton cœur visible à tous venants
> Comme une poche sur la tunique
>
> Tu auras une boîte de chocolat

(Jesus Jesus / your eyes are big like two / soldiers / You'll have a bouquet of flowers / to stick in your heart / In your heart visible to all comers / like a pocket on your tunic / You'll have a box of chocolates)

The two explicit similes, although elemental in structure, present comparisons that are peculiar, to say the least (eyes like soldiers, a heart like a pocket). Yet the reader would be hard put to reject them for they are almost as commonplace as they are unusual: first, because they are recognizable variants of linguistic ready-mades (*grands soldats*, *mettre dans la poche*); and second, because they are ensconced in a grammatically 'correct' series of interconnected phrases. The studied discon-tinuity of the Cubist system gives way here to a word flow that is syntactically supportive of what is semantically subversive. Altering just a single term in a seemingly predictable word pattern creates a disjunction that takes the reader by surprise: 'tes yeux étaient grands comme deux *soldats*'. Soldier is clearly not the anticipated completion of the comparison; nor, in the poem's other explicit simile, are flowers normally stuck in one's heart. By slipping the unconventional into otherwise conven-tional contexts, the poet eases the reader into the realm of the extraordinary, momentarily making it seem plausible. Here, in the example thus far discussed, the Second Advent is contemporized, made over into a social call, complete with flowers and a box of chocolates.

This kind of poetry differs from Cubism both in how it is composed and in how it is to be read. In the earlier poems, 'distant' ideas were spatially juxtaposed for a studied effect; now the dissimilar is blended together through the conduit of sound and syntax. For one kind of writing the reader must be active, so as to perceive the juxtapositions; for the other, passive, so as to allow the cross-overs to take him into the realm of the marvellous. One kind of writing appeals to reason; the other defies it.

Poem 6 best illustrates the generative nature of this process, starting off quite simply (and familiarly) with an image of butterflies whose folded wings visually suggest hands folded in prayer. The sound of this word in turn leads to prairie; the prairie, the sky; the sky, both (blue) water and God; God, a church; and finally, when the sequence comes to a close there is an explicit comparison as bizarre as it is natural: butterflies soaring up like Gothic church windows:

> Cinq papillons s'envolent en disant ces prières
> Aimez-vous les prières dans la prairie
> L'aurore fragile sans étoiles régulières
> Pourraient bien se casser à la sortie
>
> Dans le ciel traversent de jolis ruisseaux
> Seigneur dis-nous qui a bu le bleu du ciel
> Les papillons s'envolent comme des vitraux

(Five butterflies spread their wings on saying prayers / Do you like prayers in the prairie / The fragile dawn without regular stars / Might well break into pieces on the way out / In the sky lovely streams go every which way / Lord tell us who drank all the blue from the sky / The butterflies rise up like stained-glass windows)

Two elements seem to be in conflict here: the structured circularity of the sequence and the seemingly spontaneous nature of much of the word-play within the hermetic frame. It would seem that chance and design share an equal role in the making of a poem such as this.

Yet the volume opens with a somewhat cryptic statement with regard to chance: 'Les deux ou trois charmes des escaliers du hasard sont incontestables' (The two or three charms of the ladder of chance are undeniable, Poem 1). An assertion that is further mystified in Poem 28, where Huidobro seems to be qualifying Tzara's croupier-call (*Faites vos jeux*) to join in the game of art: 'Apportez des jeux / des petites distractions pour l'infini' (Bring along some games / some amusements for infinity). And in *Manifestes*, written against Surrealism, there is the same ambivalence regarding the place of chance in art:

> Obviously chance can create some things, but it can also create others. We ought not give any more importance to the *imprévu* than to the other elements of poetry.
>
> One time, as an after-dinner amusement, Max Jacob and I did a poem together (a poem I still have), with each one of us writing down the first thing that came to mind. The result is not unlike the poems made up of newspaper clippings, and it has the same defect. ('Je trouve')

The text referred to is among Huidobro's papers, and begins thus:

> Sur le cheminée la gondole porte des fleurs naufragées
> Le portrait de Marie est fait par l'Homme Noir
> Le soleil caressera les lèvres
> Mais c'est pour moi la bouche de la mort . . .

(On the chimney the gondola bears shipwrecked flowers / The portrait of Marie is done by the Black Man / The sun shall caress her lips / But for me it is the mouth of death)

What is remarkable is that the poem, although consciously done, is charged with a certain dreamlike irrationality. In this particular case the why and how is known: an expedient use of syntax, word order, and conjunction oblige the reader to accept two separate trains of thought as though they were one. And again there is a tension between chance and design, a tension that is quite effective in taking the reader beyond reality. Huidobro spoke slightingly of this poem mostly because of the way it was made. Interestingly enough, his disapprobation of Surrealism was similarly motivated: 'Personally, I cannot accept Surrealism because to my way of thinking it cheapens poetry by opening it up to everybody like a simple after-dinner game.' ('Je trouve')

The root of his reservations regarding both approaches to poetry (Dada and Surrealism) is not so much chance but its corollary: anyone can play the game. The basic antinomy of the voluntary as opposed to the involuntary, coupled with Huidobro's long-standing commitment to the idea of the artist as creator, forces him to take a stand. Again and again in *Manifestes* we find him returning to plea that poetry should not be cheapened and that it should remain the exclusive prerogative of poets. For him a poet is one who, besides being inspired, is also one who 'takes an active and not a passive role in putting a poem together and making it work' ('Manifeste manifestes'). Breton's idea was just the opposite, asking that the poet be not the inventor of the poem, but simply its recorder, an 'appareil enregistreur' for what was then being called 'la pensée parlée', the unarticulated flow of subconscious thought. The method of recording this psychic flux, as articulated in the Surrealist manifesto of 1924, was 'l'écriture automatique', automatic writing. Questioning the method, Huidobro placed the creative faculty of the poet over automatism; and instead of the subconscious he exalted something he called the 'superconscious'. Basically though, terminology aside, he was against improvisation:

Following these theories will lead us to an art of improvisers. They are the only ones who do things this way. And they are not the masters but the slaves of their mental imagery. They give themselves over to some internal dictate and the result is a stream of swamplights. No, that is too easy, too banal. Poetry is something much graver, more formidable and it arises in our superconscious.   ('Manifeste manifestes')

Huidobro was especially troubled by the secondary role Surrealism assigned the creative act. The image seems less important than the state of mind that produces it. Automatic writing implicitly challenged a basic assumption dear to the modern writer: his role as creator. Huidobro was particularly sensitive to this ramification of Surrealism's unique approach to literary composition. Not surprisingly, he came up with a two-pronged assault on the movement in 1925, questioning the system in *Manifestes* and trying to go it one better in *Tout à coup*.

The title of this book of poems, alluding to the rapidity of its execution, is not insignificant. Nor is the fact that the little volume contains just thirty-two poems, a number that coincides exactly with the thirty-two of Breton's *Poisson soluble*. And while the issue of automatic writing is no longer important today (it was dropped from the second Surrealist manifesto in 1930), what is, is the fact that a new and radically different sort of writing did begin to emerge in the mid-1920s, a writing that employed a kind of double vision, using the real to make the reader's imagination accept the unreal, the marvellous.

To do this, the text was treated not as a construct, but as a vehicle, a verbal conduit which could connect and hold connected what reason might find incompatible. In the process, spontaneity, or rather the appearance of spontaneity, took on an importance it had not enjoyed since the early days of Romanticism.

Writing from entirely different theoretical bases, both Huidobro and Breton authored texts that are stylistically similar and exercise the same strange power over the reader, moving us beyond the rational. Breton though, had persuaded himself that he was on to something new; Huidobro, on the other hand, was aware that in art it is technique that makes the old seem new. He as much as says so in Poem 21:

> Les voyages des somnambules en lumière de finesse
> Respirent mes divagations
> Quand viennent les poètes avec les fleuves amis
> Apporter les coussins de la tendresse
> Je mets des souliers neufs à mes chansons

(The voyages of sleep-walkers in a glow of finesse / Breathe in my wanderings / When the poets come with their friendly rivers / To bring the pillows of tenderness / I put new shoes on my songs)

Surrealism was but one more development in the avant-garde search for new dimensions of poetic experience; and, in the case of Huidobro, it led to other, more unorthodox kinds of writing in *Altazor* and *Temblor de cielo*. But these texts did not appear until 1931. In the meantime the poet would return to Chile to try his hand at another game and take up another career: politics.

VI
Politics (and Theatre)

Man is man and I am his prophet.   1933

Successful as a poet, Huidobro assumed that anything else he
set his mind to should turn out equally well. So, in 1925,
when Chile is at a political turning-point, following the Army's
ousting of Alessandri, the poet is convinced that he is just the
man for the presidency. He campaigns and loses. A lack-lustre
bureaucrat wins, and Huidobro — after a brief mid-life crisis —
goes back to Europe. A few years later he is again in Chile,
drawn perhaps by the temporary success of his former supporter,
Marmaduque Grove, at setting up a Socialist Republic in 1932.
This time though he stays on and participates in the political
manœuvring that eventually installs the Popular Front. It is
difficult to be precise about what generates these moves: a
belief in himself as a leader, a vision of change, or simply the
joy of being involved? Whatever the motivation, when things are
happening in Chile, he is there; and when the action is else-
where, he manages to place himself in the thick of it, as for
example his participation in the Spanish Civil War and the
Allied liberation of France. Moreover, when nothing grand
seems to be happening around him, he is adept at creating his
own little scenario. The political for him is always somewhat
theatrical. Right from the beginning.

In 1924, following the publication of a political tract, *Finis
Britannia*, he has himself kidnapped, supposedly by British
agents acting in defence of the threatened empire. The whole
event has the air of a Dada spectacle: handbills are distributed
all over Paris, and polite notices of the book are followed by a
three-day press search for the missing Chilean author. The text
that was at the centre of all this was excluded until recently
from Huidobro's *Obras completas*, and remains unknown and
little understood today. It was a cheaply printed pamphlet of
some ninety-odd pages, containing the lofty pronouncements of
one Victor Haldan — a fictional ringer for Huidobro — who
glosses the ideas of Ghandi, Atatürk, and other liberation
leaders of the time. The speeches, self-consciously rhetorical,
are partially framed by the narrative device of a train ride on
the Orient Express. The hero and other agents are on their way

to Istanbul to attend a secret meeting:

That afternoon, Victor Haldan and Miss MacKenzie, a lovely Irish lass who had a kind of mystic adoration for him, had taken their seats aboard the Orient Express. They were going from Paris to Constantinople, where in five days there was to be a General Assembly of the Alpha Society. Other members of this secret society were also on the same train, but these Cavaliers of Liberty were pretending not to know one another; they exchanged not a word because they knew themselves to be under surveillance by agents of the British police and it was necessary to avoid arousing the slightest suspicion.

Victor Haldan was plunged in thought as the sun went down over the countryside, when suddenly, lifting his head, he exclaimed:

— The blow must be struck in a decisive manner, so as not to fail. If all the colonies were to rise up on the same day, at the same time, England would be doomed. There is no other way . . .[1]

The final solution though is not to be rushed, for Haldan goes on to envisage the schedule for this general uprising as some five years distant, in 1929. Actually, the mock-heroic thrust of *Finis Britannia* is signalled in the subtitle: *Une redoutable Société Secrète s'est dressée contre l'Impérialisme Anglais* (A Formidable Secret Society Rises Up Against English Imperialism). To further highlight its zaniness, the original pamphlet carries this finishing touch, blocked out as a colophon (and inadvertently dropped from the version in the latest edition of the complete works): 'Un soir en passant près d'ici, quelqu'un se rapprocha de ces pages et il vit que l'auteur dépassait de toute sa tête le livre qu'il avait écrit' (One evening, passing near here, someone came over to these pages and noticed that the author was head and shoulders above the book he had written).

More interesting than the text is the context Huidobro created for it: his own kidnapping. Paris newspapers of the time are filled with articles detailing the strange case of the abducted Chilean. But once he turns up and the story is analysed by the international press, the farce is out in the open. The *New York Herald* account is typically tongue in cheek:

Señor Vicente Huidobro, Chilean diplomat, man of letters and author of *Finis Britannia*, who disappeared three days ago, leaving a disconsolate wife and four children, and causing a good deal of trouble to the Paris police, returned home in the small hours yesterday. Though still dazed by drugs, he related how in keeping an appointment at the Porte d'Auteuil given him by a mysterious telephone call, he was met by three men in an automobile who carried him off to a strange place, where he was made to write the English, French, and Spanish equivalents of 'Deutschland über alles', substituting 'England' for 'Deutschland', 100 times in each language.

The kidnappers were 'English Fascists', and the motive of the adventure, or farce, according to Señor Huidobro, was English vengeance for his attacks on 'British Imperalism' in his *Finis Britannia*.[2]

The hoax was so transparent that the worldly Paris police investigating the case came up with a more practical explanation for the poet's disappearance: he had simply wanted to get away from his wife for a few days. This interpretation caused Huidobro considerable embarrassment, particularly as imaginative journalists elaborated on the theme. A Brazilian newspaper, picking up the story from its wire service, reports that the poet was the victim of an 'emboscada' (ambush), and concludes with some *risqué* verses:

> Tomai a lição, maridos
> Amigos da bilontragem!
> Tirai do caso a vantagem!
> Que aproveita aos mais sabidos
> Si acaso andastes . . . perdidos
> En qualquer 'zona estragada'
> Não vos desculpeis, qual nada!
> Fazendo cara de victima
> Dizei à esposa legitima:
> — Ai, meu amor, que emboscada![3]

(Take up the lesson, married men / Fond of whoring around! / Take advantage of this case! / Learn from those in the know / If by chance you get . . . lost / In some 'red-light district' / Don't apologize, act natural! / Putting on your best victim's face / Tell your wife: / Ay, my love, what an ambush!)

What Huidobro learned from all this was the extraordinary power of the press to create as well as spread the news. Thus, when he returns to Chile the following year, he wastes no time in setting up his own newspaper, *Acción*, as a vehicle to project himself on the national scene. Again, he manages to draw attention to his person almost immediately, getting front-page coverage in practically all the nation's dailies. On 8 August 1925, just three days after the inaugural issue of *Acción* had called for a political clean-up, Huidobro is reportedly mugged at the portal of his family house on the Alameda. The public outcry is immense, and overnight the poet is a national political hero. Some felt that this was a put-up job and that Huidobro was acting as a political front for Ibáñez and a progressive faction of the military. In fact, one political cartoon of the time, doing a take-off of Picasso's portrait of Huidobro, shows him standing before a manifesto-bedecked screen behind which lurk a bevy of easily identifiable conspirators.

Acción lasted little more than three weeks; it was shut down on 29 August by the provisional government interested in promoting a single united-front candidate of the major political parties. Huidobro, undaunted, prints up another paper, *Reforma*, a broadside which calls for removing the ban on *Acción*, and resumes his long-shot bid for the presidency. Throughout the campaign he styles himself as a South American Atatürk, Chile's man of the hour, whose mission is to rally the country's youth to forge a new nation. An extravagant posture, by any measure. Yet, while the British empire could afford to ignore the pranks of a Victor Haldan, the Chilean establishment did not feel so secure with regard to Huidobro. The problem was that he was one of them — scion of an old and powerful family. Furthermore, his almost daily release of exposés and denunciations were all generated from within, laying bare the secrets of political compromise and profiteering among the country's leading politicians.

Just before the elections, in October, his candidacy is hastily legitimated, through a rigged Convention of Chilean Youth. Huidobro's old friend, the apolitical Alone, chronicled this manœuvre:

As in any convention, before it got under way, many names were whispered about; some were challenged and others were offered in their place. It all began well enough. Once the conventioneers were seated, a young man stepped out of the darkness of the proscenium and read out the 'Youth Programme'. A splendid programme: 'corral and expel lobbyists, arrest and exile of venal magistrates, mass execution of the corrupt, stimulate immigration to repopulate the country . . .'. Long applause. Suddenly, another orator steps forth, a real orator, one of those who knows how to whip up 'storms of enthusiasm'; and he begins to say that this Youth Convention is ridiculous. A wave of satisfaction passes through the crowd. Crowds enjoy being worked: like circus animals and women, they adore their masters. The speaker borders on insult: 'What is this Youth Assembly? Youth includes everyone, oligarchs, democrats, priests, atheists, the ignorant and the wise, the clever and the foolish. Among the young there are old people just as among the old there are those who are young, such as Anatole France who just died at eighty in full bloom.' The Convention would seem to have no other possibility than to dissolve itself. But there is salvation, there is a way to unite all interests and reconcile the most remote things, there is a magic key: the candidacy of Doctor Salas! Enormous, thunderous applause. The hall trembles. Will he be elected by instantaneous acclamation? Perhaps he would have, had not

Vicente Huidobro got up from his seat and, from the convention floor, launched into a violent speech against 'the unidentified individual who had just spoken.' A speech in which he protests against the attempt to distort this Assembly, which is not oriented toward any particular candidate, but rather to affirm the existence of Chilean youth. The crowd listens to him, it smiles, it applauds. Now it has changed its mind. It no longer wants Doctor Salas. It wants Vicente Huidobro.[4]

With little real chance of winning, Huidobro seems to have been politicking for the sheer joy of it, the exhilaration of being in the public eye. How else to explain his enthusiasm for a doomed cause? The elections of 1925 were won handily by Figueroa Larraín, the official candidate of a coalition of the major political parties. Two years later he resigned, turning power over to the ever-ambitious Ibáñez. But by then Huidobro was in the United States, in self-imposed exile.

He had evidently acquired a taste for politics though, for in a 1927 interview in New York, he is speaking out against Latin America's dependent status vis-à-vis the United States. He comes down particularly hard on the Pan-American Union, claiming that its headquarters ought to be in South America rather than in Washington.[5] Over the years this theme takes on a greater urgency, and by 1933 he is speaking of the need to create regional blocs to protect Latin America's interests from being co-opted by the United States. Always the poet, he dreams of an ideal Republic of Andesia, named after the Andes and comprising Argentina, Bolivia, Chile, Uruguay, and Paraguay. In an interview of the time he defends this project: 'Don't get the idea that this is just another utopia. Tomorrow will bring a collectivist world, without any of the old bitterness, nor narrowness of criteria, and this project will come to pass, since this is the way things must turn out in a world that controls its own destiny. How much time could be gained if we set ourselves to building it today!'[6]

The confident determinism of this internationalist view should not be surprising, for by this time Huidobro was a member of the Communist party. Just when he joined is not known; although in his library there is a 1929 edition of a *Manuel élémentaire du Communiste* and in a 1931 squabble with Buñuel he boasts of his militancy:

With regard to my revolutionary work and whether or not I am a Communist, you have no right to speak. As long as you don't sign up in the party you shouldn't be saying anything to me. Besides, my revolutionary work is much prior to yours and sufficiently proven in several countries.

Just now in Spain, in January of this year, still under the danger of the other regime, I carried two manifestos to Madrid, one of which was published and the other was not because it was considered to be *too* revolutionary. I crossed the frontier with both of them in my bag and risked spending my life in jail. Would you do the same?[7]

As always, he dramatizes his own actions. Communism, however, was not a passing fancy for him; he remained a militant in the party until well into the 1940s. His involvement does nevertheless follow a trajectory, a trajectory of disillusionment not unlike that of other intellectuals of his generation.

Through his private papers, interviews of the time, and the public record it is possible to piece together some idea of this trajectory: its beginnings, its high points, and its end, which came, not unexpectedly, in 1947, as the Cold War was developing. Huidobro then came out with a public statement: 'Por qué soy anticomunista' (Why I Am an Anticommunist).[8] Back in the beginning, everything was secret, and he threw himself into the movement with the ardour of a schoolboy discovering a new subject. Among his papers there are numerous book catalogues from the early 1930s in which he has checked off literally hundreds of items dealing with Russia and the theme of social revolution. Many of these, some with copious marginalia, became a permanent part of his library: books and magazines with titles like *La Révolution mondiale, La Scène ouvrière, Organización y constructores de Rusia, Teatro soviético, Cuadernos de la economía mundial*, to name but a few. Some of the publications he received seem ludicrous today: *Vida nueva* for example, combining an advocacy of free love with admiration for the Soviet Union, was printed in Santiago and distributed free to the unemployed so that they could earn a few cents selling it! Others, like the speeches of Luis Emilio Recabarren, founder of Chile's Communist party, are well thumbed and must have been the object of serious study and frequent consultation by Huidobro.

His ideological outlook shaped by the party, he is back in Chile in 1933, seeking once more to change the system. Shortly after his arrival he is interviewed by *Síntesis*, a Santiago news magazine. Declaring that any young person who is not already a Communist is simply an 'idiot', Huidobro speaks of the need for taking a stand:

As you can see by what I have already said, it is my conviction that artists and intellectuals must get involved in the social struggle and that they ought to be on the side of life, not death. Let's leave death to the dead while we the living stand up for life. And, just as there are cadavers that must constantly be slain, there are also the living who must be vivified. For this reason, in order to awaken the living, to raise them up to life, we [artists] are obliged to take part in the struggle.[9]

And take part he did, adding a certain imaginative flourish to the party's policies. In October of 1933, when he is interviewed by *Hoy*, he attempts to set forth a rather orthodox analysis of the political 'crisis':

It is impossible to get out of this crisis without a total change of the political and economic system. This change is foreseen by Marxist–Leninism, in other words, a socialist economy. There is no other way.

The essential factor is to adopt the principles of a revolution that is both agrarian and anti-imperialist. Social revolution in our Latin American countries can not be communist as in the major industrial countries, but rather an anti-imperialist agrarian revolution, in other words, nationalization of wealth, expulsion of the imperialists, and redistribution of property. According to historical materialism, this is the evolutionary step that corresponds to us.

His imagination leads the way however, and political jargon cedes to a more vivid expression:

The socio-psychological factor is an epiphenomenon of the economic factor and derives from a crisis of authority, the advance of social ideas and the backwardness of the people in government. The political demagogues of America are still sleeping in the feudal area. While the world moves forward, they go right on sleeping in the shade of a coconut tree, waiting for a coconut to fall on them, like a bomb.[10]

Huidobro's way with words could sometimes be too vivid, moving people to violence. In 1935, for example, he caused a near riot with some extemporaneous remarks when Enrique Molina, rector of the University of Chile, was giving a series of public lectures on the Russian Revolution. According to one newspaper account, Huidobro's critique split an otherwise sympathetic audience, provoking catcalls and a shouting match. The police were called in and the result was mayhem.[11]

He must have been a stirring speaker though, for when he was in Spain to defend the Republic, the military authorities found it useful to send him out on speaking forays. The procedure seems rather risky. A United Press dispatch, datelined 30 June, reports Huidobro at the front lines addressing Franco forces from a loudspeaker-equipped armoured vehicle. The idea was to persuade them to change sides.[12]

In politics, as in literature, he was always trying to persuade others of the rightness of his views. These views for a time were dictated by his party, which sometimes put him in a difficult spot; as in 1938, when the Chilean Popular Front was searching for a compromise candidate. The Communists had decided to back Ibáñez, the same army officer who had wrested power from Huidobro's former rival, Figueroa Larraín, back in 1927. The poet is called upon to defend the choice. He does, with an article titled 'Unidad' (Unity). In this carefully worded piece, Huidobro points out how the party, collectively reassessing the former caudillo's actions, now realizes its error in not getting behind him before. According to this forced reasoning, Ibáñez was really rather benign: 'During his government workers were not killed. Repression was limited to banishment, which was really a white-glove procedure compared to other governments before and after him. Under Ibáñez there were jobs and the right to work was protected more than before.'[13] Shortly after writing this, Huidobro finds himself out on a limb, when the party suddenly changes tactics, backing Aguirre-Cerda instead.

Much the same kind of thing happened to him in 1940, at the time of the German–Soviet non-aggression pact. Then, responding to an interviewer's question about the mixed-up state of the world, he had this to say:

— I think that one man happened to stand up in a world where everyone was sitting down. Suddenly, history began to move to his rhythm, dangerous for some, fascinating for others, particularly for those of us who were yearning to do something else rather than just 'mark time'.
— Undoubtedly, you are referring to Hitler. Do you admire him?
— I admire a country that is racing into history at a thousand kilometres an hour. If the driver happens to be Hitler, why not admire him too?[14]

Huidobro was far too independent a spirit to accept for long such a hold on what he could think and say, and his personal correspondence of the time shows him chafing against party discipline. In October 1938, shortly after the Ibáñez fiasco, he confides to a friend:

Among Communist officialdom, the fools — and there are a lot of them — may be annoyed by my independent attitude, because I never relinquish my personal thinking. But they ought to understand that a writer, a man of learning and culture, is not the same as any semi-literate militant. In this world there are foot soldiers and captains, everyone is not the same, nor can we make the same demands on everyone. It would be ridiculous if a thinking man were not allowed to question anything. And it would be the height of slavery. Those who think that way are bad Communists. I have the right to make known my points of disagreement with the party's directives. Spiritual slavery is Fascism, not Communism.[15]

Despite this attitude, he stuck with the party and did not allow his misgivings to become public. In fact, it was not unil after the Soviet Union was invaded, in the summer of 1941, that he spoke out against Hitler, calling for his defeat, which then, in a neat reversal of rhetoric, was to signify 'the triumph of history'.[16] The party's new friend and ally was to be the United States of course, and Huidobro promptly penned a series of 'Letters to Uncle Sam', laying down some of the preconditions.[17]

All this manœuvring evidently did not sit well with him, for only a few weeks afterwards, he is talking once again to Vattier, the same reporter to whom he had earlier expressed an admiration for Hitler. This time he is lambasting everything: politics for him now is a 'contagious disease', and politicians are 'more dangerous than rats'. He leaves little doubt about the depth of his disillusionment:

Politics is the art of lying, camouflaging, falsifying, dirtying lives, buying and selling minds, speculating about ideas that are little understood, and opinions that rise and fall in a thermometer of saliva. In order to keep a political party going enormous sums of money must be spent. You have to have radio stations, newspapers, public halls. Money, lots of money. Truth is not enough. The truth doesn't count.[18]

What first drew Huidobro into politics was the opportunity it afforded of putting himself before the public as a paladin of truth, and his early campaigning was outspokenly combative. Huidobro loved to stand up and give directives; as a Communist he was obliged to lie low and follow them. Too undisciplined for the party, for any party, it is not surprising that he drops out in the 1940s, but rather that he managed to stay in for more than a decade.

Eager to get back in the thick of things, his chance comes in 1944 when he is permitted to enter France as a war correspondent with the Allies. Yet even there his personal concerns are made to outweigh all others. Quite literally: one of his problems at war's end was how to transport several hundred kilos of excess baggage back to South America. Characteristically, he expects special treatment:

My general: An order from you would straighten out my difficulties. In the military plane to Brazil they won't allow me any excess baggage and I am carrying movies and things (. . .) that are indispensable for my lectures on the war. I am willing to pay for the excess, which amounts to some 200 kilos or more, but they won't accept it without an order from above.[19]

Back home (without films), he lectured mostly about his own exploits, showing off a German telephone supposedly ripped out of Hitler's bunker. Few were willing to believe him, then or now. His military papers neither confirm nor deny this particular episode; they do however show him moving with the troops through Germany, first in Bavaria, later along the Elbe, while broadcasting intermittently for the Voice of America from Paris. Wounded twice, in April and again in May, he was sent to London in June, and from there he was discharged. When he finally returned to Chile, late in 1945, it was with a new companion, Raquel Señoret, a young Chilean whom he had met at the Embassy in London.

As though beginning a new life, he declares himself to be above politics, but as the Cold War gets under way he is among those who line up against the Communists, publicly denouncing the party in 1947. What determines his new attitude is what the party had allowed itself to become under Stalin:

Communism has become a political party like any other, as sinuous and zigzagged as any political conglomerate. But with a single difference: it demands of its members fanaticism, that they believe whatever the supreme chief or the central committee decrees to be infallible, conforming to some reason beyond appeal, even though the very next day the decree is just the opposite.[20]

Huidobro would not have thought himself a reactionary, rather a fighter for what was then being called 'intellectual freedom'. His death, early in 1948, saved him from a final disillusionment on that score.

Looking back on the poet's involvement in politics, two things seem clear: the enthusiasm he brought to his beliefs, and his theatrical sense of timing. Indeed, Huidobro, while ineffectual as a politician, was splendid as a performer. He knew politics was a show, a Grand Guignol. And nowhere is this more evident than in his writing for the theatre.

In the early 1930s, while still in Paris, he seems to have renewed his interest in the stage. *Gilles de Rais*, his surrealist-styled play on the Bluebeard theme, was published there in

1932 and portions of it were staged the following year at the Théâtre de l'Œuvre.[21] Drama was not a new endeavour for Huidobro. Some of his earliest artistic efforts were for the stage. When he was barely twenty, a drawing-room comedy, *Cuando el amor se vaya* (When Love Goes), had a brief run in Santiago's Palace Theater before folding in May of 1913. His best play however was political, *En la luna* (On the Moon), and although published in Chile in 1934, it was not staged there until some thirty years later.

Ahead of its time, *En la luna* is an outsize farce in the modern tradition of the absurd. Holding up to ridicule the puppet democracies of Latin America, it sharpens its point about political manipulation by having the actors portray puppets, moving themselves about the stage with the exaggerated jerkiness of marionettes on a string. The puppeteer for this 'pequeño guiñol' is one Maese López, whose imagination, like that of Cervantes's Maese Pedro, lets things get out of hand. *En la luna* climaxes with a revolt; the puppets, 'freed', dance wildly. The show must be forcibly stopped:

MAESE LOPEZ: — Please, Colorín, cut my inspiration short. Stop these puppets for me; they're capable of going on like this for ever. Kill the show!

COLORIN: — All this shouting for that? [*He takes a pistol from his pocket.*]

MAESE LOPEZ: — [*Raising his pistol and shooting it into the air.*] This show is over.

[*CURTAIN*]

At the outset, this same Maese López sets things in motion; like any fast-talking circus barker he lures passers-by into his side-show with the promise of cheap thrills:

MAESE LOPEZ: — Ladies and gentlemen: Stop, let no one pass by. Here I am. One moment, please. You have here Maese López, the great showman of marvels; here is López, with his show (. . .). Everything I bring you is new and even more extraordinary than before. Nothing like this has ever been seen on the moon. You know that López kids you not. I am not bringing you the giant lady who looked like she could grab the Earth and Venus in her hands; nor am I bringing you the little rubber boy who could turn himself inside out (. . .); and neither do I bring you that man who could squeeze his tummy so as to fart out the national anthem (. . .). What I am bringing you is a piece of true theatre, in other words, pure fantasy. You are about to see something that has not happened anyplace. Nor shall it ever happen anywhere.

There is an echo of Huidobro's poetic credo here, and well there might be, for he is now using the theatre to create the new reality called for by his political beliefs.

En la luna contains the scenario for total revolution, for tearing down the old order and building up the new. The play's four acts, roughly equal in length, detail the progressive deterioration of a state moving backwards through rigged elections, military *coups*, and anarchy, before blundering into the absolute tyranny of a theocracy. It is only in the last act that this antihistorical process is suddenly reversed, when workers and intellectuals unite to create socialism. Everything in the play is overblown: its plot, its characters, its dialogue. Huidobro, in a prefatory note to the director, stressed the need to stylize the performance as much as possible:

> The actors have to bear in mind that this is a puppet-play and they should employ an exaggerated manner, grand gestures (. . .). It is recommended that the scenery be of an extremist taste, either very simple or very elaborate. The politicians are to wear satin cut-aways, in striking colours: red, green, purple, blue, yellow, or perhaps red and yellow or blue and green squares, etc. Contrasting pants. The military should be *theatrically* military. All the characters ought to be turned out in the most conventionally theatrical way, along the lines of an operetta.

Thus, in the first act, when a new president takes office he appears on stage 'draped in a sash containing all the colours of the rainbow' and proceeds to mouth an inaugural speech that, although it reads like Spanish, is untranslatable nonsense: 'Señores y conciudadanos: la patria en solemífados momentos me elijusna para directar sus destídalos y salvantiscar sus princimientos y legicipios sacropanzos . . .'.

Even when the dialogue makes linguistic sense, it is nonsensical. In one scene the Finance Minister is proposing to the Cabinet his brainstorm for economic recovery. To get money back into circulation the government ought to make begging obligatory:

PRESIDENT: — Let's hear your idea.
FINANCE MINISTER: — Quite simple and quite easy. We shall declare begging to be obligatory. We shall all become beggars.
PRESIDENT: — And I am to preside over a country of beggars?
FINANCE MINISTER: — We shall all be beggars . . .
INTERIOR MINISTER: — And so?
FINANCE MINISTER: — You still don't see the solution? Think about it a bit. It's not so hard. We are all beggars . . . My colleague then gives a

coin to a beggar, any beggar, who in turn gives it to another. Someone gives it to me, I give it to you, and so on. Money is circulating again . . .
PRESIDENT: — From hand to hand. Magnificent. Stupendous!

But before they have time to put any programme into effect, there is a military *coup*. Coronel Sotavento (*sotavento* = leeward) and his toy soldiers break down the door and call for the President to resign. The Army's *coup* is followed by the Navy's: Admiral Estribor (starboard) seeks to board the ship of state. Then the firemen revolt. Anarchy soon results and a succession of special-interest groups appear, each one seeking to redefine the government in its own image. The dentists seize power to fight 'decay'. They are followed by the typists with their dictates; then the tailors enter, carrying scissors a yard long:

PERMANGANATO: — We tailors can't be pushed around; we know what power is. [*Opening his enormous scissors.*] Careful about conspiracies. Let me warn you right now that conspirators are risking their heads. Nobody can trick a tailor. We know what measures to take; we know how to cut for the best . . .

What makes all these antics cohere into a play that will work on the stage is a sophisticated utilization of techniques at the disposal of the theatre. Huidobro's stage directions are expertly detailed with regard to space, movement, and timing. The second act, for example, is to close with an elaborate multi-level contrivance showing four separate rooms of conspirators plotting to topple the government. So as to allow time for this to be set up, Huidobro devises an open-ended mime sequence to be played out in front of the drawn curtains:

This scene takes place in front of the curtains and is preparatory to the next. There should be a backdrop painted to look like a tree-lined boulevard. In the sky these words: 'DO YOU HEAR FLOWERS GROWING INSIDE YOUR HEAD?' A beggar stands at the left with his palm extended. From the same side Fifí Fofó and Lulú Lalá come on stage.
BEGGAR: — Can you spare anything?
FIFI FOFO: — [*Giving him a coin.*] — Here you go, good fellow. [*To Lulú Lalá.*] It is such a pleasure for me to give.
LULU LALA: — Giving is indeed a great joy. [*They exit.*]
BEGGAR: — Even in that they are lucky. Our misfortune is a source of their satisfaction.
General Sotavento, Admiral Estribor, don Fulano de Tal, Pipí Popó, some Captains and the Commodore all enter.
BEGGAR: — Can you spare anything?
General Sotavento gives him something and moves over alongside the

beggar, sticking out his hand; Admiral Estribor then moves over next to
the General, sticking out his hand as well. Pipí Popó, the Captains, and the
Commodore all do the same. The beggar starts to move off-stage; and
passing in front of Sotavento he gives him a coin. Sotavento does the same,
giving it to Estribor, who passes it on to Pipí Popó, she to the Captain,
and so on until they all work their way off-stage. All without speaking.
The lights then dim and the curtain goes up. In the middle of the stage is a
huge prop consisting of four identical rooms: two above, two below. In
each of these rooms there is a table around which are seated several
hooded conspirators. As each group speaks up a red light should go on in
the appropriate room.

3	2
1	4

VOICE IN ROOM 1: — Here is our plan. Tomorrow at 2:30 we gather at
this corner and from there we march on the Palace.
VOICE IN ROOM 2: — Listen carefully now. This is where the main
gate is located. Tomorrow, at 3:15 . . .

No amount of stagecraft, however sophisticated, can overcome some of the awkwardness occasioned by the demands of
social realism. While *En la luna* is stylistically poised between
Jarry and Ionesco in the brilliance of its dialogue and the out-
rageousness of its scenario, it is still a play of the 1930s, dog-
matically upbeat with regard to its social mission. Accordingly,
in the final act, there is a 'realistic' scene where students (not
puppets) despair over how and what they can do to save the
country from further ruin. The white knight of social realism,
a worker, fortuitously appears, 'his shirtsleeves rolled up to
show his bulging muscles'. A stereotype, if ever there was one,
he literally gushes with optimism:

WORKER: — I am your hope. What's all this pessimistic talk? Come
on, join in the struggle! I know the outcome. My moment has arrived;
this is my day (. . .). I am a worker, the new man. The future is ours.
Join our struggle. Look at my muscles! Don't they give you confi-
dence?

Workers and intellectuals do band together, carrying the play to
its ideologically logical conclusion. But while Huidobro's heart
and mind were committed to his party's cause, his view of the
working class was a poet's abstraction.

This is really a minor flaw to an otherwise major work. The play
in fact ends masterfully, setting forth its thesis in a theatrically

spectacular way. From *coup* to *coup*, the moonland of *En la luna* slides backward, reaching its lowest and most ridiculous state when a court jester siezes power and has himself crowned Nadir I. From act to act and scene to scene, the turmoil on stage is punctuated by the people's off-stage cry for 'pan y trabajo' (bread and work), a background detail whose full dramatic function is reserved for the finale. In the closing scene, Nadir assembles his court to watch a puppet play (with real puppets). In this play within a play, significantly called *En la tierra* (On Earth), there is another tyrannical king, North-South III, who, muttering 'Tatarantulas', is to be seen as a direct descendant of Ubu. As the miniature play gets under way Nadir sees himself:

NADIR: [*Speaking to his court*] — What a poet and what a philosopher that king is! By the horns of the earth, I'd love to meet him!
PUPPETEER: — Praise to our king!
NORTH-SOUTH: — Tatarantulas! Let me be! I want to gaze upon my own greatness. Hand me a mirror!
PUPPETEER: — Oh, mirror of powers! Contemplate your power in this mirror. [*Stepping out, he hands him a mirror.*]
Voices off-stage: 'Bread. We want bread!'
NADIR I: [*From on stage.*] — This 'bread-bread', is it coming from here or the court of the earthly king? Is it my moon-people or your earth-people who are shouting?
NORTH-SOUTH III: — Just what is the meaning of this 'bread-bread'? Who dares to beat on the gates and disturb my sleep?
NADIR I: — Is it the 'bread-bread' of the moon that he is hearing on earth, or is it the 'bread-bread' of the earth that we are hearing on the moon?
NORTH-SOUTH III: — Tatarantulas! I am the King of the Universe!
NADIR I: — This king is getting on my nerves.

With both lines of action thus enmeshed, the people's revolt in the miniature play becomes one with the student-worker revolt of *En la luna*, doubly reinforcing Huidobro's internationalist thesis that all peoples must and will unite to set things right in the world. As both puppet tyrannies collapse, a stirring voice is heard over a loudspeaker:

VOICE: — It would take just one night to rid the world of injustice, of parasites, of octopuses and vampires. Just one night to cleanse the world of corruption. And the sun of the following day would brighten the smile of a new world, a world reborn.

This is the vision of a poet, not a politician. A poet who always viewed politics as a kind of theatre.

Fittingly, his last writing for the stage was both poetic and political. In the newly liberated Paris of 1945, Pierre Darmangeat reportedly staged a reading of a play by Huidobro called *Deucalion*.[22] The text has been lost; but the title is clue enough to its contents: Deucalion is the Noah of Greek mythology who repopulates the earth from Parnassus. A poet's last attempt to give dramatic shape to a new world order.

VII
Novel and Film

Man begins life by seeing, then he can hear, later he is able to speak, and finally he begins to think. In his inventions, man has followed this selfsame order. First he invented photography, a mechanical eye; then the telephone, a mechanical ear; later the phonograph, a mechanical voice; and ultimately, the cinema, mechanizing thought.   1921

Even before the poet's involvement in politics, he was seeking a wider public through the mass-oriented art of the cinema. An entertainment column in *Paris-Journal* (20 April 1923) reveals that Huidobro, 'one of the luminaries of literary Cubism, is secretly at work on a film that will revolutionize viewing habits'. A decade later, trying to revolutionize political habits, he would turn to the stage and the novel: 1934, along with *En la luna*, would see the publication of *La próxima*, a prescient prose narrative whose subject was the next world war. While Huidobro's career as a film-maker was cut short by the emergence of the 'talkies' and his political novel just as quickly outdated by the thrust of history, true popular success came to him when his efforts at novel and film were combined, creating, almost by accident, a filmic novel; what he himself called a 'novela-film'.

In this somewhat hybrid genre he produced two masterworks: *Cagliostro* (1934) and *Mío Cid Campeador* (1929). Both, like *En la luna*, are conceived as entertainments: one updates the story of the medieval hero of Castille; while the other deals with the larger-than-life adventures of an eighteenth-century mesmerizer. In both cases Huidobro borrowed freely from a variety of sources and made up the rest. The idea was not to tell an original story, but to retell the familiar in an original way. A kind of *re-escritura*.

The impetus to do a novel probably came from Joseph Delteil, a now-forgotten French novelist who was all the rage back in the 1920s. The fact is that when Huidobro returned to Paris in 1928, Delteil's *Jeanne d'Arc* (1925) had already gone through several editions and was still a runaway best-seller. Lives of other heroes were soon to follow (*La Fayette*, 1928; *Napoléon*, 1929). Essentially, Delteil brought these figures back to life by re-telling their stories with the metaphoric verve of the avant-garde. Huidobro, ever the competitor, was anxious to try his hand at such a novel, but in Spanish (Delteil was his friend), and with the even more extravagant culture heroes of that world. What is more, the year before, in 1927, he had met Douglas Fairbanks and was encouraged to do a filmscript with a swashbuckling hero. Not surprisingly, Huidobro in 1928 is writing to his friend Larrea, then in Madrid, asking for books on the Cid and Cortés.[1]

Yet, there was perhaps another, more personal factor motivating his final choice of subject: a romantic attachment to a young woman named Ximena, a circumstance which must have prompted him to see himself as being somehow connected to the Cid. To this end, he consulted experts in heraldry (one of Huidobro's ancestors, the first Marqués de Casa Real, had actually come from Burgos), and at one point he even wrote to Menéndez Pidal seeking to connect the Cid's line of descent with his own.[2]

Whether actually believing himself a descendant, or simply feigning belief, the result was the same: an impishly arrogant present-day narrator, anachronistically at ease with the past. Regarding the 'Afrenta de corpes' incident in the medieval poem, Huidobro has this to say: 'I just can't see my grandfather the Cid allowing my aunt Mary and my grandmother Christine being thrashed without eating their husbands alive. This incident never occurred. I swear it. If it had we would know about it in the family, and then you would see how I would have made mincemeat out of such scoundrels in these pages.'[3]

This glib self-confidence is part of what makes Huidobro's novel so unique, permitting the author to 'improve' upon his source materials at will; and, in so doing, to surpass his literary models. While Delteil had breathed new life into Joan of Arc by retelling her legend in contemporary language, Huidobro decided to carry the process much further, updating not only the *Cantar* but also the manner of its formation. For example, the circumstances casting the Cid as something of an outlaw are conveyed through a use of anachronism that borders on the ludicrous: the *jongleurs* of yesteryear as newsboys hawking an 'extra' in today's Madrid. Thus, when the news of Count Lozano's murder breaks, the narrator is able to conjure up a scene like the following:

The cafés in the Puerta del Sol are literally filled with people. Not even a pin can get inside (unless it is a tie-pin, pocketed by a pickpocket). The evening papers hit the streets with their huge headlines, those headlines that devour everything around them, that swallow up people, cars, houses and tramways. Those enormous headlines dominate all, with newsboys shouting:

> COUNT LOZANO MURDERED MONTES D'OCA SEIZED CRISIS BETWEEN KING AND POPE
>
> Suspicions of guilt in the murder of Count Lozano today centre upon Rodrigo Díaz de Vivar. The alleged assassin is said to have fled from his house, with a band of relatives and friends, seeking asylum elsewhere.
>
> The Count's body was horribly mutilated, one hand having been cut off. According to the police, bruises on the body indicate that the murderer repeatedly kicked the victim after he had fallen to the ground.

Oh, how deplorable!
Fortunately though, back in those crude times, there were no newspapers, nor even cafés in the Puerta del Sol. The earth, spinning in its chaos, rotates on the daily news of banal hearsay. In the old days it rolled out on its elliptic orbit a poem that is now legend. Let's return to those days. But first let's shake out the dust, for Rodrigo kicked up a lot of it when he and his men took flight.   (89-90)

The aside to the reader, although a borrowing from the rhetoric of radio drama, bears a functional comparison to the formulaic modes of address found in the *Cantar* where the narrator clues the public to what it is about to hear, reminding the listener that he is present at a narration about something that has already happened and that is being artistically retold. Huidobro too feels the need to frequently remind the reader that *Mío Cid Campeador* is a retelling, *his* retelling. The literary convention informing this work is not unlike that of Huidobro's poetry at its most inventive level: whatever is said is real, or at least functions as though it were. The threshold connecting words with the reality they can evoke is regularly crossed, often flamboyantly. Thus, following a particularly emotional moment for Ximena when tears well up in her eyes, the narrator informs us that one of those tears he has just described, 'trembles briefly before falling into the novel and I am helpless to stop it from rolling across this page' (42).

Huidobro never lets the reader forget that it is he who is writing what is being read and that he feels no constraints whatsoever on his imagination, especially when it comes to altering history so as to make it more entertaining. Sometimes though he makes imaginative use (and abuse) of historical fact for the same purpose. At one point, after detailing the preparatory manœuvres for what is to be a decisive battle between the Cid and his arch-enemy García-Ordóñez, an unexpected twist is given to the narration when it turns out that the battle cannot take place as anticipated. A small fact of history thwarts Huidobro's plans:

> The hour of justice is near. All of Spain eagerly awaits this moment. The Chronicle fixes its anxious eyes upon it; the Legend rises to attention. Oh, with what gusto are we going to witness and describe the battle in which the Cid will once more pluck the beard of his mortal enemy!
> Unfortunately, we cannot describe the battle: that scheming García-Ordóñez has tricked us. He went off with his troops; he retreated without even getting near the site where the Cid was waiting for him.
> In vain my pen had been rinsed in rose-water getting ready to give a few good pricks to that miserable Count, take him prisoner and rub his face in a manure-heap. But he doesn't show. There is no sign of the Count at all. He leaves me with my pen in my hand, he snatches the honey right out of my mouth, he robs me of the joy of vengeance.
> So, you don't dare to show your face? Alright; you'll be exposed as a coward, a vile and insidious schemer. Here I pillory you before the world, I run you through on this page, and I myself pluck your beard. You swine! (368)

Playfulness of this sort within a text is one of the mainstays of children's literature, and so it is not surprising that Isabel Shepard, an enterprising author of children's books, wrote to Huidobro proposing an abridged edition of his *Mío Cid Campeador*. He was of course delighted at the prospect of reaching those 'virginal minds'.[4]

In *Altazor* (1931) he would portray himself as an anti-poet, 'a savage who was parachuted one morning into the landscaped garden of literary precepts'; here, in his first novel, the pose is similarly irreverent: an anti-novelist gleefully trampling on the conventions of literary realism. Writing this highly personal account of the Cid some eight hundred years after the fact, Huidobro has occasion to mock traditional authorial modes of 'seeing' into the past. In one scene, in which Ximena is described

as either embroidering or spinning ('bordando o hilando'), Huidobro blurts out that 'at this distance, at the distance of all
these years, I really can't make out if she is spinning or embroidering; she is working at something though' (65). The seeing
convention, and its limitations, descend to slapstick for a
moment when the narrator teams up with a reader to focus in
on the year 1081. This of course is the year of the Cid's major
campaigns; he then seems to be all over Spain:

> Reader, to follow the Cid at this frenetic stage, we must get a telescope
> of long — centuries-long — range and focus it on the year 1081. Here we
> go. Put your eye up to the lens and focus it. What do you see?
> — I see Cleopatra on the Nile.
> — You made a mistake; you went too far back. Focus it nearer. Here, let
> me do it. I have a knack for this.
> — No, no. Leave it to me. Ah, now I have it right. I am coming in on the
> year 1081, 1081 on the roads of Spain.
> — What do you see there?
> — I see the Cid Campeador, the one who was born at the right moment,
> the one who took up the sword . . .   (301–2).

Here, as throughout the novel, the language is intended to
allude to the *Cantar*: 'el que en buen hora nació y en mejor hora
ciñó espada'.

The literary tradition of the Cid is always present; sometimes
the allusion is to the *Cantar*, at other times to the *Romancero*
or any of the many rewrites they have spawned. In a whimsical
reversal of chronology, Huidobro has the hero operate with an
awareness that he is the source of this long tradition and must
therefore live up to it. Early in the novel, there is a childhood
contest over who can leap farthest. When the turn comes to
Huidobro's Cid, the young man 'thinks first of the *Cantar*,
then he thinks of the *Romancero* and the epic, of Guillén de
Castro, of Corneille, and of me; gathering his strength, he
leaps' (30).

Other works of literature also weigh heavily in the novel,
complementing those on the Cid. While the telescope scene
alludes rather indirectly to the famous opening of Clarín's *La
Regenta*, other allusions are more explicit. Valle Inclán for
example: when an old hag appears at a window, 'en una ventana
asoma la nariz de alcuza una vieja de Valle (81). Even the
Quijote is present when the Cid, faced with a field of wind-
mills, 'feels some crazy urge to spur his horse on, to attack them
with his lance, riveting them to the sky. But he holds himself

back and I hear him exclaim — "Let's leave that to someone else".' (303)

Tradition is an important informing principle in just about every work of literature, with the author usually writing against it or within it. Huidobro, though, does things somewhat differently. A good portion of his novel consists of slightly altered borrowings from familiar sources. Not plagiarisms as someone has recently suggested,[5] but artful remakes. The *Romancero*, itself a compendium of remakes, is present on practically every page. When Huidobro calls attention to such an obvious source it is often with a humorous intent. In one of the central chapters, the Infanta de Zamora becomes so enraged at the sight of the Cid at her palace gates, that she spews out a *romance* ('Afuera, afuera Rodrigo'), inadvertently 'forgetting its assonant rhyme scheme' (223). Even when the borrowing is quite literal, as when the Cid is forced to leave Burgos, Huidobro cannot refrain from artful intrusion:

Just when the Cid is about to break down the door, a nine-year old girl steps out of the *Cantar* and going up to him she speaks with a frank and charming verse rhythm:

> Campeador, que en buen hora ceñiste espada,
> no podemos, Mío Cid, darte asilo por nada;
> el rey nos lo ha prohibido con severas amenazas.
> Si te abrimos perderemos los haberes y las casas,
> perderemos nuestros ojos, nuestros cuerpos y aun las almas.
> No podemos albergarte, ni tampoco venderte nada,
> ni trigo, ni pan, ni viandas, ni la ración más menguada.
> Cid, en el mal de nosotros vos no ganaréis nada.
> Seguid y que Dios os proteja y la tierra os sea ancha.*

Having thus spoken the child hurried back inside her strophe. (288)

The impact of this most famous of scenes is enhanced by the closing metaphor: 'la niña volvió a meterse corriendo dentro de su estrofa'.

It is this dynamically inventive use of language, forging a new myth out of the old, that makes this book of fifty years ago

* Campeador, who at the right hour took up the sword, / we cannot, my Cid, give you any help at all; / the king has forbidden us under heavy penalty. / If we open the door to you we shall lose our possessions and our homes, / we shall lose our eyes, our bodies and even our lives. / We cannot lodge you, nor can we sell you anything, / neither grain nor bread, nor meat, not even the meagrest ration. / Cid, you have nothing to gain with our misfortune. / Go your way and may God protect you and make the world wide for you.

seem so alive today, pertinent to the experimentalism of what
has come to be called the New Novel. Alejo Carpentier, dean of
Latin America's 'new novelists', recognized as much when he
reviewed *Mío Cid Campeador* back at the time of its original
publication: 'Huidobro has given us a mythic biography of the
Cid that will forever fix the hero in our minds — how could
History ever pretend to have more authority than the Novel?'[6]
What most delighted Carpentier, and was largely responsible for
Huidobro's success as a modern mythmaker, was the novel's
highly charged language; *Mío Cid Campeador* is the novel of a
poet, an avant-garde poet. In his fertile imagination, the most
prosaic scene can lead into the most extravagant scenario.
Simply paying homage to Babieca (the Cid's horse), the narrator
can get carried away:

> Babieca would make any poet soar higher than Pegasus. She hears me
> and stamps her hoof. She is pleased with me. I thank you Babieca.
> There, at the extreme edge of fable, Babieca prances, she rears up on
> her hind legs in order to nibble on a star; she lifts up her tail and breaks
> wind on History, letting cascade a stream of golden verses, and in a bound
> she is galloping off to the other side of the world.   (176)

Sometimes though, this overwriting gets out of hand and the
author must be restrained. On one occasion, the Cid himself
steps into the novel to straighten things out. The poet, waxing
eloquent over Ximena's beauty — her long neck, her lily-white
skin, her coral lips — heaps up literary clichés, making her into a
goddess; the ghost of the Cid then appears at his writing-table:
'Poet, you are dead wrong. Ximena was not Greek, she was
Spanish (. . .). If you want to make things up about me, I don't
care; but I can't allow you to lie like this about Ximena. She
had a wonderful [Spanish] body, broad hips and big breasts,
without any of that business of amphoras and marble.' (63-5)
Mío Cid Campeador was Huidobro's first novel, and it shows
him at his most playful. Using and abusing the conventions of
the serious novel of his time, he succeeds in creating a work
that is highly original and broadly entertaining. Although avant-
garde, it is still accessible to the common reader. The reason
for this is less ideological than circumstantial: Huidobro originally wrote the novel to serve as the basis for a film. The cinema
is the most popular of the arts, the spectacle appealing to almost
everyone. Paradoxically however, the most cinematic portions
of the text are those which are least appealing today: scenes of
individual derring-do originally conceived for the likes of a

Douglas Fairbanks, great battles laid out along the epic lines of D. W. Griffith, cliffhanging rescue situations, and a variety of special visual effects. Some of the visual effects became a problematic concern for the author because the publisher decided to bring out a de luxe edition with illustrations. Their correspondence on this gives us an inside view into Huidobro's thinking with regard to the functioning of his text.

Having decided to fill in where the *Cantar* was blank, with the birth, childhood, and adolescence of the Cid, Huidobro not only lengthened the story considerably, but also created some special difficulties for himself. How does one portray a hero in diapers? Huidobro's Cid, born with an awareness of his epic obligations, simply refuses to be diapered, letting out a universe-piercing wail:

At that moment an enormous storm shakes the firmament, making the air shudder and shattering all the windows in heaven. A blinding flash of lightning shoots across the sky writing in billboard-size letters:

CAM
P
E
A
DOR.

In correcting the page-proofs, Huidobro objected to the line-drawing for this chapter. In his view, the artist had stolen the thunder from his text: 'There is one sketch that must be corrected. It's the one on page twenty-five which shows the new-born Cid. The word Campeador that falls from the sky must be erased because it completely destroys the ending of the chapter and kills the surprise I had planned for the reader. This should be easy to fix up: just leave the lightning bolt without the word inside.'[7]

Despite Huidobro's cavilling, the visual qualities of the novel were really interpreted quite well by Ontañón, a Spanish set-designer who did the illustrations (thirty-one line-drawings and seven in colour). Nor did its filmic qualities go unnoticed by critics in Spain. Fernando Mantilla, reviewing the novel for the cinema section of *Atlántico* magazine, called for it to be made into a movie right away: 'The novel is better than Douglas Fairbanks deserves. It should go to launch a new star (. . .) in a Spanish superproduction. The Cid, with his powerful lance could ride through our borders and Babieca's hooves could bring to the talkies an as yet unheard success among the sounds of the silver screen.'⁸ The review is so gushy that it could have been ghosted by Huidobro himself. Publicity is but another dimension of art, and not the least creative. We know for certain that he did coach the publisher on promotion:

For bookstore placards and newspaper ads you might want to use something like this:

HERE THE CID IS REBORN
AND THE GREATEST EPIC OF HIS PEOPLE.

But if you prefer to use the inflated style of Yankee books, we might as well go all out and simply announce:

THE BOOK OF TODAY . . .
AND OF THE CENTURY.

Although one should be modest, it doesn't really affect me since all this is just a question of commercial puffery (and only the two of us are in on the secret).⁹

Modesty notwithstanding and all secrets aside, the book was a great success in Spain. So much so that it was quickly translated and published in England under the title *Portrait of a Paladin* (1931); and so successful was it there that the translator (Warre B. Wells) obtained contract for other, unpublished manuscripts from Huidobro.

It was in this roundabout way that *Cagliostro* came into print in English several years before being published in Spanish.¹⁰ When the original finally did appear, in 1934, it was billed as a 'novela-film'. The novel did in fact have its beginnings as a filmscript, a scenario for a silent movie. It will be recalled that in April of 1923 *Paris-Journal* reported Huidobro to be at work on a Cubist film that was to 'revolutionize viewing habits'. Yet another newspaper, a month later, contained further details on the project: 'Vicente Huidobro, the pure poet of *Horizon carré* and *Tour Eiffel*, has completed the scenario of a film *Cagliostro*, in which the specifically cinegraphic action is "visualized" with an acute sense of optic rhythm.'¹¹ The film must have already been shot, for among Huidobro's papers there is a memo in which the writer and director jointly declare their dissatisfaction with the 'découpage'.¹²

This film of 1923, to my knowledge, was not released nor have any copies survived. The script however did resurface in 1927, when it won a prize in New York from the League for Better Pictures. The *New York Times* for 23 July 1927, under the heading 'Chilean Gets Film Prize', reports the following:

'Vicente Huidobro, young Chilean poet and novelist, was announced yesterday as the winner of a $10,000 prize offered by
the League for Better Pictures for the book of the year having
the best possibilities for moving-picture adaptation. The book,
still in script form in the hands of Paris publishers, is called
Cagliostro and is based upon the life of the eighteenth-century
necromancer and popular mystic.' *Cagliostro* was truly ill-fated.
The book that was so promising in July was outmoded just a
few months later when, in October of 1927, Warner Brothers
released *The Jazz Singer*, the talking picture that turned the
film world upside down. Especially the New York film world,
bumping it off to Hollywood. Huidobro's *Cagliostro* was left
behind, an instant relic of the past; it was written in the language of the silent film.

By design its imagery was created in the filmic tradition of
the great German silents of the 1920s, the Expressionist-
Cubist world of the studio-filmed horror tale. Even the classics
of the genre, such as *The Cabinet of Dr Caligari* and *Nosferatu*,
are gimmicky films by today's standards, their horrific impact
the result of a deliberate unnaturalness. Still-shots, painted sets,
stilted acting, and Gothic subtitling were all systematically used
to create the illusion of an otherworldly reality. And Huidobro's
novel, concerned with the exploits of an eighteenth-century
master of the black arts, was equally contrived so as to make
the greatest use of the possibilities of the genre. Accordingly,
scenes of levitation, spatial projection, hypnotism, and black
magic abound.

Huidobro's interest in film was not unique. Like other writers
of the avant-garde, he was intrigued by this modern form of
illusion that relates motion, time, and space in a new kind of
composition. In fact, as early as 1916, there is a poem in *El
espejo de agua* whose subject is the magic of the Newsreel:

El sueño de Jacob se ha realizado
Un ojo se abre frente al espejo
Y las gentes que bajan a la tela
Arrojaron su carne como un abrigo viejo.

La película mil novecientos dieciséis
Sale de una caja.

La guerra europea

Llueve sobre los espectadores . . .

(Jacob's dream has been realized / An eye opens in front of the mirror / And the people who come on screen shed their skin like an old overcoat / The movie 1916 / Comes out of the box / The European War / Rains down over the viewers . . .)

The jumpy discontinuity of the poem is not unlike that of the early one-reelers, whose compressed treatment of time derived from the sequential montage of separately filmed scenes. It should be remembered that the rise of literary Cubism is intertwined with the development of film as an art form, and that both rely on essentially similar compositional techniques: montage and cutting. Montage is metaphor. Even the theory is the same. The most effective metaphor, according to Reverdy, the principal theoretician of Cubist poetry, was that produced by the juxtaposition of 'distant realities'; similarly, the most effective montage, according to Eisenstein, the principal theoretician of the silent film, was that produced by the 'collision' of conflicting shots. In both cases the result was the same: a new and dynamic reality created by the unexpected association forced to take place in the mind of the reader, or viewer.

There were important differences however. Film was public and narrative, while poetry was personal and lyrical. One was commercially oriented toward a mass audience and the other was the artistic property of an élite. Huidobro in the 1920s was searching for a wider public. Unable to bring out a film, he was forced to settle with bringing film to the novel. In this regard, the preface to the English-language edition of *Cagliostro* contains an important statement:

As for the form of this book, I have only to say that this is what may be called a visual novel, with a technique influenced by the cinematograph. I believe that the public of today, which has acquired the cinema habit, may be interested in a novel in which the author has deliberately chosen words of a visual character and events that are best suited to comprehension through the eyes (. . .). Character drawing today has to be more synthetic, more compact, than it was before. Action cannot be slow. Events have to move more rapidly. Otherwise the public is bored.

Huidobro was concerned with the cinema's influence on the novel. Contemporary criticism looks at the problem from the other end, focusing on the literary properties of cinema: the director as author, the film as narrative, even the camera as pen. Obviously, things were not always this way. For Huidobro exactly the reverse was true. For him, the cinema was the new art form, hence his effort to bring out a novel utilizing the procedures of film for readers who had picked up the 'cinema habit'. The informing principles of *Cagliostro*, as outlined in the 1931 preface, were four; they refer to plot, character, style, and language. Essentially, the plot is to be fast-paced since the reader habituated to film will not tolerate much descriptive exposition. Characterization likewise is to be rapid, 'four strokes of the brush', Huidobro says, 'and a living being is painted'. Furthermore, the style is to be visual, that best suited 'to comprehension through the eyes'. And, finally, the language is to be of a 'visual character'. An examination of *Cagliostro* in the light of these principles of composition should permit us to appreciate the uniqueness of Huidobro's literary hybrid, the 'novela-film'.

With regard to plot and character, history tells us that Cagliostro was a famous Italian adventurer, magician, alchemist, and protagonist of many scandals in Europe during the late eighteenth century, the age of the Enlightenment. Huidobro focuses on his adventures in France on the eve of the French Revolution. When the reader first 'sees' the protagonist he is disembarking from a carriage in the dead of night. Draped with a cape only his eyes are visible. The narrator rhetorically draws our attention to those eyes:

> The strange door of the strange coach creaked as it slowly opened, and a man, wrapped in a cape that left nothing visible save his eyes, protruded his head from the night within the coach into the night outside to find out what was going on.
> Did you see those eyes? Those eyes phosphorescent as the streams that run through mines of mercury; those eyes suddenly enriched the night, they are the only light emerging from the depths of his existence. Take a good look at them, for they are the centre of my story.[13]

This kind of rhetorical persuasion, with direct authorial intrusion, might seem a bit overwrought to readers accustomed to the objectivity of the modern novel, but in the convention of the visual language of the silent film the eyes told all. There was a kind of filmic physiognomy, whereby the facial features of an individual were supposed to reveal qualities of mind and character: the shifty eyes of the untrustworthy, the flashing eyes of the lover, and here the phosphorescent eyes of the mesmerizer, Cagliostro. Other characters in the novel are typed with equal rapidity. So rapidly, in fact, that the narrator on occasion avoids all description and asks the reader to fill in with a familiar stereotype. For example, when Lorenza, Cagliostro's mistress and medium appears for the first time she is described in this way: 'She is beautiful, a brunette with great dark eyes full of light and grace. (Reader, just think of the most beautiful woman you ever saw and apply her beauty to Lorenza; that way you'll save me and yourself a lengthy description).' (38) Such descriptive shorthand takes advantage of the avant-garde's re-discovery of the expressive power of cliché when transferred to a new context.

As for plot, it is so slickly contrived for special effects that it is almost impossible to summarize. Suffice it to say that Cagli-ostro is a magician, so all sorts of tricks and magic effects come into play. At the outset he is seen arriving in France, putting his occult powers to good use, raising the dead, healing the sick, and so forth. His fame soon spreads and he is asked to perform before the court of Louis XVI. This gives rise to a flash forward, a vision of the guillotine, with powdered heads tumbling to the ground. The plot, although streamlined, is not without compli-cations: the prefect of police, for example, is determined to put Cagliostro away for practising black magic; certain of the rich and powerful want him to use his power to their advantage; while others, more scientific-minded, like Rousseau, Marat, and Sade, seek to persuade him to establish a secret sect (this per-mits a flashback as Cagliostro recounts for them his own ini-tiation into the occult). And as though all this were not enough, everything functions contrapuntally, balanced out by the con-flicting forces of love and greed, good and evil. In tune with the moralizing stance of American movies, Huidobro's Cagliostro has a tragic flaw: driven by ambition and bloated with his own importance, he abuses his power, utilizing it for personal gain. Good can then struggle with evil, and Marcival, a rival magician, steps in to undo Cagliostro's magic. Lorenza, medium (and lover), apprised of Cagliostro's wrongdoing, kills herself. Only then does he realize the error of his ways (and his true love for her), but it is too late of course, and the novel ends with his going off into the darkness from whence he came, carrying the limp cadaver of Lorenza. Before leaving though, he dutifully sets fire to his laboratory and library, salvaging two potions: one marked life, the other death. Supposedly, he will try to revive Lorenza and true love will triumph; or, failing at that, he will join her in death:

Cagliostro appears in the doorway, bearing in his arms the body of Lorenza. He goes down the steps and gets into his coach. The coach starts off at a trot, pulled by the horses of history. Behind him the house is burning. Huge flames gobble up everything and a dark cloud rises up into the sky. In front of him, a long road leads off into the horizon. The carriage reaches the end of the road. In the distance its rear-window winks like an almond-shaped eye. A cloud sinks slowly to the ground. The great mage is lost to the eyes of the world behind that mysterious cloud.

* * * * * * * * * *

What happened afterwards? Where did he find refuge? Was he able to conquer death? Does he still live somewhere with his beloved?

THE END

The rhetorical finale, holding out the possibility of the hero's return, is styled to read like the closing titles of a serial.

While rapid characterization and a fast-moving plot were once the qualities that made *Cagliostro* a prizewinner, of more enduring value has been its cinematic texture: fifty years later the novel still reads like a movie. It was Huidobro's original intention to organize the action around what was best suited to 'comprehension through the eyes', and to this end he sometimes used even the most restrictive of filmlike procedures. Perspective, for example: fixed for the movie-house spectator it is fixed for the reader of the novel, as though the camera-eye recording the action were also fixed:

Cagliostro appears on the path leading toward his coach. As he approaches, he gets incredibly bigger. He arrives, boards, and the coach sets off at a gallop. At the end of the road, when it is very far away, nothing can be seen of it except the little rear-window, almond-shaped, like a smiling eye between heaven and earth. Then a cloud, fulfilling its mission drops to the ground so as to hide everything from the curious eyes of men.   (29)

The scene closes with a standard cinematic device: the gradual dissolve. Corresponding to a fade-out, in which the last frames go out of focus, is the dark cloud dropping to the ground. The novel, it will be recalled, ends with a similar cloud blacking out everything.

The reader is always aware of the text's visual dimension. To get at the contents of a purloined letter, Cagliostro does not break it open, but resorts to Lorenza, his paramour and medium. Huidobro makes this rather simple act of clairvoyance visually spectacular through a quick-paced sequence involving close-up, dissolve, and superimposition:

Cagliostro examines the letter. He holds it up to the light, then he places it on Lorenza's forehead, commanding her.

— Read this message to me!

Lorenza's head grows in size before our eyes, blown up by our common curiosity. Her brow dissolves and in its place appears the letter so that its text can be plainly read:

'To M. Sardines, Paris Police: In accordance with your wishes, I have taken certain steps (. . .)'.

The letter thus read, thanks to the special vision of Lorenza, her head returns to its normal size, scaled down five times.   (57)

As in film montage, separate image sequences are joined together so as to create a single narrative flow. A flow, needless to repeat, specifically designed for 'comprehension through the eyes'.

But a novel's imagery is generated by words, and comprehension, however oriented, necessarily begins at the lexical level. Hence Huidobro's concern with 'words of a visual character'. The highly stylized language of the novel, and its visual impact, is enhanced for the reader through a clever set of framing devices. The front matter alerts us to the idea that reading *Cagliostro* may be an unusual experience: following the subtitle 'novela-film', there is a prefatory page with a discursive aside:

FROM AUTHOR TO READER

Let the reader suppose that he has not bought a book in a bookstore, but rather a ticket to the movies. So, reader, you are not coming out of a store but going into a theatre. You take a seat. Some music is being played that gets on your nerves. It is so ridiculous. Yet it must be so to please the crowd. The orchestra stops. The curtain goes up; or, rather, the curtains part and there appears on the screen:

CAGLIOSTRO
by
Vicente Huidobro

After the credits there is a brief . . .

And on the very next page the 'film' begins, prefaced in turn by some frames of high-sounding historical summary:

PREFACE

Towards the end of the reign of Louis XV, there sprang up all over France and most of Europe many secret sects, whose activities, although ignored by the masses, had an enormous impact on the events of the time.

How many events whose origins we ignore were perhaps hatched underground by these persecuted souls over the half-light of a candle!

These sects had their beginnings in the mysterious Orient; the power of the occult sciences concerned the greatest minds of the West who feverishly studied Alchemy, Magic and the secrets of the Kabala, drawn by the beauty of this arcane knowledge.

Among the adepts there were some who had truly extraordinary power.

Admission to these sects entailed oaths of secrecy. Woe to him who violated this trust!

This highly stylized opening, with its ominous clue as to what is to follow, is in the best tradition of the early cinema. Once the narrative begins, the film has supposedly begun to roll and the novel's language changes accordingly. Rolling forth from every sentence on every page there is a most extravagant series of visual metaphors which 'collide' and run into one another sparking a sense of the visual. By way of illustration there follows a passage from the beginning of chapter one:

An eighteenth-century storm broke that night over Alsace, over Alsace so blond from her turning leaves and her lovely daughters ['la dulce Alsacia rubia a causa de sus hojas y sus hijas']. Great clouds, black and bulging like seals' bellies, swam in the wet winds toward the west. From time to time a well-aimed lightning bolt made the warm blood of a pierced cloud drip over our stricken panorama. It was a night for the hammering of counterfeit coins and the galloping of History's wolves. To the reader's right there is rain and the source of the storm; to his left, forests and hills. The magnificent forest moans like an organ or a sea-cave as the wind passes through, it moans as though all the world's children were calling for their mothers. This page I am now writing is crossed by a trail of mud, the muck and mire of legend. At the end of the road there suddenly appear two lanterns balancing themselves like a drunkard singing to the horizon. A coach, of strange shape and colour, advances toward the reader, the heavy thud of the horses' hooves making the whole novel shake. The coach is coming right at us, it is just a few feet from our eyes. The rain beats meanly down upon the driver. All my readers, men and women, must now step back a pace or two so as not to be spattered by the wheels of this strange vehicle as it passes by.   (21–2)

And so the action goes, careening from page to page. Scenes common to the movies of the time are transformed into the boldest of verbal images. The reader–spectator is thus made to 'see' things that, although impossible to occur in reality, became possible to present visually through the cinematic art of illusion. For example, Cagliostro makes flowers bloom in midwinter with the 'magnetic heat' of his hands (a standard film trick created by shooting separate frames of film over a long period of time). In another scene Cagliostro's spirit takes leave of his

body in the middle of a Paris seance so that he can slip off to
snow-stricken Russia to save a maiden whose runaway coach is
nearing a precipice (a trick achieved by superimposition, expos-
ing the film twice).

The novel, like the movies it emulates, was conceived as an
entertainment. Huidobro, ever the performer, was prepared to
go to any lengths to make his fictional construct engaging. And,
just as in *Mío Cid Campeador* he posed as a descendant of the
hero, in order to promote this novel he prepared a preface with
the unlikely title 'I Was Cagliostro'. Evidently intended for the
English language edition, this preface was never used; probably
because it was so patently preposterous. Here too, he has the
protagonist step in, correcting the author where necessary:

I am sure the magician came in the night to read the day's work, and to
approve or disapprove when my fancy led me too far astray. In reality the
magician did not come, but quit my own body and divested himself
powerfully. If it were not himself, it was surely a kindred spirit of his.
One morning I found a line written on the back of my manuscript. This
line read: 'False and without grace', referring to a passage in the work. The
writing was not mine, and certain experts that I consulted declared, after
having compared the lines, that it was that of Cagliostro, the type of each
letter being exactly his. I have kept this page and it is at the disposition of
those who wish to be convinced of the truth herein set down. The life of
Cagliostro is a novel, or a marvellous film. It is not for this reason that I
call this work a film-novel, but because it is written as if it were a film. I
wished the scenes to unfold themselves to the reader as the scenes in a
moving picture. I have selected the most visual words, I have tried to give
the characters the greatest possible amount of life without the aid of long
commentaries, or heavy descriptions, as on the screen. I have followed a
movie technique throughout, because I believe the picture-going public of
today cannot only understand it, but would prefer novels of this kind.
And so I present you with my old life, made flesh and blood and dressed
in the linen of the screen.[14]

The mixed metaphor which closes this aborted project for a
preface synthesizes better than any words of mine the exact
nature of Huidobro's attempt to create a filmic novel, as well as
his success in doing so.

By the early 1930s, Huidobro had branched out into many
careers: art, politics, theatre, and the novel. But he was fundamentally a poet, and it was at this time that he saw into print a
long poem that many consider to be his masterpiece, *Altazor*.

VIII
Altazor

Poetry must challenge Reason.　　　　1931

Around 1930, at the peak of his literary prestige and encouraged by his near success in other endeavours, such as film and politics, Huidobro put the finishing touches to two long poems, one in verse, the other in prose: *Altazor* and *Temblor de cielo*. When he travelled to Madrid in January of 1931 to talk to publishers, his old ultraist friends hailed him as a returning conqueror, and González Ruano, interviewing him for *El Heraldo de Madrid* (6 January 1931), headlined his article, 'Vicente Huidobro: el que trajo las gallinas'. In this ambiance it is not surprising that Plutarco and C.I.A.P., then Spain's most dynamic publishing houses, contracted these latest works under generous terms for the author and even arranged to bring them out right away, within a few months.[1] The conditions seemed optimal for the poet to repeat his Spanish triumph of 1918. Yet, once this new writing was actually in print it did not generate much critical enthusiasm, at least not immediately.[2] In fact, it is only with the passing of time that interest, especially in *Altazor*, has grown — so much so, that there is a general consensus today that it is his major work, his masterpiece. Indeed, critics almost casually refer to Huidobro now as 'the poet of *Altazor*'.

The book, like its author, has been variously interpreted, and misinterpreted. For one set of readers it is an intense metaphysical work, while for another it is just a clever word-game. For some it represents the culminating point of Creationism, and for yet others it deals with the failure of the system. For all readers though, old and new, *Altazor* is an intricate, often baffling high point to Huidobro's career as a poet. And this is both its charm and its challenge.

One of the problems it poses is intrinsic to the genre, the problem of unity in what Poe first called the 'long poem'. Most long poems in our time are not epic but lyric and thus lack any kind of narrative cement to hold them together. *Altazor* is no exception. Huidobro sought to get around this problem through a patchwork combination of external ordering devices: its division into seven cantos presenting a rough trajectory from order to disorder, and its thematic billing as a voyage poem, all stressed in the rather fulsome title to the original edition: *Altazor, o el viaje en paracaídas: Poema en VII cantos*. The result though is mostly an illusion of unity, with the title holding together, what Pound called his own *Cantos*, 'a tangle of works unfinished'.

Huidobro, like Pound, was a pioneer of the twentieth-century long poem. As such, he could not shake himself completely free from the nineteenth-century notion that the poem must somehow cohere. The problem of course is that *Altazor*, like the *Cantos*, was an ongoing project, a poem that was not composed under the impulse of a single lyric moment, as say, Neruda's *Tentativa del hombre infinito*, but rather was made up of many separate epiphanies, or moments of inspiration. Therefore, what is known of its genesis is important for an understanding of its final form.

The earliest reference to the project dates from 1919 when Huidobro was passing through Spain on his way back to Paris. He then stopped off to see Cansinos-Asséns, who reported on their meeting in Madrid:

> Huidobro is once again among us, on his way to Paris. The poet who, even more to his own credit, repeats the Darío miracle, has gone way beyond the lyrical fantasies of *Ecuatorial* and *Poemas árticos*, avoiding the danger of regression, shakily presaged by some, and now carries with him the manuscript of an unpublished book, *Voyage en parachute*, in which the most arduous aesthetic problems are resolved.[3]

Judging by the title (*Voyage en parachute*), the new work was in French. More important though at this juncture is the indication regarding its thematic purpose, that it was to be a poem resolving 'the most arduous aesthetic problems'. What aesthetic problems?

The answer becomes clear remembering that it was in *Poemas árticos* (1918) that Huidobro first employed in Spanish the techniques of literary Cubism worked out with Juan Gris and the *Nord-Sud* group. The result then was an engaging series of poems based on the principle of word-collage. In *Ecuatorial* (1918), he applied many of these same compositional techniques to a long poem on a serious theme, the European War. The imagistic layering that was so strikingly effective in the shorter texts was confusingly kaleidoscopic in the longer poem; even Juan Gris declared it beyond his comprehension.[4] As a consequence, it is not surprising that Huidobro was anxious to resolve this 'aesthetic problem', and that he could conceive of

Altazor as a follow-up to the earlier poem. In fact, the first canto contains a clear allusion to *Ecuatorial*:

> Hace seis meses solamente
> Dejé la ecuatorial recién cortada
> En la tumba guerrera del esclavo paciente
> Corona de piedad sobre la estupidez humana
> Soy yo que estoy hablando en este año de 1919
> Es el invierno
> Ya la Europa enterró todos sus muertos
> Y un millar de lágrimas hacen una sola cruz de nieve

(Only six months ago / I finished ecuatorial / In the war-tomb of the patient slave / Crown of piety upon human stupidity / I am the one who is speaking now in 1919 / It is winter / Europe has already buried its dead / And a thousand tears make up a single cross of snow)

The narrative posture here is similar to that of *Ecuatorial*, as is the compressed conceptualism (e.g. tears > snow, bypassing the intermediate image of a field of white crosses in a military cemetery): 'Y un millar de lágrimas hacen una sola cruz de nieve'.

Another, more general relationship stems from the astral nature of both poems. The speaker of *Ecuatorial* assumes a god-like vantage point, permitting him to observe the world at war as though from another planet; in *Altazor* the speaker is in outer space, engaged in a free fall toward earth. There is even a certain astrological underpinning, with passages of the poem reading like a horoscope, as for example the following fragment of Canto II:

> He aquí tu estrella que pasa
> Con tu respiración de fatigas lejanas
> Con tus gestos y tu modo de andar
> Con el espacio magnetizado que te saluda
> Que nos separa con leguas de noche

(Your star is passing by / With your breathing of distant fatigue / With your gestures and your way of walking / With a magnetized space that greets you / That separates us with leagues of night)

The allusion is there, although it is not known that Huidobro ever really gave much credence to astrology.

It is known however that he was an accomplished amateur

magician, and like other artists of his time, an occasional student of the occult. Not a real believer it would seem, but rather an admirer of the strange power of magic and the black arts on the imagination of the credulous. This accords with the tongue-in-cheek humour of *Cagliostro*, as well as the jocular thrust of the preface to *Altazor*, a portion of which was first published in Chile as early as 1925.

Jean Emar ('J'en ai marre', a parodic pen-name for Alvaro Yáñez), a friend of Huidobro, and something of a spokesman for the avant-garde in South America, celebrated the poet's return to Chile in 1925 by including in his popular 'Notas de Arte' column for *La Nación* (29 April 1925) his own translation of a work in progress, significantly titled, '*Altazur*: fragmento de *Un viaje en paracaídas*'. The title, incidentally, contains the earliest mention of the protagonist's name, an evident bilingual compound (*alto/azur*), while the text itself is an early version of what would eventually become the Spanish-language preface to *Altazor*. Between 1925 and 1931 there were some changes however which seem more than stylistic. The earlier text is shorter and more humorous, although in a slapstick sort of way.

A brief comparison, by way of illustration: in both texts, when Altazor's parachute gets tangled in a star he uses the break in his fall to toss off what are billed as 'profound thoughts'. Among them is this admonition in the 1931 text: 'Huye del sublime externo si no quieres morir aplastado por el viento' (Avoid the superficially sublime if you don't want to die flattened by the wind). In 1925, the humorous intent of such a 'profundity' was much more explicit: 'Huye de lo grandioso si no quieres morir aplastado por un merengue' (Avoid the grandiose if you don't want to die flattened by a meringue). A more detailed comparison of both texts would show this to be a typical pattern of change, for while Huidobro has retained most of the original wording he has diluted its humorous thrust by adding in a good amount of serious-mindedness. Thus a deadpan declaration of 1925, such as 'My parachute dropped 3,200 metres' is puffed up to the following in 1931: 'My parachute began to drop vertiginously. Such is the force of attraction of death and the open sepulchre. You can believe it, the tomb has more drawing power than a lover's eyes. The open tomb with all its magnets. And this I say to you, to you whose smile makes one think of the world's beginning.' This is the kind of involuted reasoning on love as a metaphor for life and death that forms and informs *Temblor de cielo*; there it is the inspirational nucleus of the work, here it seems more like an afterthought, a late graft on a text begun with a wholly different intent.

Strangely enough, the humorous thrust of the preface scarcely extends to the other cantos of *Altazor*, not even to the fragments of the poem that were first published in 1926. For the second issue of *Favorables-Paris-Poema* (October 1926), a Paris-based literary review of Larrea and Vallejo, Huidobro copied out a section of what would later form part of Canto IV, titling it 'Venus':

> Noche trae tu mujer de pantorrillas que son floreros
> de hortensias jóvenes remojadas de color.
> Como el asno pequeño desgraciado la novia sin flores
> ni globos de pájaros.
> El otoño endurece las palomas presentes. Mira los
> tranvías y el atentado de cocodrilos azulados que son
> periscopios en las nubes del pudor. La niña en
> ascension al ciento por ciento celeste lame la perspectiva
> que debe nacer salpicada de volantines y de los guantes
> agradables del otoño que se debatía en la piel del amor.

(Night bring on your woman with calves that are like flower pots of young hortensia wet with colour. / Like the little disgraced donkey the fiancée without flowers nor globes of birds. / Autumn stiffens the pigeons who are still around. Look at the streetcars and the assault of bluish crocodiles that are periscopes in clouds of modesty. The little girl in ascent at one hundred per cent celestial licks the perspective that ought to emerge bespattered with kites and the sweet gloves of autumn that went on debating over the skin of love.)

Noteworthy is the run-on quality of the discourse and its many discontinuities. Not all of Canto IV is like this, although this fragment as well as another, more simply titled 'Poema' and published in a Chilean avant-garde magazine (*Panorama*, April 1926), are *intentionally* muddled. What permits this assertion is the fact that when Huidobro revised these texts for inclusion in the final version of *Altazor* he muddled them even further, dropping all punctuation, breaking the lines in an arbitrary way, and even removing some of the verbal connectors. Just why he did this becomes clear in the total context of Canto IV where these fragments function as an example of Surrealism, serving as a preamble to go beyond the illogical concatenation of words.

This he eventually did. And in the very next published fragment of *Altazor*, also from Canto IV, there is the earliest record
of Huidobro's experimenting with non-words, or rather with
totally new words made up out of recognizable segments of the
lexicon:

> A l'horitagne de la montazon
> Une hironline sur sa mandodelle . . .

This anticipation of *Altazor*, consisting of some forty-five lines
in all, was first published in *Transition* (June 1930), the 'orphic'
review founded by Eugène Jolas on the principle that poetic
autonomy obliged writers to defy the rules of grammar. The
fragment, in French, raises again the question of the language,
or languages in which the poem was created.

It would seem that the project was conceived in French and
worked on sporadically in both French and Spanish, with one
language, or a segment in one language serving as a generative
impulse for the other. The *Transition* text reveals that although
the principle of assemblage was the same in both languages
(e.g. *l'horizon* and *la montagne* (horizon, mountain) giving
l'horitagne and *la montazon*, and correspondingly *el horitaña*
and *la montazonte* in Spanish), French served as the base text.
Which came first is evident when both are compared. In the following example, a Hispanized spelling of *rossignol* (nightingale),
preferred over the Spanish *ruiseñor* is clue enough, since the
structuring principle of both verse sequences is the musical
scale:

Mais le ciel préfère la ro*DO*gnol	Pero el cielo prefiere el ro*DO*ñol
Son enfant gâté le ro*RE*gnol	Su niño querido el ro*RE*ñol
Sa fleur de joie le ro*MI*gnol	Su flor de alegría el ro*MI*ñol
Sa peau de larme le ro*FA*gnol	Su piel de lágrima el ro*FA*ñol
Sa gorge de nuit le ros*SOL*gnol	Su garganta nocturna el ro*SOL*ñol
Le ro*LA*gnol	El ro*LA*ñol
Le ros*SI*gnol	El ro*SI*ñol

(*Transition* and *Altazor*, emphasis mine)

(But the sky prefers the *rodognol* / Its spoiled child the *roregnol* / Its
flower of joy the *romignol* / Its flesh of tear the *rofagnol* / Its throat of
night the *rossolgnol* / The *rolagnol* / The *rossignol*)

Writing in both French and Spanish evidently made the aesthetic
problems of such a linguistically daring poem even somewhat
more 'arduous' than those Cansinos-Asséns had anticipated way
back in 1919.

Altazor was a long time in the making, some twelve years, and in its final form was published only in Spanish. In contrast, its companion-piece, *Temblor de cielo*, seems to have sprung forth full-blown in both languages. Again, its French title, *Tremblement de ciel* (a catachresis for 'tremblement de terre'), seems to suggest it was conceived in that language. All were published within months of one another: *Altazor* and *Temblor de cielo* in Madrid in the summer of 1931; *Tremblement de ciel* in Paris in January of 1932. Where *Altazor* is a linguistic extravaganza, *Temblor* and *Tremblement* are rather tame. Tamed would be an even better descriptive term, for both versions are rendered into an almost absolute equivalency. Huidobro's view on the interrelationship of these works can be gleaned from the draft of a letter to Miró Quesada, dated 11 June 1931:

> In today's mail I am sending you *Altazor* and *Temblor de cielo*. *Altazor* is already quite old and you surely know some of it, since fragments have been given out in French and Spanish to newspapers and reviews over the past ten years. This, aside from the readings, three or four, that I have made from the poem. But it was necessary to publish it once and for all; my friends were constantly asking me to do it, and finally the poor thing has found a publisher. How many times it has been turned down! It is a book that has, no doubt, some historic importance because in it are traced out all the paths I have followed and perhaps I'll never be able to leave some behind. This is the importance it has to me, besides that which the poem itself might have and might have had for others. *Temblor de cielo* is perhaps more mature, more solid, more finished. It has produced a lot of enthusiasm among my friends — so much that it frightens me — they take it for something enormous, greater than Lautréamont and Rimbaud. Really, I tell you, I am afraid . . .[5]

Setting aside for a moment the question of Huidobro's sincerity (always difficult to assess when he is referring to himself), this document reveals several facts: the author's awareness of the incongruities of *Altazor*; his recognition of some enduring aspects in his writing style; and, perhaps most importantly, his view of himself as being in the tradition of the *poètes maudits* rather than at the cutting edge of the avant-garde. These are important clues to an understanding of his aesthetic evolution between 1920 and 1930, and prompt complementing what is already known of the elaboration of *Altazor* with what is known of Huidobro's personal development during this same period.

The cross-overs between art and life are many, and in the preface to *Altazor*, first published in 1925, after the poet had entered his thirty-third year, there is this birth-chart beginning: 'I was born at 33, the day Christ died; I was born in the Equinox, beneath hortensias and airships of heat.' Other references, equally co-ordinated to his person, time, and place are in the first canto, probably begun in 1918, just after the publication of *Ecuatorial* and when Huidobro was twenty-five:

> Soy yo Altazor el doble de mi mismo
> El que se mira obrar y se ríe del otro frente a frente
> El que cayó de las alturas de su estrella
> Y viajó veinticinco años
> Colgado al paracaídas de sus propios prejuicios

(It's me Altazor the double of myself / The one who looks at himself working and laughs at the other face to face / The one who fell from the heights of his star / And travelled twenty-five years / Hanging from the parachute of his own prejudices)

And, in Canto IV, when his name comes up it is with the force of an epitaph: 'Aquí yace Vicente antipoeta y mago' (Here lies Vicente anti-poet and mage).

The poem was written at different times and under varied circumstances, hence its anachronisms and inconsistencies. And as is logical, Huidobro's own thinking about the project went through many transformations during the long period from its initial conception in 1919 to its final publication in book form in 1931. The earliest samplings of the work in progress, which date from 1925-6, are conflicting, and well they should be for they emerge during a period of momentous change for him, coinciding with his return to Chile, his abortive involvement in national politics, and his fateful encounter with Ximena Amunátegui, for whom he would leave his wife of fifteen years and their children. Such a mid-life crisis has come to be a predictable part of modern culture. Then the situation was much different, particularly in the tight-knit social world of the Chilean upper class. Such things were not supposed to happen, and when they did they were inevitably hushed up. Huidobro, in his typically rebellious way, did not go along with this; he did quite the opposite, publicly announcing his passion for Ximena, then a mere schoolgirl, in the pages of *La Nación*. On Good Friday (2 April 1926) he published 'Pasión y muerte', a long personal confession which begins in the following uninhibited way:

Señor, perdóname si te hablo en un lenguaje profano,
Mas no podría hablarte de otro modo pues soy
    esencialmente pagano.
Por si acaso eres Dios, vengo a pedirte una cosa
En olas rimadas con fatigas de prosa.
Hay en el mundo una mujer, acaso la más triste, sin duda
    la mas bella . . .

(Lord, forgive me if I speak to you in profane language, / But I really can't speak to you in any other way since I am essentially pagan. / Just in case you really are God, I want to ask you a favour / In rhymed waves with the fatigue of prose. / There is in this world a woman, perhaps the saddest, certainly the prettiest . . .)

Part of the problem was that the woman in question was not only pretty, but a minor — and, to make matters worse, the daughter of a powerful political figure. Neither the Huidobros nor the Amunáteguis would allow the romance to prosper. The poet's wife, for her part, refused to continue with a sham marriage, and so Huidobro was obliged to leave Chile, alone. He returned to Paris to close up the family house in Montmartre before proceeding on to New York to maka a new start for himself. It was there, in 1927, that he won a film prize for his Cagliostro script and wrote occasionally for newspapers and magazines, such as *Vanity Fair*. He seems though to have been biding his time until Ximena came of age, for in 1928, in an episode worthy of a *feuilleton*, he travelled clandestinely to Chile, kidnapped his beloved, and spirited her off to Paris, where they set up house in the Montparnasse district, 16 rue Boissonade.

It was in this exultant mood that he envisaged himself as a Tristan figure and wrote *Temblor de cielo*. Hence the significance of the year of composition, 1928, carried on the title-pages of *Temblor/Tremblement*. In this same vein of using literature to organize his life, he was inspired to rewrite the Cid legend as a filmic novel, seeing himself and Ximena as a modern-day incarnation of the medieval couple. This was a period of culminating activity for Huidobro. Chance and circumstance led him to new projects and enabled him to carry old ones to completion, among them *Altazor*. Influencing his decision to finish this work, so often begun (and abandoned), was another factor, also circumstantial: the publication in 1928 of Rolland de Rénèville's study, *Rimbaud le Voyant*, setting forth the thesis, novel for the time, of the visionary poet's quest as a failure, a noble failure. For Huidobro, formed in the aesthetic mould of later Modernism and a true believer in the redeeming mission of poetry, this was the sort of break-through idea that could permit him, like Rimbaud, to aban-don the search for a new poetic language, and to recognize without shame the impasse of the literary avant-garde, publicly setting its goals behind him. That Huidobro was pleased to see himself as a failed artist, as a *great* failed artist, comes through quite clearly in his letter to Miró Quesada — and in another letter, to Buñuel over politics. In the Spring of 1931, when *Altazor* and *Temblor de cielo* were about to appear, Huidobro responds haughtily to some perceived insult from Buñuel: 'You may be right that I am a failed artist, but in my failure I am with Rimbaud and Lautréamont.'[6]

Having detailed the genesis of *Altazor* and the shifts and changes in the poet's thinking during the long period of its elaboration, it is time to take up the text itself, the final version of the poem as it was first published in 1931. The original edition contained the following clarificatory note: 'This poem has been published in various newspapers and reviews in disperse fragments and without order; this is the first time that it is published complete and in book form.' The order and completeness that this seems to promise is not borne out in the text itself, whose disparities of tone, style, and content were undoubtedly an obstacle to a satisfactory reading of the book when it first appeared. And although there have been many partial readings of *Altazor* over the years — some quite brilliant — the poem as a whole has consistently eluded interpretation. So much so that while there is consensus today regarding the book's importance, there is disagreement as to why. This is unfortunate but understandable, given the fact that *Altazor* is not a 'finished' work in the traditional sense of the term. It is rather a text in discontinuous progress, suddenly brought to conclusion, frozen as an 'open work' at the moment of being turned over to the publisher.

The prose preface and the first canto record two different conceptions of what the work was to be, two approaches aesthetically separate and separable. In contrast Cantos III–VII do cohere somewhat in their progressive pattern of disarticula-tion. Canto II is a case apart, although related to other con-stants in Huidobro's work. Thus, between the covers of *Altazor* there are really several different beginnings with one common ending: failure. For this reason, an examination of the unique-ness of each canto is perhaps the most appropriate way to approach the total richness of the book.

Canto I, the longest at almost seven hundred verses, is also
the most tightly structured. It begins with a series of speculative
questions posed by the speaker, Altazor, to himself, Altazor/
Huidobro. The central concern is metaphysical: the urge to
arrive at the meaning of life, metaphorized here and throughout
the poem as a fall into oblivion:

> Cae en infancia
> Cae en vejez
> Cae en lágrimas
> Cae en risas
> Cae en música sobre el universo
> Cae de tu cabeza a tus pies
> Cae de tus pies a tu cabeza
> Cae del mar a la fuente
> Cae al último abismo de silencio
> Como el barco que se hunde apagando sus luces

(Fall in infancy / Fall in old age / Fall in tears / Fall in laughter / Fall in
music over the universe / Fall from your head to your feet / Fall from
your feet to your head / Fall from the sea to the fountain / Fall into the
last abyss of silence / Like a ship that sinks putting out its lights)

Prompting this soul-searching there are many biographical,
generational, and cultural imputs, none extraordinarily unique:
a personal loss of faith, the so-called decline of the West, the
Rimbaldian legacy of the poet as visionary . . . What is unique in
all this is Huidobro's use of the long poem as a means of carrying on what is essentially a lyric dialogue with himself, an
anguished and vacillating dialogue that transcends the pompous
prophetic modality then current in the Spanish metaphysical
poem. The result, even in the most reasoned segments, is a kind
of inconclusive musing:

> Abrí los ojos en el siglo
> En que moría el cristianismo
> Retorcido en su cruz agonizante
> Ya va a dar el último suspiro
> ¿Y mañana qué pondremos en el sitio vacío?
> Pondremos un alba o un crepúsculo
> ¿Y hay que poner algo acaso?

(I opened my eyes in the century / In which Christianity was dying /
Twisted on its agonizing cross / It will now give out its last sigh / And
tomorrow what will we put in its place? / We'll substitute a sunrise or a
sunset / But must we substitute anything at all?)

The canto has a dynamic internal development. Once the pre-
liminaries are handled and Altazor/Huidobro is situated as the
protagonist, the thrust of the speaker changes from one who
questions his fate to one who wants to do something about it,
to break out of the pattern of cultural givens. Thus, a litany of
the familiar, faith in the allness of God, welling up as though
from the subconscious, is given free reign for a time, only to be
summarily ridiculed and rejected:

> Dios diluido en la nada y el todo
> Dios todo y nada
> Dios en las palabras y en los gestos
> Dios mental
> Dios aliento
> Dios joven Dios viejo
> Dios pútrido
> lenajo y cerca
> Dios amasado a mi congoja
>
> Sigamos cultivando en el cerebro las tierras del error
> Sigamos cultivando las tierras veraces en el pecho
> Sigamos
> Siempre igual como ayer mañana y luego y después
> No
> No puede ser Cambiemos nuestra suerte

(God diluted in all and nothingness / God all and nothing / God in words
and in signs / God mental / God breath / God young God old / God putrid /
distant and near / God moulded to my grief / Let's go on cultivating in our
minds the fields of error / Let's go on cultivating in our breasts the true
fields / Let's go on / Always the same like yesterday tomorrow and now
and later / No / No it cannot be / Let's change our lot)

Variants of this formula of negation occur several more times
in the wake of other commonplace ideas: the need to suffer,
'No / No puede ser / Consumamos el placer' (No / It cannot be /
Let's devour pleasure); the need to persevere in the face of
adversity, 'Seguir / No / Basta ya' (Go on / No / It's already
enough); the need to accept life as a preparation for death, 'No /
Que se rompa el andamio de los huesos' (No / Break down the
scaffolding of bones). Having rejected the hand-me-down
explanations for life's meaning, the speaker cries out for a
miracle of vision, a new 'bateau ivre':

Todo en vano
Dadme la llave del naufragio
Dadme una certeza de raíces en horizonte quieto
Un descubrimiento que no huya a cada paso
O dadme un bello naufragio verde

Un milagro que ilumine el fondo de nuestros mares íntimos
Como el barco que se hunde sin apagar sus luces

(All in vain / Give me the key of a shipwreck / Give me some certainty of
roots on a calm horizon / A discovery that doesn't slip away at every step /
Oh give me a beautiful green shipwreck / A miracle that lights up the
bottom of our inner seas / Like a ship that sinks without losing its lights)

That Canto I is very carefully, indeed elaborately patterned is
evident by the fact that here, at its mid-point, the speaker's
thought progression is signalled to the reader through the
altered simile of life as a sinking ship ('como el barco que se
hunde apagando sus luces' > 'como el barco que se hunde sin
apagar sus luces'). Not surprisingly, to take up this challenge in
the second half of Canto I, another persona emerges as the
speaker's voice takes on a new vigour:

> Soy todo el hombre
> El hombre herido por quién sabe quien
> Por una flecha perdida del caos
> Humano terreno desmesurado
> Sí desmesurado y lo proclamo sin miedo
> Desmesurado porque no soy burgués ni raza fatigada
> Soy bárbaro tal vez
> Desmesurado enfermo
> Bárbaro limpio de rutinas y caminos marcados
> No acepto vuestras sillas de seguridades cómodas
> Soy el angel salvaje que cayó una mañana
> En vuestras plantaciones de preceptos
> Poeta
> Antipoeta
> Culto
> Anticulto

(I am all of man / Man wounded by who knows who / By an arrow astray
in the void / Disproportionate human terrain / Yes disproportionate and I
proclaim it without fear / Disproportionate because I am not a bourgeois
nor from a dying race / I am a barbarian perhaps / A disproportionate
infirm / A barbarian without routines and trodden paths / I don't accept

your seats of comfortable securities / I am the savage angel that dropped one morning / Into your garden of precepts / Poet / Anti-poet / Civilized / Anticivilized)

The speaker's Luciferian tone is noteworthy, vividly conveying an entire generation's realization that the old order was no longer meaningful. Yeats, writing from within the tradition, seems to have inspired the sacred image for the change that was to come: 'after our own verse, after all our subtle colour and nervous rhythm . . ., what more is possible? After us the Savage God.' Little wonder that the new order envisaged by Huidobro's 'angel salvaje' is a millenium, a Black Advent:

> Yo poblaré para mil años los sueños de los hombres
> Y os daré un poema lleno de corazón
> En el cual me despedazaré por todos lados

(For a thousand years I will people the dreams of man / And I shall give you a poem full of heart / In which I will tear myself to pieces)

Evidently, the early scheme for *Altazor* was religious and Rimbaldian, an anguished visionary poem in which the speaker's various personae were to beat their way toward redemption through the text.

The first canto must have been composed when Huidobro still had faith in the redeeming power of poetry, for he even appropriated the language of the Psalms to give his claim a more persuasive ring:

> Mas no temas de mí que mi lenguaje es otro
> No trato de hacer feliz ni desgraciado a nadie
> Ni descolgar banderas de los pechos
> Ni dar anillos de planetas
> Ni hacer satélites de mármol en torno a un talismán ajeno
> Quiero darte una música de espíritu
> Música mía de esta cítara plantada en mi cuerpo
> Música que hace pensar en el crecimiento de los árboles

(But don't fear me for my language is different / I do not try to make anyone either happy or sad / Nor to unfurl flags from chests / Nor to give rings to planets / Nor to create marble satellites around a strange talisman / I want to give you music for the spirit / My music from this cithara of my body / Music that makes one think of trees growing)

Driven by optimism, the canto anticipates a triumphant closure. Hence its structured symmetry. Towards the end, a refrain, 'Silencio la tierra va a dar a luz un árbol' (Silence the earth is about to give birth to a tree), is repeated several times, escalating with each repetition the speaker's heady claim to be conjuring up something new:

> Silencio la tierra va a dar a luz un árbol
> Tengo cartas secretas en la caja del cráneo
> Tengo un carbón doliente en el fondo del pecho
> Y conduzco mi pecho a la boca
> Y la boca a la puerta del sueño
>
> El mundo se me entra por los ojos
> Se me entra por las manos se me entra por los pies
> Me entra por la boca y se me sale
> En insectos celestes o nubes de palabras por los poros
>
> Silencio la tierra va a dar a luz un árbol . . .

(Silence the earth is about to give birth to a tree / I have secret letters in the strong-box of my head / I have a painful coal in the depths of my chest / And I lead my chest to my mouth / And my mouth to the gate of dreams / The world comes into me through my eyes / It comes into me through my hands and through my feet / It comes through my mouth and it leaves me / In celestial insects or clouds of words through my pores / Silence the earth is about to give birth to a tree . . .)

The refrain is a standard device for accumulating force and intensity. Huidobro uses it to advantage, introducing a variation of it to close the canto, rendering the final assertion somewhat momentous:

> Silencio
>   Se oye el pulso del mundo como nunca pálido
> La tierra acaba de alumbrar un árbol

(Silence / One hears the world's pulse pallid as never before / The world has just given birth to a tree)

Thus ends Canto I; and what is titled Canto II, an ode to woman, has little if any direct relation to the first.

A possibly rejected fragment of *Altazor*, a text which may at one time have been composed as a follow-up to the momentous finale of Canto I, is found instead in *Ver y palpar*. In this collection of 1941 Huidobro included a piece called 'Poema para hacer crecer los árboles' (Poem to make trees grow). That this text — whose generative word-play is similar to that of the later cantos of *Altazor* — may once have formed a part of the long poem is mere speculation, and is reported here merely as a matter of curiosity. The fact of the matter is that Canto I is complete unto itself, stating the need for a new kind of expression and announcing its imminence.

While the second canto may not be the logical outcome of the first it nevertheless merits an eventual consideration on its own merits. Here though, I would only like to point out its relationship, its ambiguous relationship not to *Altazor*, but to other works, both prior and later. In 1913, in *Las pagodas ocultas*, a volume of later Modernist prose dedicated to his wife ('A la hermana de mi espíritu', To my spiritual sister), there are these versicles:

> Oye, Amada, tus ojos son dos santos que absuelven
> mis acciones y aprueban mis designios.
> ¿Irías a ser muda que Dios te dio esos ojos?
> . . . .
> ¿Irías a ser ciega que Dios te dio esas manos?

(Listen, Loved One, your eyes are two saints that forgive / my actions and approve my plans. / Were you to be mute that God gave you those eyes? / (. . .) / Were you to be blind that God gave you those hands?)

The same imagery is repeated in Canto II with the intriguing time tag, 'otra vez' (again):

> Heme aquí en una torre de frío
> Abrigado del recuerdo de tus labios marítimos
> Del recuerdo de tus complacencias y de tu cabellera
> Luminosa y desatada como los ríos de la montaña
> ¿Irías a ser ciega que Dios te dio esas manos?
> Te pregunto otra vez
> . . . .
> Te pregunto otra vez
> ¿Irías a ser muda que Dios te dio esos ojos?

(Here I am in a tower of coldness / Wrapped up in the memory of your maritime lips / In the memory of your complacence and your hair-do / Luminous and loose like mountain streams / Were you to be blind that God gave you those hands? / I ask you again / (. . .) / I ask you again / Were you to be mute that God gave you those eyes?)

Unfortunately, not enough is known regarding the circumstances of this canto to account for its place in *Altazor* nor its place in the eventful life of the author. However, the cross-overs between Huidobro's art and life are many, and it does not seem unreasonable to assume that Canto II, like *Temblor de cielo*, was prompted by his emotional renewal in the mid-1920s. Its plain lyricism may indeed be the stylistic constant Huidobro had in mind when he told Miró Quesada that perhaps he would 'never be able to leave some [paths] behind'.

Thus far I have been stressing the book's inconsistencies, its diverse expressive moods; but now I would like to draw attention to a common point of departure: the search for a new expressive system. The theme, introduced in the first canto, is picked up in the third, where the efficacy of poetry itself is questioned:

> Manicura de la lengua es el poeta
> Mas no el mago que apaga y enciende
> Palabras estelares y cerezas de adioses vagabundos
> Muy lejos de las manos de la tierra
> Y todo lo que dice es por él inventado
> Cosas que pasan fuera del mundo cotidiano
> Matemos al poeta que nos tiene saturados
>
> Poesía aún y poesía poesía
> Poética poesía poesía
> Poesía poética de poético poeta
> Poesía
> Demasiada poesía
> Desde el arco iris hasta el culo pianista de la vecina
> Basta señora poesía bambina

(Manicurist of language is the poet / But not a mage who turns off and on / Stellar words and cherries of wandering goodbyes / Very removed from earth's hands / And everything he says is invented by him / Things that can only occur outside the everyday world / Let's kill the poet who has us satiated / Poetry still and poetry poetry / Poetic poetry poetry / Poetry poetic by a poet poetic / Poetry / Too much poetry / From a rainbow to the pianist's ass of the lady next door / It's enough childish Madame poetry)

From this point on *Altazor* assumes a clear direction of movement, beginning a process of disarticulation that culminates in the primal scream closing Canto VII and the book. The latter cantos (III–VII), taken together, form something of a unit containing a trek through the blind alleys of linguistic experimentation, a literary 'quest' in which the speaker wrests with one new combinatory device after another, leaving each behind once its limitation becomes apparent. In this scheme of successive change only the procedure is constant: a particular linguistic possibility is used and abused, pushed to its limits, eventually exhausting it and the reader. *Altazor* in this way transcends its own form as it passes from being a text that discourses on the limits of poetry to one that actually demonstrates those limits, and goes beyond them: a verbal *tour de force* that in the reading becomes a performance, a lingustic 'happening'.

Huidobro clears the stage for this event by tearing down the supposed 'advances' of modern poetry. He begins, appropriately enough, denigrating the alogical simile associated with Lautréamont ('beau comme'):

> Basta señora arpa de las belles imágenes
> De los furtivos 'comos' illuminados
> Otra cosa otra cosa buscamos
> Sabemos posar un beso 'como' una mirada
> Plantar miradas 'como' árboles . . .
>   (emphasis mine)

(It's enough Madame Harp of beautiful images / Of those sly illuminated 'likes' / Something else something else are we searching for / We know all about casting a kiss 'like' a glance / About planting glances 'like' trees . . .)

Some thirty-seven crossed similes later, the series is finally abandoned in a string of weary etceteras: 'Colgar reyes como auroras / Crucificar auroras como profetas / Etc. etc. etc.' (Hang up kings like dawns / Crucify dawns like prophets / Etcetera etcetera etcetera).

The purpose of all this is to create a separate literary space, testing and discarding procedures identified with the avantgarde; procedures that, according to the text, have cuased the 'death' of language and 'el entierro de la poesía' (the burial of poetry). By the end of Canto III, Huidobro has not only wiped out his own poetic system, but others as well. The context for the portion of the poem appearing below is Breton's 1924 evaluation of the Surrealist image (a modification, in turn of Reverdy's on Cubism): 'Its value depends on the beauty of the spark it gives off, which is a function of the difference of potential between the two conductors':

Y puesto que debemos vivir y no nos suicidamos
Mientras vivamos juguemos
El simple sport de los vocablos
De la pura palabra y nada más
Sin imagen limpia de joyas
(Las palabras tienen demasiada carga)
Un ritual de vocablos sin sombra
Juego de ángel allá en el infinito
Palabra por palabra
Con luz propia de astro que un choque vuelve vivo
Saltan chispas del choque y mientras más violento
Más grande es la explosión
Pasión del juego en el espacio
Sin alas de luna y pretensión
Combate singular entre el pecho y el cielo
Total desprendimiento al fin de voz de carne
Eco de luz que sangra aire sobre el aire

Después nada nada
Rumor aliento de frase sin palabra

(And since we are to live and don't commit suicide / While we are living
let's play / The simple sport of words / The pure word and nothing else /
Without imagery clean of adornment / (Words are overcharged) / A ritual
of words without shadow / An angel's game out there in infinity / Word by
word / With the light of an astral body that a collision makes live / Sparks
fly from the collision and the more violent they are / The greater is the
explosion / Passion for a game in outer space / Without the wings of the
moon and pretension / Singular combat between breast and sky / A total
setting loose finally of voice from flesh / An echo of light bleeds air upon
air / Later nothing nothing / Rumour breath of a phrase without a word)

Thus ends the canto; its one hundred and sixty verses presenting, and representing a kind of literary history, the cyclic death
of poetry from Modernism to Creationism, from Symbolism to
Surrealism.

Canto IV presents the other side of the story, the cyclic
revival of poetry. Hence the rescue tone of its leitmotiv: 'No
hay tiempo que perder' (There is no time to lose). This verse is
repeated some fifteen times through the canto as Huidobro
rushes us through various kinds of post-Surrealist expressive
techniques, ranging from psychic word flow to a kind of syllabic
trans-sense breaking down words into their component parts so
as to suggest other words and other meanings.

> Aquí yace Raimundo raíces del mundo con sus venas
> Aquí yace Clarisa clara risa enclaustrada en la luz
> Aquí yace Alejandro antro alejado ala adentro
> . . . .
> Aquí yace Altazor azor fulminado por la altura*

This technique of artistic distortion, cited here at its entry level, goes on to seemingly endless complications. Rather than analysing their mechanism, it is more important at this point to anticipate the curious cumulative effect they exert on a reader, obligating an aesthetic appreciation of a text that is not only destructive, but self-destructive.

In the following fragment, the fact that reading is essentially sequential is utilized to occasion a misreading:

> El meteoro insolente cruza por el cielo
> El meteplata el metecobre
> El metepiedras en el infinito
> Meteópalos en la mirada
> Cuiadado aviador con las estrellas

The trans-sense arising from utilizing a common word like *meteoro* (meteor) as though it were a compound (*mete-oro*: stick in, gold), produces a humorous effect that would seem to be related to that of the preface. But effects are not causes, and here humour functions to point up the polyvalent nature of language, its potential for generating meanings according to context. Having found this 'key', the reversible *eterfinifrete*, Huidobro hastens to end the canto on this falsely triumphant note:

> El pájaro tralalí canta en las ramas de mi cerebro
> Porque encontró la clave del eterfinifrete
> Rotundo como el unipacio y el espaverso
> Uiu uiui
> Tralalí tralalá
> Aia ai ai aaia i i

The irony of this finale is that it foreshadows the inarticulate wail that closes out Canto VII, and *Altazor*.

Trans-sense will ultimately be little more than a prelude to

* It is impossible to provide English equivalents for the latter cantos of *Altazor* since the author's purpose was to defy language; the defiance is meaningful only in the context of the sounds and rhythms of Spanish.

nonsense. But before that dead end is reached Huidobro presents a dazzling array of new verbal schemes in Canto V, whose opening line reads like a warning posted at the frontier: 'Aquí comienza el campo inexplorado' (Here begins the unexplored terrain). Altazor will be the reader's guide through this linguistic wonderland where all the rules are either ignored or violated. The result is a festive liberty, whose aftermath will be anarchy. At first though, the new freedom is as engaging as it is simple; poetry is an invitation to play with language. In the following example, the simple expedient of shifting gender markers about creates a fresh sort of expression:

> La montaña y el montaño
> Con su luno y con su luna
> La flor florecida y el flor floreciendo
> Una flor que llaman girasol
> Y un sol que se llama giraflor

In another, rhyme is intense, as in a children's song; the auditory pattern heightening the reshuffling of meaning as the same words are changed about:

> Nos frotamos las manos y reímos
> Nos lavamos los ojos y jugamos
> El horizonte es un rinoceronte
> El mar un azar
> El cielo un pañuelo
> La llaga una plaga
> Un horizonte jugando a todo mar se sonaba con el cielo después
> de las siete plagas de Egipto
> El rinoceronte navega sobre el azar como el cometa en su
> pañuelo lleno de plagas

These procedures are not arbitrary. The system of 'de-writing' varies considerably, but there is always a system. In general, Huidobro establishes poetic tension by defamiliarizing what is familiar. In one sequence this is done by holding the vocabulary constant while the word order is changed:

> La herida de luna de la pobre loca
> La pobre loca de la luna herida
> Tenía luz en la celeste boca
> Boca celeste que la luz tenía . . .

Finally, words themselves are transformed, nouns becoming verbs, and verbs becoming nouns:

> La cascada que cabellera sobre la noche
> Mientras la noche se cama a descansar
> Con su luna que almohada al cielo
> Yo ojo el paisaje cansado
> Que se ruta hacia el horizonte
> A la sombra de un árbol naufragando

Everywhere though, the emphasis is the same, on poetry as play. However, it is play that is not just meant to be amusing, but ultimately tiring; and so that the reader will be properly fatigued, a windmill of images is set in motion, a mill that whirls on and on, page after page, for several hundred verses:

> Jugamos fuera del tiempo
> Y juega con nosotros el molino de viento
> Molino de viento
> Molino de aliento
> Molino de cuento . . .

The effect on the reader is predictable, leading to fatigue and an awareness that a variety that is endless is also meaningless. To close the canto the speaker admits as much, falling back on reality with a single declarative verse, typographically set apart: 'Y yo oigo la risa de los muertos debajo de la tierra' (And I hear the laughter of the dead from beneath the ground). Poetry is a game, but a meaningless game when it is solely concerned with form.

If Cantos IV and V were worked up to clear away the past and present of the avant-garde, levelling it to a senseless formalism, the sixth, along with the last, delineates a future that is equally vacuous: a blind alley in which all combinatory devices having been exhausted, poetry is reduced to sounds devoid of meaning. The process is stepped from canto to canto. In Canto VI the lexicon is somewhat recognizable, although meaning is not. This portion of the poem cannot be 'read', only pronounced. But it is in the process of enunciation that one perceives vague echoes of tradition. In the following fragment, for example, it is the octosyllabic measure of the Spanish *romance* and its patterned repetitions which serves to create the illusion of the poetic, the echo of something familiar that sounds like what is traditionally called poetry:

> Ancla cielo
>   sus raíces
> El destino tanto azar
> Se desliza deslizaba
> Apagándose pradera
> Por quien sueña
> Lunancero cristal luna
> En que sueña
> En que reino
>   de sus hierros
> Ancla mía golondrina
> Sus resortes en el mar

From non-sense with standard vocabulary in the sixth canto, the poem passes on to an invented language in the seventh, where the only recognizable element to remain is the sound system of Spanish:

> Tempovío
> Infilero e infinauta zurrosía
> Jaurinario ururayú
> Montañendo oraranía
> Arorasía ululacente
> Semperiva
>   ivarisa tarirá
> Campanudio lalalí
>   Auriciento auronida
> Lalalí
>   Io ia
> i i i o
> Ai a i ai a i i i i o ia

Altazor is without doubt Huidobro's most intriguing work. An incomplete fragmentary package of diverse attempts to write the total poem, it is unmatched in Spanish for the boldness of its execution and for the frankness of its conclusion. After publishing this book in 1931, Huidobro's career as a vanguardist was over. His writing took on a more human dimension as he himself became more involved with the here and now. A glimpse into what is behind this change is afforded by *Temblor de cielo*, the companion volume to *Altazor*.

The prose text, like its verse counterpart, is elusive. It too is divided into seven canto-like fragments, hinting at some symbolic framework for its loose and rambling discourse on life,

love, and death. An extended prose-poem, its form of delivery is
that of a speech with numerous asides, some to a personage
significantly named Isolda, some to the supposed audience, and
some acted out in a kind of dialogue presentation. It is only
toward the end of the last section that a form and theme are
explicitly identified:

> Just a few words more, my friend, before I finish up: — Vain are your
> quarrels and your battles, vain is the glow of your swords and your words.
> Only the grave is right. Victory always goes to the cemetery. Triumph
> flourishes only in the implanted mystery.
> Thus was the speech that you called macabre without any reason at all,
> the beautiful speech of the presenter of nothingness.

Death is the dominating idea in this work, with love, or
rather love-making as a metaphor for life's final act. The argument is minimal and developed in spurts, moving from a notion
that all is not right with the world to a cataclysmic sky-quake
whose outcome is dual: the narrator's meeting with Isolda and
the death of God. While it is easy to appreciate the extent to
which *Temblor* is a literaturized Tristan/Isolde account of
Huidobro's mid-life crisis, it must be remembered that it is not
only this, but also something else: a piece of sustained lyric
writing unlike anything he had ever done before. It is no
wonder then that he boasted of his awe over the result to Miró
Quesada, implying a comparison with Lautréamont's *Chants de
Maldoror*.

Right at the beginning of *Temblor* there is a portrayal of God
as a Satanic figure who combats boredom by working miracles:
rendering the deaf blind and the blind deaf. And, lest the
Luciferian–Maldororian intent be missed, the reader is reminded
at poem's end that transgression means freedom: 'Crime is
needed if you want to fly again.' In this topsy-turvy scheme of
things it is the pleasure principle that prevails with woman as
the object of desire, the life force that pulls toward death. As
though infused with the power of the author's vision, stock
metaphors take on a new life. Woman as a temple of love, for
example: 'Lying on her back she is like a temple. Rather,
temples are like women, with their towers like breasts, their
cupola like a head, and their door like a sex organ through
which one enters in search of the life inside the nave, and
through which one exits when life is finished.' The game of love
as a kind of ritual death: 'And this game that you thought was
the game of life is really the game of death. There it is, man

over woman from the world's beginning to its end. Man on top of woman eternally like the stone on a tomb. This is nothing more than death over death.' These ideas are not new. What is new is Huidobro's ability to recharge them, making them speak out with renewed persuasive power. A power that is not ultimately dependent on the sort of verbal collisions which animated his avant-garde writing. On the contrary, this is writing at its most simple, relying on a straightforward syntax and lexicon. Hence the reason for its absolute equivalency in both versions, the French and the Spanish.

Altazor and *Temblor de cielo*, taken together, complete the record of Huidobro's artistic passage from the 1920s to the 1930s, from the celestial poetics of the avant-garde to a concern with the emptiness of the world in which one must live, and die. Both volumes contain the same myth-shattering message: God is dead, and so too is the poet's singular career as a little god.

Notes

Unpublished material, unless otherwise indicated, is conserved by the Huidobro family in Santiago de Chile. The Huidobro-related material facilitated by Juan Larrea now forms part of his estate in Córdoba, Argentina. Other unpublished items relating to Huidobro and the avant-garde in France and Spain are conserved at the Bibliothèque Littéraire Jacques Doucet in Paris and by Gerardo Diego in Madrid.

INTRODUCTION *(pp. 1-6)*

1 Julio Molina Núñez and Juan Agustín Araya, *Selva lírica: Estudios sobre los poetas chilenos* (Santiago: Universo, 1917), p. 294.

2 'Búsqueda de Huidobro', *Ercilla* (Santiago), 7 February 1968. This and other texts of Neruda on Huidobro are reproduced in 'Posdata: Sobre Huidobro y Neruda', *Revista Iberoamericana*, xlv, 106-7 (April-September 1979), 379-86.

3 Unpublished letter (Paris, 18 May 1922), conserved by Larrea: '(. . .) Me parece que deben Uds. fundar esa revista que piensan hacer les traerá ella mucho bien y les hará respetar. Hagan una cosa pequeña de cuatro páginas u ocho a lo más pero muy escogida, muy de élite. Sean muy difíciles para aceptar la colaboración a ella de manera que todo el mundo codicie aparecer en vuestra compañía y que sea como un timbre de honor, como un certificado el ocupar plaza en esas páginas y para que no les dé mucho trabajo háganla mensual y de formato pequeño. Un artículo de prosa, dos a lo más y el resto poesía pura. Pienso que si realizan esta idea deben poner como título a la revista algo que sea como nuestra bandera para España y la América Española y que se relacione con lo que nosotros más podemos amar en el mundo. Sería un hermoso título CREAR o algo por el estilo (. . .).'

4 Interview: César González Ruano, 'Vicente Huidobro, el que trajo las gallinas', *El Heraldo* (Madrid), 6 January 1931.

I. THE LITTLE MAGAZINES *(pp. 7-19)*

1 'Rubén Darío', *Musa Joven* (Santiago), i, 5 (September 1912).

2 *Nord-Sud* (Paris), i, 1 (15 March 1917).

3 David Bary, 'Vicente Huidobro, agente viajero de la poesía', *La Cultura y la literatura en Iberoamérica* (Berkeley, Univ. of California, 1955), pp. 147-53.

4 'Vicente Huidobro en vanguardia', *Revista Iberoamericana*, xlv, 106-7 (April–September 1979), 222.

5 'Conferencia de Vicente Huidobro', *Ultra* (Madrid), i, 20 (15 December 1921), s.p.

6 Amédée Ozenfant pointed out the similarity of their thinking in a dedicatory note to *Après le Cubisme* (1918): 'Mon cher Huidobro, "Rien d'anecdotique ni de descriptif. Faire un poème comme la nature fait un arbre." Vous pensez en cela très justement. Recevez cet essai datant de plus d'un an déjà, et fait surtout en tête de chapitre pour mettre de l'ordre dans nos idées, qui depuis se sont precisées. Bien sympathiquement. A. Ozenfant. 16 janvier 1920.'

7 *Comœdia* (Paris), 13 February 1924.

8 Politics was in the air, for according to the printed invitation Alessandri was to have been present. Vallejo, out drinking with yet another Latin American politico then in Paris (Haya de la Torre), did not make the lecture, although he reports it as a success in a letter to Larrea (Paris, 23 February 1925): '(. . .) Antenoche, con motivo de la llegada a París de un amigo mío, Victor Raúl Haya de la Torre, nos hemos emborrachado mucho. Hoy he pensado en mí, en ti, en tantas cosas graves y hermosas (. . .). Huidobro ha dado una conferencia en la Sorbona. Yo no estuve, pero me dicen que hubo gente y alcanzó éxito. Habló de lo inconsciente, subconsciente en la inspiración artística (. . .).'

9 'Vicente Huidobro habla para *Síntesis*', *Síntesis* (Santiago), i, 2 (April 1933), 4.

10 The manifesto 'Total' was first published in French in *Vertigral* (July 1932), around the same time as Huidobro joined the Communist Party. A Spanish version later appeared in Argentina (*La Nación*, June 1933). This version, with slight variants, was the lead text in *Total 1*; the second manifesto, 'Nuestra barricada', is evidently a more updated measure of Huidobro's thinking with regard to the artist's role in the social revolution.

11 Unpublished letter from General Lister to Huidobro: 'Frente de Aragón a 24 de octubre de 1937. Querido Huidobro: Recibo tu carta y el recorte de periódico y por todo ello veo que has llegado a tu tierra sin novedad y que estás trabajando; creo innecesario decirte la alegría y la satisfacción que ello me causa y aunque me guardes un poco de rencor me siento satisfecho de no haberme dejado convencer por tus discursos, cuando a todo trance, querías marcharte a las trincheras a combatir; pues hoy más que nunca, estoy convencido que ahí en América, tu pluma y tus palabras, pueden hacer por la libertad de España mucho más do lo que hubieres hecho en las trincheras. ¿De acuerdo amigo? Las fotos que me pides están en Madrid y te las

mandará en cuanto tenga ocasión, pues yo como ya te habrás enterado por la prensa me encuentro en Aragón, donde como en nuestro gran Madrid, hemos hecho morder el polvo de la derrota a los españoles traidores y a los italianos que han corrido delante de nuestros bravos combatientes como en Guadalajara. Querido Huidobro, espero me mandes prensa y todo lo que tu escribas sobre nuestra lucha. Te saludan todos tus amigos de la 11ª División a los cuales les leí tu carta y yo te mando un abrazo fuerte, como mi odio al fascismo, que te ruego hagas llegar a todos nuestros amigos antifascistas de ese gran pueblo de Chile. Lister.'

12　'En una interesante conferencia expuso V. Huidobro el tema: Introducción a la poesía', *La Mañana* (Montevideo), 8 November 1944.

II. MODERNISM *(pp. 20-40)*

1　*Pasando y pasando* (Santiago: Imprenta Chile, 1914).

2　Newspaper clipping in Huidobro's scrapbook: 'El decadentismo obliga a los que lo sigue a pasar de la razón al delirio. Ahora estamos en la mitad de la gruta. En la parte más tenebrosa. Todo huele a humedad y hasta se siente el chapoteo de una laguna cercana. El poeta dice entonces: "En el estanque azogado / que está de estrellas florido, / una rana masca nueces / y un sapito raspa vidrios". Una rana mascando nueces nos hace el mismo efecto que ver a una ostra escarbándose los dientes. Si no estuviéramos en la Gruta del Silencio reiríamos a gritos (. . .)' (Nadir, '*La gruta del silencio*').

3　Unpublished manuscript: '(. . .) Yo he recorrido todas las escuelas. He hecho poemas clásicos, románticos, decadentes, simbolistas, panteístas (lo más burro de todo), modernistas, unanimistas, simultaneístas, etc. etc. Todos los en *ista* imaginables. y esto aunque a cualquier imbécil debe parecer lo contrario, es la prueba de mi absoluta seriedad. Además, figuraos el *métier*, el *savoir faire* que me ha dado tal ejercicio y el cúmulo de conocimientos que así he adquirido. Soy uno de los pocos poetas de hoy que lleva tras de sí una verdadera y enorme labor artística. Puedo desafiar a cualquiera a haber profundizado el Arte más que yo y a poderse considerar verdaderamente como un iniciado del divino misterio de la Poesía. Cuando se ha penetrado a la sinagoga de los iniciados, cuando se conocen todas las leyes de los excepcionales y se sabe matemáticamente cómo trabajaban sus obras los viejos maestros, que risa produce leer los estudios de ese hato de imbéciles que en el mundanal ruido se llaman críticos. ¿Cuándo se penetra al Misterio de los Iniciados? Cuando no se les invita, cuando se hace como ellos, o sea se crea una cosa nueva (. . .). Figuraos el placer que hubiese sentido un hombre que hubiese podido contemplar el momento en que Dios creaba los mundos y las cosas. El placer que hubiese sentido ese hombre es el que yo desearía poder dar algún día

a mis lectores, con la sola diferencia que el placer que yo querría darle
no sería como aquel, un placer esencialmente dinámico sino pura-
mente poético: El poeta debe ser un pequeño Dios (. . .). Esto es lo
que debe hacer el poeta, hacer una cosa que no sea ni imitación ni
exageración de la realidad. Hacer un poema que no sea otra cosa que
un Poema. Sin ningún elemento extraño, completamente puro, absolutamente desligado de todo: Un poema es una página en el cielo. Una
vez estudiado todo esto viene el ponerlo en práctica. El hecho: Al
querer realizar lo que era el fruto de largos estudios y meditaciones, al
hacer el primer poema, que podríamos llamar puro, tratando de que
cada verso fuera una cosa creada por mí, me encontré con enormes
dificultades. Hice un poema; no me gustó. Hice dos, tres, cuatro, lo
menos diez, pero había algo que fallaba. Ninguno me satisfacía. Creí
haber caído en un error y quise volver máquina atrás y enviar todo a
paseo, pero era inútil. Quise hacer poemas como antes, pero sentía
una repugnancia enorme a esa poesía inferior y felizmente sentía en el
fondo de mí como una voz que me decía: Sigue adelante! Y después
de días terribles de un gran abatimiento, sin saber cómo, una noche,
repasando los últimos poemas que había hecho, caí, de un golpe de
luz, en la cuenta de por qué razón no me gustaban. La razón era sen-
cillísima, como pasa con toda cosa nueva, había exagerado la nota y
caído en el otro extremo. Por crearlo todo, por alejarme de la realidad, había caído en la pura fantasía, en lo Fantástico, tan repugnante
y tan peligroso como lo Realista, y generalmente grotesco. Entonces
vi que tenía que bailar entre esas dos cloacas: lo Fantástico y lo
Realista sin caer en ningúna de ellas. Y el problema principal estaba
resuelto (. . .).'

4   Frédéric Lefèvre (the first critic to apply the term Cubism to literature),
     attributes this expression to Paul Dermée, who, in a 1917 lecture on
     Max Jacob, 'nomme son maître: le Mallarmé du Cubisme' [*La Jeune
     Poésie française* (Paris: Rouart, 1917), p. 201].

5   'Au poète Vincent Huidobro qui a inventé la poèsie moderne sans
     connaître les resultats de l'effort européen, et dont la place était
     marquée d'avance parmi nous. Max Jacob.' In Huidobro's autographed
     copy of *Le Cornet à dés.*

III. THE AVANT-GARDE (CUBISM) *(pp. 41–70)*

1   Unpublished postcard (Madrid, 11 January 1917) to Huidobro in
     Paris: 'Mi querido amigo: Mucho me alegro de tener al fin noticias de
     Uds. Sean muy felices en el nuevo año y recuérdennos como nosotros
     a Uds. Ya contará Ud. sus impresiones de París. Muy suyo, Alfonso
     Reyes.'

2   Unpublished letter: 'Estimado señor: Recién hoy he estado por *La
     Prensa* de vuelta de un viaje y me apresuro a escribirle para que

charlemos larga y amablemente ya que siendo amigo de Amador le considero como amigo mío. Estoy en mi casa: 38, rue Eugène-Carrière, Nord–Sud, Lamarck, todo el día de hoy, martes, hasta medianoche. Mañana salgo para Verdun y créame que Ud. haría un gran placer viniendo hoy a la casa de su Affmo. Alejandro Sux.'

3   Unpublished letter (Paris, 8 January 1917): 'Estimado señor: Si no tiene Ud. nada mejor que hacer el lunes próximo (15 de enero), tendré mucho gusto en que venga a esta su casa, por la noche, a las 9, para proponerle un trabajo que tal vez le interesará. Aprovecho la oportunidad para ofrecerle las seguridades de mi consideración más distinguida. V. García Calderón.' In a previous letter to Fernán Félix de Amador (Paris, 1 January 1917), García Calderón detailed his project: '(. . .) Entre mis proyectos figura una antología que se titulará por ejemplo, *Los más recientes poetas de América*, y en donde el joven poeta más celebrado de cada país presentará y seleccionará poesías de sus jóvenes compatriotas. Ud. se encargará de la Argentina (. . .), Prado o Huidobro de Chile (. . .).' A facsimile of this letter is in Federico Fernández de Monjardín's *Fernán Félix de Amador* (Buenos Aires: Ediciones Culturales, 1973), p. 64.

4   'Mon cher Pierre Reverdy . . .' in *Pierre Reverdy* (Paris: *Mercure de France*, 1962), p. 304.

5   'Un gran poeta chileno: Vicente Huidobro y el Creacionismo', *Cosmópolis* (Madrid), i, 1 (January 1919).

6   *Correspondance de Max Jacob*, edited by François Garnier (Paris: Éditions de Paris, 1953), volume 1, p. 144.

7   Angel Cruchaga, 'Conversando con Vicente Huidobro', *El Mercurio* (Santiago), 31 August 1919.

8   In *Manifestes* (Paris: *Revue Mondiale*, 1925), he points out: 'Vers la fin de 1916 je tombais à Paris dans le milieu de la revue *SIC*. Je connaissais très peu la langue . . .' (pp. 45–6). And in a draft of a letter (in French!) to Angel Flores regarding the flap over *El espejo de agua* (*Herald Tribune Books*, 29 November 1931), he states: 'Ma plaquette: *Espejo de agua*, que vous n'avez évidemment jamais lue, n'a pas été publiée à Paris (nouvelle erreur dans laquelle vous tombez), mais à Buenos-Ayres, en 1916. Elle a été traduite par moi-même et par Juan Gris et forme la première partie de mon livre: *Horizon carré*. Celui-ci publié à Paris en 1917.' The complete text of this letter was published by Nicholas Hey in his review of Hugo Montes's edition of the *Obras completas* [*Revista Iberoamericana*, xlv, 108–9 (July–December 1979), 702–4].

9   This dedication was written in the maquette of a collaborative project with Juan Gris, where the painter was to illustrate the poems of Reverdy. Further details on the project and the circumstances of its elaboration are contained in 'Un poème inconnu de Reverdy: En marge de son amitié avec Huidobro', *Bulletin du bibliophile* (Paris), 1975–II, pp. 186–92.

10 Originally Huidobro had written in a somewhat jumbled French: 'Creer un poeme en prenant de la vie le motif et en le transformant pour le donné une seconde vie. Pour ça rien d'anecdots ni des descriptions dans le sujet, car avec ses moyens ce ne serait pas la vie que nous creons mais ce qu'on raconte qui emeura le lecteur. Faire un POEME comme la nature fait un arbre.' Gris rewrote the opening to read: 'Créer un poème en empruntant à la vie ses motifs et en les transformant pour leur donner une vie nouvelle et indépendante. Rien d'anecdotique ni de descriptif. L'émotion doit naître de la seule vertu créatrice.'

11 'Je trouve', *Manifestes*, pp. 57-8.

12 See for example: André Malraux, 'Des origines de la poésie cubiste', *La Connaissance* (Paris), i, 1 (January 1920), pp. 38-43; Jean Cassou, 'Cubisme et poésie', *La Vie des Lettres* (Paris), i, 2 (October 1920), pp. 182-5; Maurice Raynal, 'Juan Gris et la metaphore plastique', *Les Feuilles Libres* (Paris), v, 31 (March-April 1923), 63-5.

13 Jean Cassou, 'Reverdy, poète cubiste', *Entretiens sur les Lettres et les Arts* (Rodez), No. 20 (1961), 64-5.

14 Unpublished letter (Beaulieu-près-Loches, 5 August 1918): '(. . .) Me parece muy cómico lo que me dices, que gentes que no han trabajado en ello y ni siquiera aprobado ni defendido seriamente nuestro esfuerzo reivindiquen la denominación de *cubistes* y quieran conocer nuestra estética mejor que nosotros mismos (. . .).'

15 'Or, le poème de M. Reverdy est fait comme un tableau.' In 'Reverdy par Max Jacob', *Arts* (Paris) June 29–July 5 1960 — published version of Max Jacob's manuscript text of presentation for the séance at rue Huyghens in 1917 (where Huidobro first met Reverdy).

16 'Reverdy est jeune et un peu entier dans ses opinions. Néophyte de la littérature il voudrait lui faire la place d'honneur et rugit devant les fantaisies typographiques . . .' (Letter to Doucet, 31 March 1917, in *Correspondance . . .*, p. 149).

17 The allusion is to Reverdy's *La Lucarne ovale* (1916, 1918): 'Au moment de la revue *Nord-Sud* dont je fus l'un des fondateurs, nous avions tous une ligne générale plus ou moins commune dans les recherches mais au fond on était bien loin les uns des autres. Tandis que d'autres faisaient des lucarnes ovales, je faisais des horizons carrés. Et voilà la différence exprimée en deux mots. Toutes les lucarnes sont ovales, alors la poésie reste dans le réalisme. Les horizons ne sont pas carrés, alors l'auteur présente ici une chose créée par lui' ('Le Créationnisme', *Manifestes*, pp. 47-8).

18 Unpublished letter: '(Paris) 3 avril 1918. Mon cher Huidobro: Merci pour l'horizon qui repose l'œil — je voudrais vous voir. Ecrivez vite. Cocteau.' The book's title was a cause for punning among the group. Juan Gris, writing to Paul Dermée (4 June 1918), had this to say: '(. . .) terribly sorry to hear that khaki threatens on your horizon. But of course it is a very frequent colour for the horizons nowadays, especially if they are not square!' (in *Letters of Juan Gris*, Collected

by Daniel-Henry Kahnweiler and Translated by Douglas Cooper, Privately Printed, London: 1956).

19 M.C.P., 'Les Lettres', *Le Pays* (Paris), 14 June 1918.

20 *Les Écrits de Paris* (Paris), 15 July 1918.

21 '*Horizon carré* de Huidobro', *Les Lettres parisiennes* (Paris), 10 June 1918.

22 'Les Lettres', *L'Intransigeant* (Paris), 23 March 1918.

23 'En la selva lírica: aventuras y descubrimientos', *El Mercurio* (Santiago), 6 May 1918.

24 According to Huidobro's eldest son, Vicente, the noise of the bombardments had come to traumatize his sister, Carmen. For this reason, the Huidobros left Paris, going first to Beaulieu-près-Loches, and later to Madrid, where they arrived in the summer of 1918.

25 Delaunay did, however, do a preliminary design [Item # 100 in catalogue of 1957 exhibition at Musée Nationale d'Art Moderne: '*Football*, projet de décor pour un ballet, 1918', in *Robert Delaunay* (Paris: Éditions des Musées Nationaux, 1957)]. And, in a letter (Madrid, 19 December 1918), to Huidobro, then in Chile, there is this comment: 'Mon cher Huidobro: Merci pour vos 2 cartes dont la dernière ne m'a pas tranquilisée. Je crois que c'est une excuse pour le Football (. . .).'

26 Gloria Videla has detailed the poet's stay in Madrid in 'Huidobro en España', *Revista Iberoamericana*, xlv, 106-7 (January–June 1979), 37-48. His return to Chile, and the controversy he aroused there in 1919, is covered in 'Del modernismo a la vanguardia: el Creacionismo pre-polémico', *Hispanic Review*, xliii, 3 (Summer 1975), 261-74.

27 Compare: Antonio Machado, 'Sobre las imágenes en la lírica (al margen de un libro de V. Huidobro)', in his *Obras completas* (Madrid: Plenitud, 1957); Gerardo Diego, 'Posibilidades creacionistas', *Cervantes* (Madrid), October 1919, pp. 23-8.

28 'Vicente Huidobro en vanguardia', *Revista Iberoamericana*, xlv, 106-7 (January–June 1979), 217-18.

29 Unpublished letter (Beaulieu-près-Loches, 15 October 1918): '(. . .) Sobre tus libros debo lo primero decirte el gran placer que me ha causado tu dedicatoria y en seguida la gran emoción poética que he tenido leyéndolos sobre todo los *Poemas árticos*. De ellos se *dégage* algo que no existe por ejemplo en el libro de Juan Ramón que me enviaste. El lirismo y la poesía que es tan raro encontrar y que es lo único que me interesa. Y ahora como soy tu amigo y como repetidas veces me lo has pedido paso a hacerte la crítica de ellos. *Poemas árticos* yo lo considero superior a *Ecuatorial* o por lo menos lo comprendo mejor, lo poseo mejor por ser más familiar. El otro es para mi demasiado grandioso y no he llegado aun bien a penetrarlo. Los dos son seguramente mejores que *Horizon carré* pero . . . desde entonces acá he reflexionado mucho sobre ciertas cosas y si antes admitía ciertos medios literarios que tú usas ahora no los admito, me explico

mejor: Hay en tus producciones un cierto prurito por las imágenes que es exagerado y que quitan fuerza a tus poemas y a la verdadera imagen emotiva. Así cuando tú escribes, nubes hidrófilas haces una imagen ingeniosa pero seca y no poética, pero cuando escribes, pasaron las nubes balando hacia el oriente das una emoción, mientras que el ascensor como un buzo no tiene otra base que tu pura ingeniosidad. Fíjate como todas las imágenes fuertes de tu libro tienen una base sólida y común. El invierno viene etc. (cementerio frío). Atado a un barco etc. (atado a su destino) y nada más vulgar que un pañuelo que seca al sol al cual puedes añadir la luna. Seguramente, más vale un adjetivo bueno que una imagen no emotiva e ingeniosa y considerable *touffe* de Mallarmé vale más que una imagen forzada (. . .).'

30 Juan Gris, as cited in John Golding, *Cubism* (Paris, 1962), p. 103.

31 François Poncetton, 'Du dadaisme', *Clair* (Paris), 29 January 1919.

32 Rafael Cansinos-Asséns, 'La nueva lírica (*Horizon carré*, *Poemas árticos, Ecuatorial*)', *Cosmópolis* (Madrid), i, 5 (May 1919).

33 Hernán Díaz Arrieta, 'El Creacionismo', *Zig-Zag* (Santiago), xv, 755 (9 August 1919).

34 Rafael Cansinos-Asséns, 'Vicente Huidobro', *La Correspondencia de España* (Madrid), 24 November 1919.

IV. POLEMICS *(pp. 71–83)*

1 'A propósito de una acusación de plagio: Carta del señor Vicente Huidobro Fernández', *El Mercurio* (Santiago), 18 September 1916.

2 Rafael Cansinos-Asséns, in an interview shortly before his death in 1964, recalled that it was a dispute over similarities in their work that originally brought them together: 'Conocí a Vicente Huidobro a raíz de la publicación de *Las pagodas ocultas*, el libro que allá, en Chile, hubo de exaltar hasta su más crespa ola el mar rugiente entre Scila y Caribdis, entre la incomprensión ingenua y la mala voluntad; *Las pagodas ocultas* se publicó en 1914, en el mismo año que *El candelabro de los siete brazos*, y tiene con este libro una semejanza fraterna (. . .). Cuando publicó *Las pagodas ocultas*, Vicente Huidobro me escribió una bella carta comentando con ingenuidad jubilosa, no envuelta en los velos de las plañideras, estas semejanzas. Al mismo tiempo me hablaba de los tamborileos de la crítica (. . .). Más tarde, cuando Huidobro vino a España a fines de 1916, de camino para París, hablamos largamente de todo eso.' In an interview with César Tiempo, 'Vicente Huidobro y *Las pagodas ocultas*', *Zig-Zag* (Santiago), 8 May 1964.

3 Unpublished letter (Seville, 31 January 1920): 'Admirado y querido poeta: Su carta me ha sorprendido, pues, en verdad, nunca creí que la vanidad del señor Edwards llegase a extremos tan ridículos. En el

núm. XXXIX de *Grecia*, de fecha de hoy, publico, en lugar preferente, su carta, con una nota precedente donde pongo de relieve al suministrador de los datos biográficos de Edwards, que no fue otro que el desdichado señor Lasso de la Vega (. . .).'

4 Enrique Gómez Carrillo, 'El cubismo y su estética', *El Liberal* (Madrid), 30 June 1920.

5 Unpublished manuscript: '(. . .) P. S. Después de firmado este artículo se me acerca un amigo y me dice que tenga cuidado pues el señor Carrillo es un admirable duelista. Yo no lo soy tanto pero si algo se le ofrece sepa el señor Carrillo que mi dirección es Paris, 41 rue Victor Massé.'

6 Angel Cruchaga, 'Conversando con Vicente Huidobro', *El Mercurio* (Santiago), 31 August 1919.

7 Frédéric Lefèvre, 'Une heure avec M. Max Jacob', *Les Nouvelles Littéraires* (Paris), 12 April 1924.

8 Unpublished letter (Paris, 16 July 1920): '(. . .) Lee mi respuesta en los diarios españoles. Los he destrozado. Si vieras como se burla de ellos toda la gente que vale algo. Inútil decirte que toda la juventud española está conmigo. Ya verás los artículos que van y vienen en mi defensa. Aquí en París la misma cosa; todos los artistas que valen están a mi favor y este lío me ha servido enormemente de reclam (. . .).' (In Manuscript Collection, University of Florida Libraries, Gainesville, Florida).

9 Juan-Jacobo Bajarlía traces the twists and turns of this argument and offers an explanation for its motivation in *La polémica Reverdy-Huidobro: Origen del Ultraísmo* (Buenos Aires: Devenir, 1964).

10 Unpublished letter (New York, 6 June 1932): '(. . .) Yo he seguido con bastante fidelidad y mucha admiración su obra (. . .). No soy pues el terco enemigo de su estro que Ud. se suponía, y aunque nos sacamos los dientes en discusión de detalles quiero que me tome por el más humilde de sus admiradores y uno de los más sinceros (. . .). A principios de setiembre pasaré por París camino a España. Dígame si Ud. piensa estar allí para pasar a saludarle.'

11 'Les Lettres', *L'Intransigeant* (Paris), 9 December 1924.

12 Draft of an unpublished letter (Paris, 14 May 1931): '(. . .) He sabido que Ud. ha mezclado mi nombre en asuntos suyos en que yo no tengo que mezclarme y diciendo cosas absolutamente falsas. Ha dicho Ud. que yo atacaba al subrealismo porque había querido entrar en él y no había podido. Esto es una simple mentira. En primer lugar nunca he querido entrar en el subrealismo, en segundo lugar es falso que yo ataqué al subrealismo. Lo he atacado hace años y por escrito, de frente, en lo que había que atacarlo y tanta razón tenía que ellos mismos reconocen ahora que el dictado automático — justamente el punto que yo ataqué —ha sido un fracaso respecto a lo que se esperaba podría dar. (. . .) Así pues es falso que yo haya querido entrar al subrealismo y le desafío a demostrar lo contrario. He pertenecido al

movimiento más interesante de este siglo — no como uno de tantos sino entre los primeros — y jamás he tratado de sacar partido de ello, sino muy al revés he preferido retirarme y trabajar en silencio. Por el momento no me interesa la bullanguería y cuando me dé la gana de volver a saltar al medio ya verá Ud. que también sé hacerlo y conozco la técnica (. . .).'

13 Carbon copy of an unpublished letter (Santiago, 26 October 1938), here quoted in its entirety: 'Querido Poroto: Veo por tu carta que las intrigas de la Banda Negra y de su jefe el pobre Bacalao siguen su curso normal. Sabía que había mandado verdaderas circulares llenas de calumnias sobre mí no sólo a Argentina sino también a Europa. La envidia de ese hombrecito amarillo y aceitoso es algo que llega a lo patético. Te agradezco conmovido tu confianza en mi honradez y el crédito que me das. No te defraudaré. ¡Figúrate! ¡Yo fascista! Es para morirse de la risa. Lo que hay es que sigo siendo el único verdadero comunista entre todos esos falsos revolucionarios intelectuales trasnochados que se aferran hoy al comunismo por espíritu arribista como antes — sólo ayer — eran perfectos reaccionarios mientras esperaban buenos bocados de la reacción. Soy comunista y ellos no lo son. Lo soy a pesar de los virajes y contra virajes del partido, a pesar de sus marchas y contra marchas. A pesar de los pesares. Y por eso no caigo en éxtasis ante los Frentes Populares ni ante las demagogías nacionalistas, aunque las cante Dimitrof, su madre y su abuela. Lenin dice que todo comunista tiene que ser esencialmente internacionalista y que al no serlo sólo prueba que no ha comprendido nada de las doctrinas revolucionarias o que es un confusionista de la clase más peligrosa. Confieso mi pecado de preferir Lenin a Dimitrof. Por otra parte y aún dejando de lado el punto de vista revolucionario, creo que el maravilloso rol de América consiste en parir al hombre futuro, al ser humano con todo el sentido de un verdadero humanismo o sea el hombre sin distinción de razas, ni fronteras, ni provincias, ni tribus, ni color de los ojos ni forma de los pies. América tiene que dar al mundo un sentido internacional absoluto o no tiene nada que hacer, sino seguir imitando a Europa y arrastrándose penosamente detrás de esos viejos países llenos de odios ancestrales y rencores podridos . . . seguir hasta el fin de los siglos obedeciendo todo lo que le mandan los tíos ancianos y obsecados. No, mi querido Poroto, no podemos resignarnos a esa falta de libertad espiritual que parece aconsejada por los que más dicen atacar la esclavitud. Si pienso de un modo diferente a Dimitrof, lo siento mucho pero no puedo abdicar de mi conciencia. Por los dos artículos que te incluyo, verás que no tengo nada de fascista y que si apoyé a Ibáñez es porque de los tres candidatos presentados, él era el más revolucionario-siendo los otros dos perfectamente e igualmente derechistas. El hecho de mandar decir a Buenos Aires que yo he caído preso como fascista sólo prueba la canallada de un Bacalao enfermo de odios recónditos-y el hecho de que allá le creyeran tan facilmente sólo prueba que tenían ganas de dejarse engañar. En verdad es aterrador ver la soltura con que los hombres se dejan arrastrar por la calumnia. Ello

revela para un psicólogo que creer en la maldad es más agradable que creer en la bondad — porque somos inclinados al mal y nos gusta en el fondo encontrar compañeros de ruta. Nos gusta y creemos que nos justifica. Yo caí preso únicamente por haber ido de visita a la casa de Ibáñez la tarde de la masacre. Y estuve seis días preso porque el enemigo se aprovechó de las circunstancias para vengarse de mis artículos y mis opiniones mil veces manifestadas en todas partes. No es más-En saliendo de la cárcel escribí un artículo mas fuerte contra el gobierno que los anteriores. Se publicó en *La Opinion* y se titulaba "Queremos justicia". Que los nacis chilenos apoyaron a Ibáñez no es culpa mía. Luego han apoyado a Aguirre Cerda y los comunistas no han chistado ni protestado por ello, al contrario muy contentos de ver que los veintinueve mil votos nacistas daban la victoria al Frente. Y has de saber que el candidato del Frente Popular fué a visitar a la cárcel al jefe del nacismo chileno. ¿Qué tal? ¿Tienen derecho a hablar los que tanto hablan? En cambio a mí personalmente el diario nacista no ha hecho otra cosa que insultarme . . . Y yo no lo he hecho mal. Nadie les ha pegado más fuerte aquí en Chile que yo. La ola de calumnias contra mí tendrá que calmarse y volver a su seno, mejor a su hígado . . . de Bacalao. Ya todo el mundo conoce el origen y todos están cansados de tanta idiotez y tanta intriga. Aquí y en Europa y en todas partes la gente de real valer está conmigo. Entre los comunistas oficiales, los tontos-y los hay muchos — pueden estar molestos por mi actitud independiente y porque yo no abdico jamás de mi pensamiento íntimo. Pero ellos deben comprender que un escritor, que un hombre de estudio y de cultura no es lo mismo que un militante más o menos analfabeto. En el mundo hay soldados y hay capitanes, no todos son lo mismo ni a todos puede exijirse igual. Sería ridículo que un hombre que piensa no pudiera discutir. Y sería el colmo de la exclavitud. Los que así piensan son malos comunistas. Yo tengo derecho a manifestar los puntos en que no concuerdo con las directivas del partido. La esclavitud espiritual es fascismo y no comunismo. Y basta. Ya esto se alarga demasiado.'

14 Tzara's letter to both poets has been reproduced by Juan Larrea, one of the signatories, in *Del surrealismo a Machupicchu* (Mexico: Mortíz, 1967).

15 'Controversia literaria, la *Antología de poesía chilena nueva*, Vicente Huidobro responde a Pablo de Rokha', *La Opinión*, 19 June 1935; 'Controversia literaria: Carta al poeta Vicente Huidobro', *La Opinión*, 23 June 1935; 'Respuesta a la carta de Pablo de Rokha', *La Opinión*, 1 July 1935; 'El término de una polémica literaria, punto y aparte a Huidobro', *La Opinión*, 3 July 1935; 'El poeta Vicente Huidobro pone fin también a una polémica: A Pablo de Rokha para siempre y hasta nunca', *La Opinión*, 6 July 1935.

16 'Vicente Huidobro, conocido poeta y escritor de avanzada, es atacado por un empleado de la Dirección de Investigaciones', *La Opinión*, 29 March 1936; 'Vicente Huidobro, agredido anoche', *La Opinión*, 20

October 1937; 'El poeta chileno Huidobro fué asaltado en su casa por dos agentes italianos a causa de su obra poética "Fuera de aquí"', *Crítica* (Buenos Aires), 1 November 1937.

17 'Vicente Huidobro', *En España con Federico García Lorca: Páginas de un diario íntimo, 1928-1936* (Madrid: Aguilar, 1957), pp. 189–92. Maples Arce, the Mexican Stridentist, reports a similar scene when he first met Huidobro in Paris in the 1930s: 'En casa de Torres García me encontré una noche con Vicente Huidobro, quien nos estropeó la velada con sus querellas y celos literarios. Afectaba siempre un gesto de desdén hacia todos los escritores y su calificativo favorito era idiota, que repetía insistentemente, deletreándolo' (in his memoirs, *Soberana juventud* (Madrid: Plenitud, 1967), p. 232).

18 'Vicente Huidobro habla para *Síntesis*', *Síntesis* (Santiago), i, 2 (April 1933).

19 Gonzalo Rojas, marginalia in an earlier draft of this chapter (New York, November 1980): 'El fue la libertad: el que sembró más hondo. En mí, y en tantos: en la medida de nuestra propia medida. Una libertad que nos hizo hombres: poetas responsables, con utopismo y todo, con anarquismo. Pero sin servidumbre. No es que haya sido el único progenitor pero, sin él, todo hubiera sido otra cosa entre nosotros. Bebió en la roca viva del ESPIRITU NUEVO (l'esprit nouveau, de Apollinaire), y fue de veras el gran dador: el que nos lo dio todo sin que le pidiéramos nada; ni obtuviera nada de eso. Amó a la juventud y supo oirla siempre, como ninguno (. . .). No escribió halagos, ni tampoco prólogos. Pero nos enseñó a ser el ser que somos; libertad, como dije y herejía en el sentido grande: distanciamiento contra patetismo.'

20 Unpublished letter (Buenos Aires: 13 August 1940): 'Querido amigo: Excúseme el retraso y la brevedad con que respondo al amable envío de su libro *Sátiro* y de dos folletos adjuntos. Yo tambien le he recordado mentalmente en distintas ocasiones, inquiriendo sus noticias por amigos comunes. Porque olvidadas ya, al menos por mi parte, las diferencias de un día, su nombre y su figura quedaron sólo asociados en mi mente a los mejores días de mi iniciación literaria, a aquel Madrid de 1918, casi fabuloso ya ante lo que ha venido después . . . Si viene usted alguna vez a Buenos Aires — yo proyecto desde hace mucho un viaje a Chile, pero ignoro aun cuándo podré cumplirlo — no deje de avisarme. Me será gratísimo evocar con usted aquellos tiempos y confrontar nuestras posiciones actuales. Entretanto muy cordiales saludos de Guillermo de Torre.'

21 'Poco antes de morir [Huidobro] visitó mi casa de Isla Negra, acompañando a Gonzalo Losada, mi buen amigo y editor. Huidobro y yo hablamos como poetas, como chilenos y como amigos.' In *Confieso que he vivido* (Buenos Aires: Losada, 1974), p. 389.

22 'Vicente Huidobro habla', *La Tarde* (Santiago), 10 September 1946.

V. BEYOND CUBISM *(pp. 84–103)*

1   Unpublished letter, conserved by Gerardo Diego (Soria: 16 November 1921): '(. . .) Voilà l'affaire: acabo de recibir carta de Huidobro (desde Paris) en la que, con su optimismo de siempre, me habla de sus tournées artísticas. Y me dice que quiere venir a España y dar una conferencia en el Ateneo a mediados de diciembre (. . .).'

2   At least two Paris newspapers (*L'Intransigeant* and *L'Internationale* (17 January 1922)) announce such a lecture for the 21st of January at the Square Rapp. Huidobro, in 1925, looking back on his Creationist campaign, mentions 'mes conférences de Buenos-Ayres, de Madrid, de Berlin, de Stockholm et celle de Paris, au théâtre du Square Rapp' (*Manifestes*, pp. 13–14).

3   Unpublished letter (Céret, 15 March 1922), reproduced here in its entirety: 'Mi querido Vicente: Tu m'as fait un grand plaisir avec ton livre. Il y a de très belles chose que je ne connaissais pas, par ex. "Ombres chinoises". Il y en a aussi que je connaissais et que j'ai relu avec plaisir. Tu es vraiment un poète. Dis-moi lorsque tu voudras ce qu'il faut que je fasse pour ton livre. Ou bien attends que je sois rentré à Paris car nous pensons partir vers le 15 Avril. Tu n'es pas gentil de ne pas m'écrire plus souvent. Je m'ennuie beaucoup, beaucoup . . . Je doute de tout. Je n'ai aucune confiance dans mon travail ni aucune lucidité d'esprit. Ce pays est abrutissant. Je ne comprends pas très bien ce que tu me dis du Congrès de Paris car je ne suis pas très au courant. On m'avait demandé d'adhérer. J'ai vu ton nom, celui de Raymond, Waldemar, Lipchitz, etc. et j'ai envoyé mon adhésion. Lorsque je serai à Paris nous verrons . . . J'ai aussi reçu une protestation contre le Congrès signé de Satie et quelques Dadas et un imprimé de Picabia que je ne sais s'il est pour ou contre le Congrès. Tu sais, je m'en fous . . . Nos amitiés à vous tous et à toi, JUAN GRIS.'

4   His withdrawal happens to be documented. On 17 February 1922 a group of artists and writers met at the Closerie des Lilas to discuss Breton's slighting of 'foreigners', and ended up withdrawing from the upcoming Congress (the text of 'Résolution' is published in Michel Sanouillet's *Dada à Paris* [Paris: Pauvert, 1965], pp. 334–5). On the original document, now in the Jacques Doucet Library, we find that Huidobro has penned next to his signature the following declaration of personal loyalty to Tzara and disgust over the whole affair: 'Je ne trouve pas M. Tzara un imposteur.'

5   The essay, besides serving as the base text for Huidobro's speaking tour on Creationism, was also published in *L'Esprit nouveau* (April 1921).

6   Huidobro's text was published by Varèse in the score for his *Offrandes* (Boston: Birchard, 1927). A recent recording of the piece is available on Columbia, *The Varèse Album* (1972).

7   'El arte del sugerimiento', *Pasando y pasando* (Santiago: Imprenta Chile, 1914).

8 'Les robes-poèmes', *Bon Soir* (Paris), 9 July 1922.

9 The catalogue, carrying a preface by Maurice Raynal and a note on Huidobro by Waldemar George, lists the following items: 'Océan', 'Tour Eiffel', 'Arc-en-ciel 1', 'Minuit', 'Piano', 'Arc-en-ciel 2', 'Marine', 'Arc-en-ciel 3', 'Couchant', 'Kaléidoscope', '6 Heures octobre', 'Moulin', 'Paysage'. In addition to those we have already commented upon, an outline image of another can be made out as a wall hanging in a photo of the interior of Huidobro's studio.

10 Letter from Huidobro (Paris, 18 April 1922) to Larrea in Madrid; partially reproduced in 'Trayectoria del caligrama en Huidobro', *Poesía* (Madrid), i, 3 (December 1978), 42.

VI. POLITICS (AND THEATRE) *(pp. 104-119)*

1 *Finis Britannia: Une redoutable Société Secrète s'est dressée contre l'Impérialisme Anglais* (Paris: Fiat Lux, 1923), pp. 18-19. It would be more correct if the title were 'Finis Britanniae'. The author's grammatical slip was cleverly pointed out by at least one newspaper of the time: 'M. Vincent Huidobro publie, aux éditions "Fiat Lux", un petit livre, d'ailleurs intéressant, qui a pour titre *Finis Britannia*. Ces poètes d'avant-garde, tout de même, ils révolutionnent jusqu'au latin!' (*Le France* (Paris), 1 February 1924).

2 'Chilean Diplomat Was Kidnapped', *New York Herald*, 15 March 1924. Press agencies provided Huidobro with this and other newsclippings of the kidnapping and its aftermath: 'Un Attaché à la légation du Chili a disparu mystérieusement', *Petit Parisien*, 13 March 1924; 'Étrange disparition d'un attaché à la légation du Chili', *L'Écho de Paris*, 13 March 1924; 'Deux disparitions gardent un caractère des plus mystérieux', *Excelsior*, 14 March 1924; 'L'Extraordinaire aventure de l'homme de lettres Chilien', *Excelsior*, 15 March 1924; 'O Sr. Huidobro . . .', *Gazeta de Noticias* (Rio de Janeiro), 18 March 1924; Enlevement d'un écrivain Chilien par des bandits', *La Patrie* (Montréal), 14 April 1924; 'Pizzicati e anedotti Parigini', *Corriere Italiano* (Rome), 30 April 1924.

3 Larrea, who was in Madrid at the time, opts for this interpretation, asserting that Huidobro's insistence on sticking to the 'official' version of his kidnapping led to his falling out with Juan Gris (in his 'Vicente Huidobro en vanguardia', *Revista Iberoamericana*, xlv, 106-7 (January-June 1979), 213-73). Also, among Larrea's papers there is a note from Huidobro accompanying a 1924 newspaper clipping from *Paris-Journal*. Titled 'L'Étrange aventure de Vincent Huidobro', it is essentially an interview in which the poet tries to put a serious face on the whole escapade. The note (undated) confirms this intent: 'Querido Larrea: Ahí tiene Ud. la verdad de lo ocurrido y podrá Ud. desmentir todos los chismes aunque ello no vale la pena. Un fuerte y cordial abrazo. Vicente Huidobro.'

4   'La proclamación de Vicente Huidobro', *La Nación* (Santiago), 18 October 1925.

5   'El poeta, crítico y novelista chileno Vicente Huidobro pasa por Nueva York', *La Prensa* (New York), 7 July 1927.

6   'Primera encuesta internacional de *Europa*: el manifiesto de Vicente Huidobro: Jóvenes de América uníos para formar un bloque continental!', *Europa* (Barcelona), i, 1 (September 1933), 45.

7   Carbon copy of an unpublished letter to Luis Buñuel (Paris, 14 May 1931); '(. . .) En cuanto a lo de mi labor revolucionaria y lo de si soy o no comunista, no es Ud. quien puede hablar. Mientras no firme Ud. en el partido comunista no puede Ud. decirme nada a mí. Por otra parte mi labor revolucionaria es bastante más antigua que la suya y bastante comprobada en diferentes países. Ahora mismo en España, en el mes de enero de este año, aun bajo los peligros del otro regimen, yo he llevado dos manifiestos a Madrid, uno de los cuales se publicó y el otro no apareció por ser considerado *demasiado* revolucionario. Yo pasé la frontera con ambos en mi maleta, exponiéndome a ir a pasar mi vida en una cárcel. ¿Haría Ud. lo mismo? (. . .)'

8   *Estanquero* (Santiago), April 1947.

9   'Vicente Huidobro habla para *Síntesis*', *Síntesis*, i, 2 (April 1933).

10 'Las encuestas de *Hoy*: Sobre el momento político y económico de Chile y de América', *Hoy* (Santiago), 20 October 1933.

11 'A palos terminó la conferencia de Molina sobre la Revolución Rusa'. Unidentified newsclipping among Huidobro's papers.

12 'Ayer, Huidobro pronunció un discurso ante 8,000 soldados de la división Lister. Mañana dirigirá la palabra a los soldados rebeldes del frente de Madrid mediante un alto parlante instalado en un coche blindado, para pedirles que se pasen a las líneas leales.' Unidentified newsclipping among Huidobro's papers. Further reports on his activities are found in: 'Vivimos por España y para España: Una interviú con Vicente Huidobro, excelso poeta|chileno', *Las Noticias* (Barcelona), 6 June 1937; 'El gran escritor chileno, Vicente Huidobro, está entre nosotros, y nos habla . . .', *El Pueblo* (Valencia), 11 June 1937; 'Mensaje a la juventud americana', *ABC* (Madrid), 23 June 1937; 'Con Vicente Huidobro, poeta y antifascista de corazón', *Ahora* (Madrid), 24 June 1937.

13 'Unidad', *La Ley* (Santiago), 1 September 1938.

14 Carlos Vattier, 'Vicente Huidobro opina', *Ercilla* (Santiago), 31 July 1940.

15 Carbon copy of an unpublished letter to 'Poroto' (Santiago, 26 October 1938); full text is given in Chapter IV, note 12.

16 Huidobro, in an interview with Georgina Durand, 'El rol del poeta en el mundo que se plasma', *La Nación* (Santiago), 24 August 1941: 'Yo no puedo ser enemigo de ningún pueblo; mis ideas sociales no me lo permiten, pero puedo ser enemigo de un régimen político, como lo soy del nazismo, y en tal sentido deseo la derrota de Hitler, que significa

para mí el triunfo de la Historia, el triunfo de la razón contra el instinto.'

17 In August of 1941, Huidobro wrote a series of 'Cartas al Tío Sam'. They were published in Santiago's principal newspapers (*El Mercurio* and *La Nación*) as well as many provincial papers; more recently, they have been included in Hugo Montes's edition of the *Obras completas*.

18 Carlos Vattier, 'Con Vicente Huidobro', *Hoy* (Santiago), 11 September 1941.

19 Unpublished draft copy on stationary marked 'Legación de Chile' (17 June 1945): Mi general: (. . .) una orden suya allanaría mis dificultades. En el avión militar para el Brasil no me permiten exceso de equipaje y yo llevo películas de la guerra y grandes [*illegible*] que hemos dibujado con especialistas para mostrar en los teatros las operaciones principales de la guerra. Todo lo cual es indispensable para mis conferencias por la causa que Ud. supo llevar al triunfo. Yo estoy dispuesto a pagar ese excedente de equipaje, que son por unos doscientos kilos o poco más. Pero no lo aceptan sin una orden superior (. . .).

20 'Por qué soy anticomunista', *Estanquero* (Santiago), April 1947.

21 *Comœdia* (Paris), 10 April 1933.

22 The late Henri Crémieux, a Comédie Française actor and contemporary of Huidobro, referred to this play in a letter to me (Cassis, 16 December 1979).

VII. NOVEL AND FILM *(pp. 120–136)*

1 Unpublished letter, conserved by Larrea (Paris, 11 July 1928): 'Querido Larrea: Gracias mil por todo lo que te has incomodado por mi, y sobre todo con el sobretodo de esas tropicalidades que me cuentas se permite Madrid. Ya no necesito sino el *Cid* de Zorrilla, que eso si lo necesito pronto, y si tu gentileza llega a tanto no te olvides de hacerlo buscar sobre todo (otro más) en las librerías de viejos. Cuando te vengas de Madrid tráeme la *Historia de la conquista de México* de Prescott, la edición Mercurio de Madrid en dos volúmenes. Y para compensar todo lo que te cargo con pedidos, pídeme tú también algo aunque sea la luna o Venus. Te abraza tu amigo, Vicente Huidobro.'

2 Among Huidobro's papers there is a long letter from Arturo García Carraffa (Ciudad Rodrigo, 22 February 1929), author of the *Enciclopedia heráldica y genealógica hispano-americana*, in which he details several lineages, concluding: 'Como su abuelo Don Domingo pertenecía a una de esas dos líneas de la Cerda, de Chile, y estas líneas procedían de la familia española del mismo linaje, que tiene por primitivo ascendiente al Infante Don Fernando el de la Cerda, hijo del Rey Don Alfonso X el Sabio, resulta clara, aunque remota, la

ascendencia que Ud. señala a su abuelo.' The importance of this infor-
mation for Huidobro becomes clear in the context of another letter,
from Ramón Menéndez Pidal (Madrid: 1 March 1929): 'Muy señor
mío: en respuesta a la pregunta de su atenta carta, tengo el gusto de
manifestar a usted que, en efecto, don Alfonso X fue descendiente del
Cid, ya que su abuelo Alfonso VIII era biznieto de una hija del Cid.'

3   *Mío Cid Campeador* (Madrid: Compañía Iberoamericana de Publicaciones, 1929), p. 9. Henceforth, all page references to this edition
will be indicated in the text itself.

4   'Qué placer más grato para el corazón de un escritor que el poder
llevar un poco de alegría y entusiasmo a esos espíritus virginales y
limpios de los niños.' Draft copy of a letter from Huidobro (Paris,
4 October 1931) to Isabel Shepard.

5   Germán Sepulveda, *'Jeanne d'Arc* y *Mío Cid Campeador'*, *Atenea*
(Concepción), 435 (1977), 59–84.

6   'El *Cid Campeador* de Huidobro', *Social* (Havana), October 1930,
p. 24.

7   Draft of an unpublished letter (Paris, 2 August 1929) to Sr. Beltrán:
(. . .) Respecto a los dibujos hay dos que no son de mi agrado pero
sobretodo uno que es preciso corregir. Se trata del dibujo de la página
25 en que aparece el Cid recién nacido. Hay que borrar en él la palabra
Campeador que cae del cielo en el fondo del cuadro pues me destruye
completamente el efecto final del capítulo y mata la sorpresa que yo
quiero dar al lector. Eso es facil borrarlo, se cuide dejar el rayo sin la
palabra escrita dentro. El dibujo de la página 119 también me
destruye el efecto de la batalla descrita pues el ponerme el ejército
contrario entre dos árboles me reduce la acción, reduce el campo en la
imaginación del lector y la batalla del Cid contra los alemanes se
convierte en una batallita de juguete (. . .).

8   '*Mío Campeador*: film de Vicente Huidobro', *Atlántico* (Madrid),
May 1930, p. 68.

9   Unpublished letter (Paris, 1 August 1929) to Manuel Ortega, here
transcribed in its entirety: Estimado Sr. y amigo: En su carta del 24
de julio pasado me pide Ud. una cuartilla en que le indique la índole
de mi obra *Mío Cid Campeador* para el efecto de la propaganda que
debe empezarse con anticipación. No sé si se refiere Ud. a pedirme
alguna fórmula llamativa para anuncios en los periódicos y para las
franjas que cubren los libros nuevos o si me pide unas cuantas frases
sobre el género particular del libro. Mi obra no es una narración his-
tórica fría y austera, no es una novela en el sentido habital de esta
palabra, ni es una 'vida novelada' como esas que éstan hoy tan a la
moda. Es un género algo diferente, es una Hazaña. ?Qué género es
éste que no se encuentra en ningún texto de literatura? La Hazaña
es una historia que se canta, una novela épica, una epopeya en prosa
en la cual el autor se toma todas las libertades que permite el poema

y acaso algunas más. Yo he cogido el Cid Campeador de la leyenda y de la historia y he tratado de darle una vida nueva, un calor nuevo, sangre y huesos de hombre y a veces hasta maneras actuales. He tratado de acercarle lo más posible a nosotros, ponerle a nuestro alcance, para hacerle comprender y amar de las gentes de mi tiempo. He querido que pierda su rigidez de estatua, su figura de museo hierática y solemne, su lejanía de crónica secular, de viejo documento de archivo sólo interesante para doctos y eruditos, e interesante no por sí mismo, sino porque a él va unido el primer poema de nuestra lengua y sobre él se discute más de filología que de su propia humanidad, que de sus propios hechos. Yo sólo he querido arrancarlo por un momento de las manos de investigadores arqueológicos y hacerlo galopar sobre su Babieca en medio del siglo XX, con toda la electricidad y soltura que debió tener en sus tiempos. Toda la naturaleza, la tierra, el universo participan e intervienen en la vida del héroe de tal manera que la figura del Cid se convierte en una figura cósmica. Al mismo tiempo que por un lado se le acerca a la tierra y hasta a nuestra época haciéndole decir de cuando en cuando frases y términos del vulgo de hoy, por otro lado se le aleja y se le agiganta sobre la humanidad haciendo intervenir el mundo total en sus acciones. No sé si he logrado lo que he querido hacer, pero eso es lo que he pretendido. Creo que con esas cuantas cosas que digo sobre mi libro se puede tejer algo mejor y basarse en ellas para hacer un pequeño artículo de propaganda. Ahora si lo que Ud. me pide es alguna fórmula llamativa para anuncios en periódicos y pancartes de librería se puede poner algo así: AQUI RENACE EL CID CAMPEADOR / Y LA MAS ALTA EPOPEYA DE LA RAZA. O bien si Uds. quieren poner esas frases rotundas de libros yankees, no andarse|con chicas y anunciar tranquilamente: EL LIBRO DEL DIA . . . / Y DEL SIGLO. Aunque la modestia debía revelarse, esto no me importa porque como se trata de réclame comercial (y Ud. y yo estamos en el secreto) ello nada significa. Se trata de que el libro se venda lo más posible y yo tengo tanto interés en su difusión como Uds. En todo caso Uds. que conocen mejor el público español verán lo que hay que hacer. Saludos muy afectuosos de su amigo de siempre, Vicente Huidobro.

10 Only a few months after *Mío Cid Campeador* was published in London by Spottiswoode, Houghton Mifflin (Boston) brought out Wells's translation of *Cagliostro* under the title *Mirror of a Mage* (1931).

11 'Les Poètes et le Cinéma', *L'Ère Nouvelle* (Paris), 6 May 1923.

12 'Nous déclarons que dans le film Cagliostro de M. Huidobro le découpage est fait contre l'opinion de M. Mizu.' The document, in Huidobro's hand, is jointly signed and dated '14-Juin-1923-Paris'.

13 *Cagliostro: novela film*, *Zig-Zag* (Santiago, 1934), pp. 22-3. Henceforth, all page references to this edition will be given in the text itself.

14 Unpublished typescript, in English, bearing revisions and signature of Huidobro.

VIII. *ALTAZOR (pp. 137–161)*

1   A receipt from Editorial Plutarco dated 17 January 1931 shows Huid-
     dobro received an advance of 400 pesetas 'por importe de su original
     Temblor de cielo que esta editorial publicará en su "Colección de
     Autores Contemporáneos"'. On 13 May 1931, C.I.A.P. (Compañía
     Ibero-Americana de Publicaciones), wrote to Huidobro in Paris, in-
     forming him 'que su libro *Altazor* está ya terminado y será puesto a
     la venta uno de estos días'. By July of 1931 both volumes were out
     and copies had arrived even in Chile where they were reviewed by
     Alone (Hernán Díaz Arrieta): 'Los últimos libros de Vicente Huidobro',
     La Nación (Santiago), 23 July 1931.

2   This statement is based on a partial check of Spanish periodical liter-
     ature for 1931; it is hoped that a more thorough and systematic
     search will turn up articles and reviews hitherto unknown.

3   *La Correspondencia de España* (Madrid), 24 November 1919.

4   '[*Ecuatorial*] es para mi demasiado grandioso y no he llegado aun bien
     a penetrarlo' (Letter from Gris to Huidobro, 15 October 1918; full
     text in Chapter III, note 29).

5   '(. . .) Por este mismo correo le mando mis libros *Altazor* y *Temblor
     de cielo*. *Altazor* es ya muy viejo y seguramente Ud. conocía frag-
     mentos de él pues se había dado en muchos diarios y revistas, tanto en
     francés como en español, desde hace más de diez años. Esto aparte las
     lecturas, tres o cuatro, que yo había hecho de ese poema. Pero era
     necesario publicarlo una vez por todas; mis amigos me lo pedían con-
     stantemente y al fin el pobre encontró editor. !Cuántas veces fue
     rechazado! Es un libro que tiene, sin duda, una importancia histórica
     porque en él están marcados todos los caminos que yo he seguido
     después y talvez nunca podré salir de alguna de sus rutas. Esa es la
     importancia que tiene para mí, aparte de la que pueda tener el poema
     en sí y de la que pueda haber tenido para los demás. *Temblor de
     cielo* es acaso más maduro, más fuerte, más hecho. Ha producido gran
     entusiasmo en mis buenos amigos — tanto que me asusta — lo han
     puesto como una cosa enorme, por encima de Lautréamont y de
     Rimbaud. Sinceramente le digo que estoy asustado (. . .)' (Unpub-
     lished carbon of a letter to Miró Quesada, 11 June 1931).

6   Unpublished carbon of a letter to Luis Buñuel (Paris, 20 May 1931):
     '(. . .) Respecto a lo de artista fracasado es posible que tenga Ud.
     razón [pero] en mi fracaso voy junto con Rimbaud y Lautréamont
     (. . .).'

Bibliography

The most complete registry of published Huidobriana is that of Nicholas Hey: 'Bibliografía de y sobre Huidobro', *Revista Iberoamericana*, xli, 91 (April–June 1975), 293–353; recently updated as 'Addenda . . .' in the same publication, xlv, 106–7 (January–June 1979), 387–98, with further revisions planned. Here, for the reader's convenience, is a shorter reference listing of books by and about Huidobro. Full bibliographic description of the published and unpublished materials informing this study is given directly in the text and notes.

BOOKS BY HUIDOBRO

Ecos del alma (Santiago, Imprenta Chile, 1911).
La gruta del silencio (Santiago, Imprenta Universitaria, 1913).
Canciones en la noche (Santiago, Imprenta Chile, 1913).
Pasando y pasando (Santiago, Imprenta Chile, 1914).
Las pagodas ocultas (Santiago, Imprenta Universitaria, 1914).
Adán (Santiago, Imprenta Universitaria, 1916).
El espejo de agua (Buenos Aires, Orión, 1916).
Horizon carré (Paris, Paul Birault, 1917).
Poemas árticos (Madrid, Imprenta Pueyo, 1918).
Ecuatorial (Madrid, Imprenta Pueyo, 1918).
Tour Eiffel (Madrid, no publisher, 1918).
Hallali (Madrid, Ediciones Jesús López, 1918).
Saisons choisies (Paris, La Cible, 1921).
Finis Britannia (Paris, Fiat Lux, 1923).
Automne régulier (Paris, Libraire de France, 1925).
Tout à coup (Paris, Au Sans Pareil, 1925).
Manifestes (Paris, Revue Mondiale, 1925).
Vientos contrarios (Santiago, Editorial Nascimento, 1926).
Mío Cid Campeador (Madrid: Compañía Iberoamericana de Publicaciones, 1929).
Temblor de cielo (Madrid, Editorial Plutarco, 1931).
Altazor o el viaje en paracaídas (Madrid, Compañía Iberoamericana de Publicaciones, 1931).
Tremblement de ciel (Paris, l'As de Cœur, 1932).
Gilles de Rais (Paris, Totem, 1932).
La próxima (Santiago, Walton, 1934).
Papá o el diario de Alicia Mir (Santiago, Walton, 1934).
Cagliostro (Santiago, Zig-Zag, 1934).

En la luna (Santiago, Ercilla, 1934).
Tres novelas ejemplares [with Hans Arp] (Santiago, Zig-Zag, 1935).
Sátiro o el poder de las palabras (Santiago, Zig-Zag, 1939).
Ver y palpar (Santiago, Ercilla, 1941).
El ciudadano del olvido (Santiago, Ercilla, 1941).
Últimos poemas (Santiago, Talleres Gráficos Ahués, 1948).
Obras completas [prepared by Braulio Arenas] (Santiago, Zig-Zag, 1964).
Obras completas [expanded and prepared by Hugo Montes] (Santiago, Editorial Andrés Bello, 1976).

BOOKS ON HUIDOBRO

Bajarlía, Juan-Jacobo. *La polémica Reverdy–Huidobro: Origen del Ultraísmo* (Buenos Aires, Devenir, 1964).
Bary, David. *Huidobro o la vocación poética* (Granada: Universidad de Granada, 1963).
Camurati, Mireya. *Poesía y poética de Vicente Huidobro* (Buenos Aires, García Cambeiro, 1980).
Caracciolo-Trejo, Enrique. *La poesía de Vicente Huidobro y la vanguardia* (Madrid, Gredos, 1974).
Concha, Jaime. *Vicente Huidobro* (Madrid, Jucar, 1980).
Costa, René de. *En pos de Huidobro* (Santiago, Universitaria, 1981).
—— (editor). *Vicente Huidobro y el Creacionismo* (Madrid, Taurus, 1975).
—— (editor). *Vicente Huidobro y la vanguardia* (special number of the *Revista Iberoamericana* (Pittsburgh), xlv, 106–7 (January–June 1979).
Goiç, Cedomil. *La poesía de Vicente Huidobro* (Santiago, Nueva Universidad, 1974).
Holmes, Henry Alfred. *Vicente Huidobro and Creationism* (New York, Columbia University Press, 1934).
Ogden, Estrella Busto. *El creacionismo de Vicente Huidobro en sus relaciones con la estética cubista* (Madrid, Playor, 1983).
Pizarro, Ana. *Vicente Huidobro, un poeta ambivalente* (Concepción, Universidad de Concepción, 1971).
Szmulewicz, Efraín. *Vicente Huidobro, biografía emotiva* (Santiago, Universitaria, 1979).
Wood, Cecil. *The Creacionismo of Vicente Huidobro* (Frederickton, York Press, 1978).
Yudice, George. *Vicente Huidobro y la motivación del lenguaje* (Buenos Aires, Galerna, 1978).

Index